Peer Supervision in Coaching and Mentoring

Supervision is increasingly required for a coach's and a mentor's professional development, and engaging in reflective practice with peers can be a valuable way of meeting these needs. Peer supervision brings unique challenges though, including the possibility of collusion or stagnating at a shared developmental level.

This book is written by practicing professional supervisors who engage in peer supervision themselves and train communities of coaches and mentors. It guides practitioners to develop and integrate their range of individual and group reflective practice activities alongside professional supervision. It draws upon essential theory and methodology, explores challenges and ethical dilemmas faced within peer supervision, and provides concrete guidance, useful techniques and helpful templates.

This practical guide will be vital reading for individual coaching and mentoring practitioners and peer learning groups including within communities, universities and/or training programs. It will also support professional supervisors and organizations developing coaching cultures.

Tammy Turner is based in Sydney, Australia and she develops leaders and other coaching professionals internationally. She has been Director, ICF Australasian Professional Standards and led the ICF's global task force on coaching supervision.

Michelle Lucas is based in Weymouth, UK and her business focus is Coaching and Coaching Supervision and the development of Internal Coaches. She is the Supervision Education Lead at the Association for Coaching.

Carol Whitaker is based in Oxford, UK and specializes in Executive and Team Coaching, Supervision and Mentoring, and is a Senior Associate Lecturer for Oxford Brookes Business School.

Peer Supervision in Coaching and Mentoring

A Versatile Guide for Reflective Practice

TAMMY TURNER, MICHELLE LUCAS, AND CAROL WHITAKER

LONDON AND NEW YORK

First published 2018
by Routledge
2 Park Square, Milton Park, Abingdon, Oxon OX14 4RN

and by Routledge
711 Third Avenue, New York, NY 10017

Routledge is an imprint of the Taylor & Francis Group, an informa business

© 2018 Tammy Turner, Michelle Lucas, Carol Whitaker

The right of Tammy Turner, Michelle Lucas, Carol Whitaker to be identified as authors of this work has been asserted by them in accordance with sections 77 and 78 of the Copyright, Designs and Patents Act 1988.

All rights reserved. No part of this book may be reprinted or reproduced or utilised in any form or by any electronic, mechanical, or other means, now known or hereafter invented, including photocopying and recording, or in any information storage or retrieval system, without permission in writing from the publishers.

Trademark notice: Product or corporate names may be trademarks or registered trademarks, and are used only for identification and explanation without intent to infringe.

British Library Cataloguing-in-Publication Data
A catalogue record for this book is available from the British Library

Library of Congress Cataloging-in-Publication Data
Names: Turner, Tammy (Master certified coach), author. | Lucas, Michelle, author. | Whitaker, Carol (Executive coaching consultant), author.
Title: Peer supervision in coaching and mentoring : a versatile guide for reflective practice / by Tammy Turner, Michelle Lucas, and Carol Whitaker.
Description: Abingdon, Oxon ; New York, NY : Routledge, 2018. | Includes index.
Identifiers: LCCN 2017048661| ISBN 9781138061293 (hardback) | ISBN 9781138061309 (paperback)
Subjects: LCSH: Personal coaching. | Executive coaching. | Mentoring. | Counselors – Supervision of.
Classification: LCC BF637.P36 T87 2018 | DDC 158.3071/55 – dc23
LC record available at https://lccn.loc.gov/2017048661

ISBN: 978-1-138-06129-3 (hbk)
ISBN: 978-1-138-06130-9 (pbk)
ISBN: 978-1-315-16245-4 (ebk)

Typeset in Avenir and Dante
by Florence Production Ltd, Stoodleigh, Devon, UK

Contents

	List of illustrations	vi
	Author biographies	viii
	Foreword	x
	Acknowledgments	xiv
	Abbreviations	xv
	Introduction	1
1	Defining peer supervision	7
2	Understanding reflective practice	25
3	One to one peer supervision	47
4	Group peer supervision	75
5	Simplifying Contracts and contracting	106
6	Exploring coaching and mentoring dilemmas	125
7	Ethics: The elephant in the room	161
8	Managing pitfalls	177
9	Accessing professional supervision	203
	Afterword	217
	Index	*225*

Illustrations

Figures

1.1	The House of Supervision	11
2.1	Model of reflective practice	31
2.2	Johari window	36
2.3	Coaching session review form	43
2.4	Writing in	46
2.5	Writing out	46
3.1	A schematic of the seven-eyed model	71
3.2	A schematic of the seven-eyed model	73
4.1	Peer supervision member details for Contract	97
5.1	The shared outcome model	118
8.1	Peer supervisee developmental stages	196
8.2	Four levels of coach maturity	197
8.3	The seven-eyed model	198
8.4	Critical areas and questions to inform a coach development plan	200–202

Tables

1.1	Factors influencing the choice of professional supervision vs peer supervision	19
1.2	Excerpt from *Standards Australia Handbook*	22
2.1	Mapping CPD to the three Cs framework	29
3.1	Benefits and limitations of one to one peer supervision	48
3.2	Clues in the dialogue that territory other than peer supervision is being covered	53
3.3	Template for personal peer supervision goals	65
4.1	Benefits and limitations of group peer supervision	76
4.2	Clues in the dialogue that territory other than peer supervision is being covered	83

5.1	Five areas for contracting and decisions to be made for a peer supervision Contract	108
5.2	Practical matters to discuss: Frequency	109
5.3	Practical matters to discuss: Time management	109–110
5.4	Practical matters to discuss: Location	110–111
5.5	Practical matters to discuss: Boundaries	111–112
5.6	Practical matters to discuss: Confidentiality	112
5.7	Practical matters to discuss: Openness and trust	113
5.8	Practical matters to discuss: Managing feedback	113–114
5.9	Practical matters to discuss: Managing peer comparisons	114–115
5.10	Practical matters to discuss: Power imbalances	115–116
5.11	Practical matters to discuss: Unconscious bias	116–117
5.12	Clues that a contracting discussion is needed	120
5.13	Language differences between below the line and above the line feedback	121
5.14	Hints and tips for developing your peer supervision contracting skills	122
6.1	Independent coaches – confidentiality: Horses for courses?	128
6.2	Independent coaches – boundaries: Coach or consultant?	130
6.3	Independent coaches – conflicts of interest: What's the real issue?	132
6.4	Independent coaches – dual relationships: Who said what?	134
6.5	Internal coaches – confidentiality: Tip of the iceberg?	136
6.6	Internal coaches – boundaries: Inappropriate contact or just different cultural practice?	138
6.7	Internal coaches – conflicts of interest: Ready, steady . . . stop?	140
6.8	Internal coaches – dual relationships: Can you coach someone you know well?	142
6.9	Line manager as coach – confidentiality: Is a little knowledge a dangerous thing?	144
6.10	Line manager as coach – boundaries: When is it too close for comfort?	146
6.11	Line manager as coach – conflicts of interest: How do you manage perceptions?	148
6.12	Line manager as coach – dual relationships: How much is enough?	150
6.13	Mentors – confidentiality: It's all hush, hush . . . or is it?	152
6.14	Mentors – boundaries: How do you accommodate cultural difference and personal values?	154
6.15	Mentors – conflicts of interest: What's really going on here?	156
6.16	Mentors – dual relationships: Is it possible for a mentor to be a friend too?	158
8.1	Motivations and potential pitfalls	178
9.1	Peer and professional supervision comparisons	207

Author biographies

Tammy Turner

Based in Sydney Australia and originally from Colorado USA, Tammy is Founder of The Centre for Coaching Development and Supervision and Managing Director of TPC Leadership Australasia. As an ICF Master Certified Coach (MCC), Tammy works globally with key industry and government decision makers and has trained, mentored, and supervised many hundreds of internal coaches, leaders and HR professionals as well as freelance coaches, mentors and consultants. As a visionary in the international coaching field, she has been a contributing author to articles and books on coaching, mentoring and the power of collaborative leadership including chapters in Coaching Supervision: A practical guide for Supervisees (Routledge, 2016) and Coaching and Mentoring in the Asia Pacific (Routledge, 2017). Since 2001, Tammy has leveraged her previous executive background in Information and Communications Technology to foster corporate social responsibility efforts for disadvantaged teenagers and develop tailored solutions for corporate transformational programs for leaders and coaches. Tammy is committed to Continuing Professional Development (CPD) being the core of a reputable, self-regulating coaching industry. She has been instrumental in engaging cross professional body discussions around coaching guidelines and in defining ICF's policy for CPD as an industry standard. Her hope is for a professional coaching and mentoring community adding compelling value to both practitioners and the people whom they support. For more information view her websites www.developingcoaching.com.au and www.tpcleadership.com

Michelle Lucas

Michelle's first interest was psychology and this quickly led to a career in HR, spanning over twenty years. It was this HR work that drew her to coaching, having spent much of her time supporting executives that were dealing with transition. In 2003 she set up "Greenfields," her coaching business, and finally cut the strings with her corporate career in 2006. Passionate about CPD, she co-founded the AC's Co-Coaching Forum in Newbury. It was this group that led her to Supervision as those establishing their own coaching practice asked for support. Along the way she has achieved an MBA at Warwick University, is a Fellow of the CIPD, and is an Accredited Executive Master Coach and Accredited Coaching Supervisor with the AC – her training was Oxford Brookes and the Gestalt Centre. She works as a Career Coach and Executive Coach and also supervises those that work in similar fields. She volunteers for the AC and is their Supervision Education Lead. She is part of the Editorial Review Panel for the EMCC journal. She has written a number of articles for academic journals publishing the results of her Group Supervision research; and she has also co-authored journal articles with Carol Whitaker regarding their co-facilitation work. In collaboration with Professor David Clutterbuck and Carol Whitaker she wrote her first academic book, *Coaching Supervision: A practical guide for supervisees*, published by Routledge in 2016. She is also an active blogger on coaching supervision topics. For more information view her website www.greenfieldsconsultancy.co.uk

Carol Whitaker

Carol brings a wealth of business experience at board level in a range of industries. The development of people's potential has always been her passion, it prompted a career in HR, and it was here that she experienced coaching. It inspired her to become a coach and she sought qualification through Oxford Brookes. As she neared completion of her Post Graduate training she was invited to supervise incoming students; this developed into a core interest and she was one of the first cohort of coaches to become a qualified supervisor with Oxford Brookes. Her links remain strong with the University; she achieved an MBA with them and is a Senior Associate Lecturer for the Business School and a Coach/Supervisor for the MA Coaching and Mentoring Practice in the UK and Hong Kong, Executive Coaching Diploma and their Internal Coaching Pool. She has written a number of articles for academic journals on aspects of Supervision and contributed to books on HR, leadership, and Diversity in Mentoring; she has also co-authored journal articles with Michelle Lucas on co-facilitation and in collaboration with Professor David Clutterbuck and Michelle Lucas she wrote *Coaching Supervision: A practical guide for supervisees*, published by Routledge in 2016. A member of both the AC and EMCC, she is an Accredited Coach with Oxford Brookes and a Fellow of the CIPD. She has been running Whitaker Consulting since 2004 offering Executive & Team Coaching, Mentoring and Coaching Supervision. For more information view her website www.whitaker-consulting.co.uk

Foreword

Peer Supervision in Coaching and Mentoring: A versatile guide for reflective practice

It is a great pleasure to have been asked to write the foreword to this much-needed book. Of course, the reader might be excused for asking why another book on supervision is needed. Libraries have been written on clinical supervision in the helping professions over the past century. This book, as far as I am aware, is the first to focus fully on Peer Supervision. As such it is a major contribution to our understanding of the breadth and role of supervisory practice.

So where does this book fit in the history of supervision? White and Winstanley (2014) have traced the origins of supervision in the helping professions back to at least 1788 in the management of services for the poor in Hamburg. However, supervision as we know it, began with Psychoanalysis in the 1920s and extended to the growing array of psychotherapeutic and social work traditions that have emerged since. Coaching and mentoring have, until now, largely been the recipients of this tradition.

In this tradition, supervisory models were, in essence, adaptations and extensions of the core model and practices of these therapeutic approaches (Bernard, 2006). Modern supervision has largely been seen as a process of mentoring or apprenticing novices into the particular tradition of practice of which the supervisor and supervisee were a part. This is perhaps not surprising, given that each of these approaches is embedded in an understanding of the human person and, therefore, has a particular view on what constitutes health and growth for the person.

Aside from being the first book on peer supervision, this book is unique in that it has imagined supervision as more than the apprenticeship model that has come down to us from the clinical or therapeutic world. It recognizes that much can be gained from the co-created journey or dance of discovery between two or more peer practitioners committed to their own and each other's growth. In doing so they not only enlarge possibilities for supervision, they provide a model from which the therapeutic traditions can learn. Just as importantly, they put practical meat on the bones of this new vision. The range of practical models, tips and questions for reflection throughout the book are testament to this.

The authors have also paid careful attention to many of the important concerns of more traditional approaches to supervision. Peer supervision here is not simply two coaches coaching each other to improve their practice. While the personal development of the partners remains a core focus of peer supervision, this book continues the tradition of ensuring the interests of the supervisee's clients (and ultimately their protection) are also key goals of the process.

This book also has a contribution to make in the growing discussion of supervision as a professional process in its own right – an intentional process with its own skill set and requirements. The emergence of bodies devoted to professional supervision (such as the Association of Coaching supervisors, AOCS and the Association of Professional Executive Coaches and Supervisors, APECS) and the development of competency models and codes of ethics aimed directly at supervision is evidence of this maturation.

In part, the professionalization of supervision has been driven by legal precedents such as exemplified by the 1976 case, *Tarasoff vs. the Regents of the University of California*, which established in law the duty to protect those potentially at risk from one's client. Anxiety raised by such cases, greater reporting and connectivity, and a more general increase in anxiety in society, have led to a focus on supervision as an important way to manage professional risk.

It is likely that there is also another set of influences at work. The growing complexity of life in the modern world is also driving the professionalization of supervision. The notion that the world can be neatly divided into clear domains presided over by an equally neat set of professions is under fire. The problems we face are increasingly resistant to the imposition of unitary definitions and singular "expert delivered" solutions, and this is weakening the hegemony of the professions in their domains of practice. There is a growing recognition of the need for more reflective and multidisciplinary perspectives to address this complexity.

Ten or so years ago I was asked to participate in a panel discussion on supervision in coaching with three other colleagues, all of whom were acknowledged experts in the field. Each of the panelists was asked to speak for a few minutes. The first three speakers (including myself) each spoke about the role supervision had played in our own personal development, its importance in ensuring the adequacy of our practice, by ensuring we were practicing within the limits of our competence. The last person to speak was Dr. John Franklin. He is a coaching psychologist of enormous experience, wisdom and learning. Indeed, he has developed important interventions for change in both coaching and clinical psychology. He began, "You know, every time I sit down in front of a client, I feel like I am on the edge of my limit of competence – because people are complex . . ."

That simple and honest statement, and the few minutes that followed, had a profound effect on me. To this day it challenges me to constantly see the newness, richness and complexity of the people with whom I work. The real importance of supervision is that it provides a method for reaching clarity about the "right way" to assist the client. It is not about avoiding confusion, uncertainty and tension. Rather, confusion, uncertainty and tension are critical doorways to bigger perspectives, where the next step of the journey can be taken.

For too long I believe we have confused predictability, stability, replicability and conformity with established processes, with rigor. These things, while often important, can equally be indicators of rigor mortis. The dynamic and emergent nature of the world in which coaches ply their trade dictates that coaching should itself be a dynamic and responsive process. Coaching supervision, as a set of methods and relationships by which coaches reflect on their practice, needs also to match this variety if it is to be responsive to the needs of coaches and their clients.

When done well, supervision offers a reflective space for "just in time" processing in a volatile uncertain, complex and ambiguous world. This book recognizes that a multiplicity of perspectives is necessary in supervision. Each of the permutations of the dimensions of supervision (peer/professional, one to one/group) has a place in reflective practice. To their credit, the authors do not seek to elevate peer supervision as the one great solution to the complexity of modern practice. They recognize that multiple modalities are needed if we are to work effectively in a rapidly evolving, uncertain and often confusing space. Their use of the Johari window (Chapter 2) and reflective questioning in each chapter is evidence of this.

This book is a welcome addition to the needed variety in supervision. The lack of attention given to peer supervision is worrying from two perspectives. First, a failure to understand and explore the dynamics of peer supervision means that much of the potential benefits of this process of supervision will remain undeveloped. Second, it also means that the potential dangers and pitfalls of this approach remain hidden. It is refreshing to see that both opportunities and pitfalls are explicitly dealt with in this book.

There exists a tension at the heart of supervision. It is a tension between the ongoing development of the supervisee and the dynamic management of risk. As practitioners, our ongoing development requires us to move outside our comfort zones, to engage with what we find confusing, surprising and humbling. It brings us face to face with failure and inadequacy. As professionals we have a duty of care for our clients (exemplified by the injunction to protect the client by acting within the limits of our competence). A way to meet these two critical goals is to enter into processes that hold the tension between challenge and support. To the degree that supervision enables us to dance in this dynamic tension, it has promise to be both developmental and ethical.

This understanding also highlights the responsibility of each person involved in the dance of peer supervision. This book's attention to contracting respects this dynamic. Contracting and the administrative elements of supervision become the structure that creates a space for the dance to take place. The processes used for exploration become the choreography – the dance steps that take us into the tension. And above all, each party to the supervision engagement must be able to reflect on, and find ways of testing, their fitness for the dance steps.

So why is this book needed? It is needed because it explicitly explores an emerging area of the dance floor, and shines a light on the practical steps of this emerging dance. Is its exploration of peer supervision complete? Of course not – no single work can ever be. But it is the most comprehensive exploration to date and it is an important contribution to the field. For this the authors are to be congratulated. Part of the challenge that remains is an empirical challenge. How do we test the boundaries of peer supervision? How do we collect, hold and apply evidence to ensure that peer coaching is helping us to enter more effectively into the dance of coaching with our clients? It is my hope that this book will stimulate that discussion, research and reflection in this important area of practice.

Michael Cavanagh
Coaching Psychology Unit
University of Sydney
November 25, 2017

References

Mernard, J.M. (2006) Tracing the development of clinical supervision. *The Clinical Supervisor*, *24*(1–2), pp. 3–21.

White, E. and Winstanley, J. (2014) Clinical supervision and the helping professions: An interpretation of history. *The Clinical Supervisor*, *33*(1), pp. 3–25, DOI: 10.1080/07325223. 2014.90522

Acknowledgments

This book has been a truly collaborative endeavor and we would like to express our gratitude to the following people, without whom the manuscript would never have been completed!

Thanks to Professor David Clutterbuck, for his years of enthusiastic contribution to the coaching and mentoring industry. David supported our ambition for the book by offering his guidance on the coherence of the content and as our internal editor.

Thanks to Sally Webb, ONZM, for co-writing the original peer supervision handbook for ICF New Zealand Northern chapter's peer supervision community, which was the genesis for this book.

Also thanks to Christiana Iordanou, Licenced Psychologist, Drama Therapist and author who provided valuable input and inspiration for the Chapter, Ethics: The elephant in the room.

Special thanks to Professor Michael Cavanagh, both for compering the seminal publication, *Australian Standards' Coaching in Organisations handbook* and his ever-present thoughts about the coaching industry in the foreword.

Special thanks to Alyson Keller of Performance Impact who as a volunteer leader has supported the ICF New Zealand Northern branch in growing their peer supervision community.

Thanks also to Cath Wilson of 720 Consulting, Christine Vitzthum of Christine Vitzthum Coaching, and Amanda Horne, of Amanda Horne Pty Ltd., who took the role of our target audience, and whose care in reviewing final drafts and offering the key learning points at the end of each chapter offered additional clarity.

Abbreviations

Abbreviation	Full name
AC	Association for Coaching
APECS	Association for Professional Executive Coaches and Supervisors
CFO	Chief Financial Officer
CPD	continuing professional development
EMCC	European Mentoring and Coaching Council
GCoE	Global Code of Ethics
HR	human resources
ICF	International Coach Federation
NZN	New Zealand Northern
360 feedback	360 degree feedback

Introduction

A shared belief of the three authors is that coaching and mentoring supervision enhances our reflective practice, which leads to increased competency, capability and capacity for practitioners. As the coaching and mentoring market matures internationally, we have noticed a drive towards consistent delivery. As a result, all the main professional coaching and mentoring bodies have competency frameworks. Some are now articulated at four levels of increasing complexity. Alongside this, professional bodies, suppliers of coaching and mentoring services and providers of coach and mentor education have responded by increasingly requiring practitioners to engage in supervision. We anticipate that regular supervision is set to become a future industry standard, yet how prevalent is this in practice?

Coaching and mentoring supervision on a global scale

Supervision requirement, purpose and uptake internationally are inconsistent. Some of this reflects the various professional bodies' positioning of supervision and their different geographical influence. Globally, there seems to be a greater uptake of supervision in those markets which are perceived to be more mature, such as the UK and Europe. This may be due to the influence of the European professional bodies, which require supervision for accreditation purposes. For practitioners in other geographies, such as Australasia, the United States or in emerging markets, such as Brazil and Mexico, where coaches and mentors often belong to non-European-based professional bodies or where there is a perceived shortage of professional coaching supervisors, the uptake seems to be less.

Additional inconsistencies may be due to misunderstanding about the terminology. For example, supervision equates to monitoring for some practitioners. To members of professional bodies, nomenclature and/or development requirements are incompatible: Supervision for accreditation (Association for Coaching (AC), European Mentoring and Coaching Council (EMCC) and Association for Professional Executive Coaching and Supervision (APECS)) versus mentor coaching for credentialing purposes (International Coaching Federation (ICF)). The ICF specifically excludes supervision in favor of mentor coaching for credentialing purposes. The thinking behind this is that the skill and consistent application of skills against the ICF 11 Core Competencies is better placed with a practicing ICF credentialed coach listening to the coach's work. In comparison, supervision is seen as developing the coach's emotional intelligence and wisdom to deliver complex coaching engagements and develops their capacity to coach.

There is also a lack of clarity about what coaching supervision is, how to prepare for it and what outcomes to anticipate. Inconsistent uptake may also have an economic factor. When practitioners are starting out or are in markets where coaching and mentoring fees are less, professional supervision is not always accessed. Training courses may provide some supervision during training, but people do not seek it out after they have completed their course or got to the next level of accreditation. Often, the costs of supervision and other forms of development are not factored in their fee structures. Given professional supervision is delivered by a qualified supervisor and is a paid service, both independent practitioners and organizations with internal coaches alike make commercial decisions about this investment. Although many universities and training organizations are committed to supervision, in providing supervision as part of their programs as we mentioned earlier the cost may be prohibitive and learning circles prevail, which predominately focus on skills. These complexities combined lead to practitioners seeking to reflect on their work, engaging in alternative forms of support. Peer supervision is a common solution.

Shortcomings of peer supervision

Working with peers brings unique challenges, including blind spots, collusion and the possibility of stagnating at a common developmental level. It may also favor the practitioner's developmental needs over the guardianship of the client. In an educational or training setting this becomes particularly challenging as students grapple both with learning coaching skills and managing peer supervision.

Some consistent peer supervision limitations include:

- Many coaches do not know how to be supervised – few coach or mentor training courses contain a module on how to be a supervisee.

- With a lack of understanding of how professional supervision could bring value to their work, it may be seen as just another expense to their bottom line. Without a comparison the practitioner may believe that working with a peer will be cost effective and "just as good" as professional supervision.
- Enthusiastic coaches and mentors may willingly engage in what they believe is coaching and mentoring supervision, but in fact be operating in a "coaching the coach" frame emphasizing the development needs of the coach rather than being in service of their clients.
- Lack of peer supervision processes can enhance difficulties in collusion, competition and avoid difficult topics such as ethics or the exploration of group dynamics.
- Peer supervision may limit coach effectiveness and negatively impact on the perception of coaching and mentoring as a professional industry.
- Practitioners are untrained, unskilled or unsure about what is useful to consider in their reflective practice. Peers are less likely to recognize systemic issues and the psychodynamics that occur in coaching or mentoring relationships.
- Issues of collusion can be a problem between peers; some subjects may be seen as taboos. While any reflective practice is likely to be better than none, we believe that working with peers requires considerable structure and capability to be done well. Peer supervision therefore works best when it is a deliberate and collaborative endeavor. Peers need to be clear on their roles, on the process and continuously contract for clarity, as complexity arises.

Where this book fits in

Our intention is to provide a versatile guide for a range of practitioners who want the benefit of reflective practice, including:

- Practicing and credentialed or accredited coaches
- Practicing and credentialed or accredited mentors
- Other professionals using coaching skills
- Those undertaking practical training courses.

We hope it provides additional collateral for existing professional supervision relationships and that it will prove useful for organizations who want to create or support a coaching culture.

As such, this guide is written as a practitioner manual and is structured in two halves. The first half of the book focuses on setting up and running both one to one and group peer supervision. The second half supports the established relationship to both working together better and to extend its usefulness. Each of the nine chapters has a particular aim:

1. To explain the basics of what coaching supervision is and what it is not – to help practitioners understand how it differs from other "helping conversations."
2. To locate peer supervision in the context of reflective practice. This includes guidance on how to become a reflective practitioner.
3. To provide guidance on how to work with peers on a one to one basis to reflect on their client work. This includes techniques to use and practical tips on every stage of the one to one peer supervision relationship.
4. To provide guidance on how to work with a group of peers to reflect on their client work – this will include techniques to use and practical tips on every stage of the peer group supervision relationship.
5. To offer a series of discussion points to help form a peer supervision Contract. Further, to give hints and tips on developing contracting skills as part of regular process reviews and in the moment feedback.
6. To provide a selection of coaching and mentoring dilemmas in short case study form along with options for managing the situation. Not only do these broaden the practitioner's thinking, but also provide material for discussion in peer supervision.
7. To offer a series of discussion points around the ethical considerations that might occur within peer supervision.
8. To identify the potential pitfalls that emerge when working with peers and to provide guidance on how to spot them, discuss them and resolve them.
9. To identify when peer supervision can be extended or is not enough and professional supervision is needed instead of, or in addition to.

We recommend this book as a resource for training programs and peer learning groups. Our ambition is that professional supervisors will recommend it to their supervisees to enhance the practitioner's peer supervision, heighten their awareness and have greater recognition of how their work would benefit from professional supervision. It could also act as a guide for organizations that want to create or support coaching cultures.

We have made the following assumptions about the specific characteristics within the peer supervision context:

- Practicing coaches and mentors, i.e. people who receive some level of compensation or reward for their services (this may include pro-bono or bartering).
- Coaching or mentoring may represent the entirety or a proportion of the portfolio of work.

- The focus of the client work may range from Individual Coaching through to Organizational Coaching and we include mentoring within this scope.
- The client is not a vulnerable person, e.g. young person, client with a clinical or mental health condition and in circumstances where either the client or practitioner are at risk. With a vulnerable client group we would recommend seeking professional supervision.
- This book is not written for the professional supervisor, although we acknowledge they may also engage in peer supervision relationships.

The nature of the practitioner's underpinning knowledge and experience:

- To have been trained specifically as a coach (or mentor), or to be in the process of doing so.
- The coach or mentor training received may come from any theoretical stance.
- The depth of experience may vary from complete novice to seasoned practitioner.
- Not trained as a coach supervisor or as a supervisor of any other profession.

Final thoughts

Our intention is to provide a strong foundation for reflective practice and discussion about best coaching and mentoring practice. We hope individual practitioners will consult this guide before they enter into peer supervision. Our aim is for the guide to be educative, however we do not propose that it is a substitute for supervision training. It may also serve as a useful reference point for reviewing existing peer supervision relationships and processes. Additionally, we would encourage training providers to incorporate components of the book into their programs, supplementing and complementing their existing content.

It is important to note that we don't see peer supervision as a substitute for professional supervision. Similarly, if you were to read this book and apply all of our suggestions to your peer supervision work, we do not believe it is a substitute for supervision training. Given the complexity underpinning the client relationship, the usefulness of professional supervision should not be underestimated. Indeed our aim is that this book prompts practitioners to consider how they can use peer supervision and professional supervision to complement each other and create a sustainable way of working that benefits both them and their clients.

We hope you enjoy reading the book and that you find it useful and it enhances your work. We suggest you start with the chapters that are of most interest to you and then stretch yourself by filling in the gaps. We do not expect the book to be read cover to cover in one go, but to be something you can dip into and refer back to on your journey. If anything is unclear or you would like to share your own best practice we would welcome hearing from you.

Tammy, Michelle and Carol

Contact Tammy: tammy@developingcoaching.com.au
Contact Michelle: michelle@greenfieldsconsultancy.co.uk
Contact Carol: carol@whitaker-consulting.co.uk

Defining peer supervision   1

Definition: Peer supervision is a collaborative learning environment created between fellow coaches, mentors or other professionals (practitioners). It is of mutual benefit to the practitioners involved as well as being of service to their clients and the wider system. Peers often have comparable levels of expertise and are without supervision training. It is a self-managed arrangement where typically the major exchange is time rather than money. What's significant is that it is reciprocal, generates the power to reflect on practice together, and peers share vulnerability and support in equal measure.

What we mean by peer supervision

As coaching and mentoring has spread globally and many practitioners are exceeding twenty years' career experience, we're making the case for supervision in all of its forms to be part of the industry's continuous professional development (CPD). The scope of this book is to offer guidance to those who are new to supervision as well as those who want to deepen their peer supervision practice. Given the scope and application of this book, we are limiting ourselves to the more practical applications of peer supervision.

We start this chapter by providing a reminder of some existing definitions of supervision for coaches and mentors. The central purpose of this book is to enable "peers" to engage in supervision and therefore we also consider exactly what we mean by the term "peer." We report back on how practitioners use peer supervision. This leads us to question what differences exist between "peer supervision" and professional supervision. We identify two key differentiators, the presence or absence of underpinning supervision knowledge and the reciprocal nature of the relationship that in turn impacts on how power is experienced in the relationship. From this base we explore other activities often mistaken for peer supervision and explain why we see them as different. We consider how different geographies and different contexts might impact on the use of peer supervision. By way of summary we list the most common reasons why practitioners see peer supervision as a positive choice and also offer some words of caution.

Defining supervision within a coaching and mentoring context

There are plenty of definitions of coaching supervision to choose from. Here is a reminder of the most commonly referenced ones:

- "Coaching supervision is a formal process of professional support, which ensures continuing development of the coach and effectiveness of his/her coaching practice through interactive reflection, interpretative evaluation and the sharing of expertise." Bachkirova, Stevens and Willis (2005).
- "A working alliance between two professionals where coaches offer an account of their work, reflect on it, receive feedback and receive guidance, if appropriate." Inskipp and Proctor (1993).
- "Supervision is the process by which a coach/mentor/consultant, with the help of the supervisor, who is not working directly with the client, can attend to understanding better both the client system and themselves as part of the client-coach/mentor system, and transform their work." Hawkins and Smith (2006).
- "Coaching supervision is a co-created learning relationship that supports the supervisee in their development, both personally and professionally, and seeks to support them in providing best practice to their client. Through the process of reflecting on their own work in supervision, the supervisees can review and develop their practice and re-energize themselves. It offers a forum to attend to their emotional and professional wellbeing and growth. Through the relationship and dialogue in this alliance, coaches can receive feedback, broaden their perspectives, generate new ideas and maintain standards of effective practice." Hodge (2016).
- "Supervision is an opportunity to bring someone back to their own mind, to show them how good they can be." Kline (1999).
- "A Supervisor is a mentor's mentor and allows a mentor a place where they can bring their mentoring experiences to be supported and engage in reflective dialogue and collaborative learning to aid development. It is often seen as a safety net to overcome or avoid potential stumbling blocks and roadblocks with minimum repercussion and risk." (OCM, 2017).

Summarizing these established definitions, we see an emphasis is on the collaborative nature of the supervision relationship. Interestingly, these definitions are generic and could equally apply to supervision from a professional supervisor or to supervision among peers. A common assumption is that a professional supervisor will have greater or deeper experience than those they are supervising. However, there is nothing within these quoted definitions that require this to be true. Therefore before we proceed to define peer supervision, we provide the following definition of professional supervision – and this will be explored more fully in Chapter 9.

Professional supervision is a reflective learning environment where the supervisor is hired by the supervisee and is specifically qualified to look at the entire system in which the work is being undertaken. Although the reflective space is co-created, the professional supervisor is purposefully of service to the supervisee and their clients and the wider system. What is significant is that the supervisor's intention is to develop the practitioner's competence, capability and capacity to become a reflective practitioner of their own work.

Defining peer supervision

So what exactly is "peer supervision"? In our research for this book we attempted to find definitions that specifically explain this term, and we discovered that such definitions are hard to come by!

We located the following explanation in Standards Australia (2011), which formed part of an exploration of the benefits and limitations of peer supervision:

> In peer supervision, two or more coaches seek to assist each other in reflecting on their practice including both case specific and coach specific reflection.

We also discovered a form of peer learning used in Holland and Switzerland, which is useful in our context:

> *Intervision*: A supervision process involving a group of peers with the same professional focus, who cooperate in a goal-driven process towards finding solutions within a shared structural design. Mutually accountable volunteers give and receive learning and teaching without compensation.
> Epprecht (2011) citing Lippmann (2009)

There are certainly parallels between the concept of intervision and the emphasis of the individual's responsibility for reviewing their own work in an unregulated market. According to two Dutch management consultants, Bellerson and Kohlmann (2016, p. 9):

> Intervision is based on the idea that you alone are ultimately responsible for your own behavior. You learn to look differently at yourself, at what you do, and search for things to improve. In Intervision you take charge of your professional development, your expertise in your field, the way you work with others, and your personal performance.

The process Bellerson and Kohlmann (2016, p. 13) describe for Intervision echoes the techniques that we outline in our chapter on group peer supervision. "A group of five to eight participants unravels a problem submitted by one participant, the case provider . . . . The participants try not to come up with solutions, but by asking questions, encourage the case provider to think up their own answers and solutions." They continue: "Intervision makes you aware of your individual style, and your personal views of your work . . . at intervision sessions you help each other to uncover and clarify hidden drivers, so that you can find and make improvements."

It would seem therefore that intervision, as described by these authors, has a primary focus on the effectiveness of a practitioners work. In comparison, peer supervision as outlined below has a broader intent and impact than this.

What was interesting in our research for this book is we did not find any definitions of "peer supervision" specific to coaching and mentoring. Let's start from first principles and consider for a moment what we mean by "peer." The Oxford dictionary definition is "A person of the same age, status, or ability as another specified person." However, in the context of coaching and mentoring it is unlikely that two coaches will be exactly the "same." Typically each person will have accumulated their own specific experiences, which inform their work. Additionally it is quite difficult to compare "ability" as so much of a coach's performance is linked to the capability of their clients and the context in which they are working. What is perhaps more useful in the context of this book are the synonyms "equal," "fellow," "co-worker." These give a sense of the collegiate nature of the relationship. This feels much more useful. When two people work together as "peers" their professional profiles could be very similar or very different. We talk about the benefits and difficulties of pairings along this spectrum in Chapter 5.

How do professional supervision and peer supervision compare?

Given the similarities outlined above, it leads to the question of whether or not "peer supervision" is any different from professional supervision? Hawkins and Smith (2006) acknowledge that there are typically three central reasons for supervision, described as Developmental, Administrative and Resourcing elements. Previously Proctor (1986), who worked in the fields of counseling identified three elements: Formative, Normative and Restorative. You will notice that throughout this book we will use these terms interchangeably. In 2015 Lucas built on this with her notion of the "House of Supervision." As Figure 1.1 below illustrates – these three pillars of supervision rest on the practitioners chosen code of ethics and are held together through the activity of guided reflective practice, which fosters our capacity to deliver the work.

In our research for this book we asked a number of practitioners to describe what they used their peer supervision relationships for.

> *Peer supervision occurs when we speak about challenges that we may have in our coaching sessions and we get the feedback of our peers. We may sometimes pick a topic and each person will contribute their knowledge and experience on the topic, the challenges encountered and their strategies. They [the peer supervisee] then benefit from the varied perspective of their peers.*
> Lola Chetti, Change Consultant and Executive Coach,
> Holding Space Coaching and Consulting, Hong Kong

> *This is about working with my colleagues and seeking and delivering feedback to ensure we are always performing at our best. This can be informal or formal and is a continuous part of what we do as coaches and leadership experts.*
> Liz Rider, Business and Coaching Psychologist, Sweden

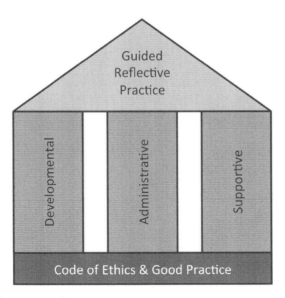

Figure 1.1 The House of Supervision
Developed by Lucas (2015)

I see peer supervision as a co-created partnership with a coaching colleague(s) where the focus of the relationship is to offer a supportive and reflective space for each person to explore their client work and personal development.

Sarah Hammond, Coach, Supervisor and Mindfulness Teacher, UK

My international virtual peer supervision group is a very accessible way to feel in touch with the coaching community, listen to questions that I could ask myself to raise my self-awareness or to perceive my current situation from a different perspective.

Nerine Gietel, Executive Coach, Hong Kong

A learning dialogue between two experienced coaches or an experienced and a less experienced coach aimed at exploring issues relating to client cases or the coaches' own development and welfare. An effective peer supervision relationship stimulates deep reflection and productive challenge in both parties.

David Clutterbuck, Mentor

Supervision by an equal or in a group of equals who are not paid to supervise. Peers offer observations and guidance.

Preeta Cooley, Executive Coach, UK

While both professional supervision and peer supervision may cover similar ground, it is nonetheless our belief that peer supervision and professional supervision are distinct from each other. We identify two differentiating factors:

1   Whether or not the individual doing the supervising is appropriately qualified to do so and as a result effectively develop the practitioner's competence, capability and capacity to become a reflective practitioner of their own work.
2   Whether or not the supervision is carried out on a reciprocal basis or money is exchanged for the services.

So why is specific coaching supervision training important?

As we will mention throughout this book, the market for coaching and mentoring is as yet unregulated. There are therefore no hard and fast rules on the profile required to work as a coaching supervisor. However, we are mindful that the interactions of a client relationship are multi-layered. For example, in supervision we can analyze the transaction utilized, we can consider the relationship between client and practitioner and we can explore how the wider system is impacting on both parties. In addition, we must also be cognizant that some of these influences will be in our conscious awareness and some will be unconscious.

As practicing supervisors ourselves, our sense is that without specific supervision training the practitioner delivering supervision will tend to focus on just the client–practitioner intervention. With respect, only the most experienced of practitioners are likely to have a working knowledge of parallel process and be skilled in identifying transference and countertransference issues. Finally, there is a subtlety and nuance among ethical issues that supervisors are trained to identify and consider – their highly specific nature means they are unlikely to have been covered in regular coach or mentor training. With this in mind we dedicate Chapter 9 to the consideration of what types of issues would be most appropriately discussed with a professional and qualified supervisor.

We believe a significant level of supervision specific training (ideally no less than sixty hours) is important and we would concur with Bachkirova, Jackson and Clutterbuck (2011) that the supervisory skill set is different from that of a highly experienced coach. They suggest that colleagues in supervision would need to be skilled in at least the following six areas:

> ... the following areas that are considered important and specific for effective supervision of coaching
> 1. Contracting and issues associated with legal and ethical arrangements of coaching in various contexts
> 2. Models of supervision with underlying theoretical background
> 3. Nature, models and dynamics of one to one relationships in the context of supervision, including issues of power in coaching and supervision
> 4. Models and theories of individual development in different contexts, including development of coaches
> 5. A range of approaches to assessment and evaluation of the coaching process depending on the context and nature of coaching
> 6. Supervision of complex coaching situations including ethical, mental health and diversity related issues.
>
> Bachkirova et al. (2011), p. 233

It is our view that unless the individual delivering supervision can evidence their knowledge in these areas (and we would add "systemic understanding" to this list), we would consider them to be offering "peer" rather than professional supervision.

So why is the reciprocal nature of the relationship important?

The practicalities of exchanging time rather than money and of greater accessibility are of course obvious features of peer supervision. Beyond these practicalities, the mutuality of the relationship impacts on how power is experienced. In 2002 Gillian Proctor wrote a book *The Dynamics of Power in*

Counseling & Psychotherapy, where she makes some important points about how certain roles in our society are afforded a degree of power, regardless of how the individual in that role actually behaves. She identifies that "role power" is bestowed on the therapist, and in our context we would suggest that the role of coaching supervisor is afforded a similar degree of role power. This becomes more concrete when the supervisor is being paid or is being asked to provide a reference for Accreditation or for CPD purposes.

However, with Proctor's assertion in mind, if it is true of the supervisory role then where the supervisory relationship is unidirectional, the person who is providing supervision or in the role of supervisor will have a tacit level of power over the other person. The only means for mitigating in-equality is for the relationship to be reciprocal because the power is bestowed to the role and it cannot be undone by individual behavior. In a reciprocal relationship at the very least the two people will both have power over the other and therefore maintain a sense of balance. Although this carries the risk of collusion in a peer relationship – for example I won't challenge you, if you don't challenge me (for more detail see Chapter 8). Ideally though when two equals come together to work in peer supervision a new kind of power can be created. French (1985) labels this kind of co-created power as the "power-to." It is described as the kind of power that combines the strength of the individual supported by its communities. "Power-to" opportunities are generative for all involved parties.

Some coaching communities organize supervision in a chain. For example, A supervises B; B supervises C; and C supervises A. After a period of working together the chain is shuffled so that people work with a different member of the community. In this arrangement the supervision is not directly reciprocal, although the chain does work on the basis of reciprocity. More has been written about working in these chain arrangements; for example see the toolbox article "To give is to receive" in Coaching at Work (2015).

What peer supervision is not: Some common confusions

Confusions with co-coaching

Many practitioners engage in co-coaching and may take the view that this is the same as peer supervision. Although both share a common developmental intention, there are some distinct differences:

- The primary reason for co-coaching is for the "coach" to hone their coaching techniques through practicing them in a safe environment. For this reason co-coaching triads are a frequently used approach to embed a new approach on training programs. The intervention is not designed for the "client coach" to resolve their issue (although this of course is a useful by-product).

- Co-coaching is often carried out in triads where one person plays the "observer" role and gives feedback to the other parties. In peer supervision there are usually no observers as everyone is encouraged to engage with the supervision issue.
- Co-coaching is often carried out in the context of a networking or community meeting. Often the whole group suggests the approach practiced. Therefore the level of autonomy of all parties is reduced compared to peer supervision where the individual is responsible for determining what they will bring.

Confusions with "coaching the coach"

We recognize that coaches engage with their peers to further develop themselves. Common motivations are:

- Learning how to attract and retain clients
- Seeking acknowledgement from their peers that their work is "OK"
- Gathering different techniques to help extend their coaching capabilities
- Sharing the self-doubt that occurs when building an independent practice or juggling day job and internal coach responsibilities.

As the above list indicates, the practitioner could bring issues from any part of their personal or professional life to work on. This has similar overtones to the normative and restorative element of supervision – as we are helping the practitioner to have good energy with which to work with their clients.

However, the distinct differences to peer supervision are as follows:

- The primary motivation for choosing the coaching topic is the individual's own personal goals. Whereas in peer supervision the motivation for the topic is more specifically linked to what they are noticing is happening (or not happening) between them and their client, or between them and the client environment. The co-coaching environment is often coming from a place of needing peer validation.
- Once the "client coach" achieves some resolution or action, the co-coach is not guided to help the "client coach" link back their insights to the impact on their coaching practice. In peer supervision one would expect that link to be made explicitly.
- The default set of tools and techniques that the practitioner uses is most likely to come from their foundational training, rather than deliberately pulling on coaching supervision models. Should the individual specifically use supervision approaches then under these circumstances the co-coaching would become peer supervision.

Confusions with coach mentoring

The term "mentor coach" is most often associated with the International Coaching Federation (ICF) and their requirement for their members seeking credentialing to have a number of hours with another member who is already credentialed, who they refer to as a "Mentor Coach." This interpretation of the words Mentor Coach is unique to the ICF context and reflects a different role than would normally be implied in mainstream mentoring. In the ICF context the supporting member needs to have a renewed ICF Credential Level of the same or above, though does not need to be a qualified supervisor. Clearly there are similarities here with peer supervision. More specifically though the purpose of this relationship focuses on the current developmental focus of the coach using the ICF core competencies as a reference point. The restorative and normative elements of supervision are excluded in the ICF's definition of the Mentor Coach relationship.

However, this approach has inspired some practitioners to set up peer groups where they use a competency framework to offer feedback on their practice.

An example of developmentally oriented co-coaching triad:

> Prompted by Clare, this triad was created as she sought to work with two other coaches who were skilled at giving objective competency based feedback and where each person perceived the others to be "as good as, or better than me as a coach." Clare knew Diane and Diane introduced her to Bernadette. All three had trained with the same provider, and were in the habit of working in triads. This is their story.
>
> To start with, we agreed that we would work together for an hour per week. We would get straight down to business – no time to waste on chitchat, that was for other meetings. We would decide who would be coach, client and observer. At each meeting we chose a competency to review and reflect on. Before starting the coaching session the coach contracts with the observer for specific feedback on the competency studied. Coach and client would work together for 30–40 minutes, and the remaining time was spent on objective competency-based feedback. We offer and receive evidence-based feedback, using this to reflect on what we did well, hear other's interpretation, notice learning and what we could do differently next time.
>
> How we work together has evolved over time, as we have become more experienced as coaches and in giving feedback. Together we have developed a richer appreciation of the core coaching competencies and consequently deepened our coaching skills.
>
> Over time, we have grown to know each other well, and we have been able to value our differences and ask for input based on each other's areas of expertise, e.g. Transactional Analysis (TA), MBTI, etc. We are now at

the point where we are working with ICF Master Certified Coach (MCC) competencies and all three of us are able to pick up on the unspoken, the slight hesitations and inferences and explore the finer nuances of what was actually taking place, what was said, and what was unsaid. This enables us to truly deepen our self-reflection and development in a safe environment where we can be open about our vulnerabilities. This is a unique opportunity for both personal and professional learning.

We have had so many aha moments since taking this approach. We've discovered that it's about being consciously competent. You might think I wrote that wrong, that being an MCC is about being unconsciously competent, no longer having to think about it. That's partly true, where coaching is so ingrained in us that we can be completely present and instinctively feel what to do or say next. But if we did not reflect on our practice, as many unconsciously competent practitioners in any field may do, we risk missing some great nuggets of learning and development. For us, this is continuous professional development on its best day. We are continuously raising our bar and challenging each other to reach ever-greater coaching proficiency.

That's why we want to share it here. It may sound simple, but it is actually quite profound.

Contributed by Clare Norman, Diane Clutterbuck and Bernadette Cass (May 2017)

As you can see from the case study above, the individuals concerned derive a great deal of benefit from this approach – and it's probably no surprise to hear that they are very experienced coaches already. However, their primary purpose is for the coach to assess their competency as a practitioner. The individual receiving the coaching will get personal development, and over time as the group experiences different ways of working they have an opportunity to debate what "good practice" looks like for them. However, these benefits are by-products. The primary focus is the skill and self-development of the practitioner. Similarly, their clients may subsequently benefit, but their clients are not the focus of their engagement. Interestingly, most supervisors do not actually experience their supervisees delivering coaching and it feels clear from this example that in the context of peer supervision, this could actually be a useful addition.

Confusions with supervision delivered by a non-qualified supervisor

As discussed above in the current market, there are no specific characteristics required to promote you as a Coaching Supervisor and similarly, practitioners are at liberty to choose whichever configuration of supervision suits their circumstances. This creates a "buyer beware" marketplace.

Where practitioners elect to work with a supervisor without coaching supervision specific training, these fellow practitioners may be regarded as "peers." However, where the responsibility lies clearly and unilaterally in the hands of one person within the relationship (particularly where a fee is also charged) – we would regard this as a professional supervision relationship. As discussed above this is because unless the relationship is reciprocal, the power bestowed to the Coaching Supervisor role prevents the sense of equity required for an effective peer supervision relationship. If we were to be pedantic we might argue that in the absence of specific Coaching Supervision training, a more accurate description of these kinds of relationships would be guided reflective practice.

Another potential confusion occurs within organizations. For example an internal coach may be buddied up with another coach with more coaching hours, either from the same or allied organization. In this scenario, the colleague may be perceived as a "peer" and the conversations may include a discussion of client work – this does not in our view create a peer supervision relationship. We would consider this more akin to a mentoring relationship. Unlike peer supervision, this type of buddy relationship will typically be set up for the benefit of the less experienced practitioner. Although the buddy may also find the relationship beneficial, that mutuality was not its original purpose.

There are many different configurations of guided reflective practice – all of which can bring value. If this is something you're interested in, we offer some suggestions in Chapter 2. However, we hope the potential confusions identified here highlight the importance for individuals to be clear about exactly what kind of supervision relationship they are engaging in and the purpose of the supervision.

Impact of geography on peer supervision

In researching this book, we found very little research to support why some markets embrace supervision and others are resistant. In our experience the value of supervision as part of CPD is strongly influenced by the geographical location of the coach, their understanding of "supervision" and/or if supervision is required as part of their training. There may also be a level of market maturity that is needed to appreciate the value of what supervision offers (Lawrence and Whyte, 2014).

Many coaches have a desire to meet face to face and may also have a need for community, regardless of supervision being virtually available. As already mentioned, in some markets, supervision is required for accreditation or to oversee the success of coaching within an organization. In others there may

Table 1.1 Factors influencing the choice of professional supervision vs peer supervision

More likely to opt for professional supervision	More likely to opt for peer supervision
Comfortable with virtual technology	Preference for face to face communication
If working in a mature coaching market and/or years of practicing	Working in a less mature market
Professional supervision adds value and is worth paying for	Limited access to professional supervisors in the locality
	Professional supervision seen as a money-making activity by more experienced coaches

also be a bias that coaching supervision is a moneymaking activity for more experienced coaches, rather than something that adds value. We think these factors influence whether coaches pay for professional supervision and/or do reciprocal work with their peers. See Table 1.1 above.

Impact of context on peer supervision

This book is written to support practitioners regardless of the context in which they work. Around the world, human resources and organization managers receive coach training to either specifically coach others as clients or use coaching communication skills as leaders. The trained internal coach is often holding multiple relationships with their colleagues or staff. We believe supervision is uniquely positioned from which to view ethical dilemmas, practitioner blind spots, collusion and bias.

Internal coaches also have more opportunity than most independent practitioners for seeking the counsel of their peers on an informal basis. Some of the processes in the book may be useful to peer supervision groups; however, we would more likely suggest professional supervision instead given the particularly complex landscape. This is covered in more detail in Chapter 9. Also Katherine St John Brooks (St John Brooks, 2014) has written a book *Internal Coaching*, which offers a pragmatic view of the complex world of internal coaching pools.

The status of peer supervision for accreditation purposes

The various professional bodies differ regarding how explicit they are about the required characteristics of the supervisor engaged to provide a supervision report as part of the accreditation process. As each professional body's requirements vary and can be updated, we suggest checking in with your professional body before making a choice to use peer supervision for accreditation.

Peer supervision in practice

In writing this book we have enquired what draws people to seek out peers for supervision, either as their primary source of supervision or as part of a blend. From those discussions we have discovered that peer supervision is most often utilized for one of the following reasons:

- Cost: This is a frequently cited reason for choosing peer over professional supervision. Often the exchange is a reciprocal one, so the only "cost" to the practitioner is that of time. This can be a practical reality for independent practitioners who are just setting up their business, those with mainly pro bono clients, or those where coaching forms the minority of what they do. Similarly cost is also a consideration for organizations. Often there has been an increase in internal coaching programs but budgets haven't stretched to externally facilitated supervision. Where there is limited or no provision of professional supervision the solution is often peer group supervision.
- Confidence: The label "supervision" is frequently lamented as having managerial overtones and due to the mandatory nature in some professions or Professional Bodies, can have appraisal overtones to it. Therefore those individuals who are still developing their self-confidence as a coaching practitioner may be reluctant to open their work to inspection to someone who clearly has more experience than themselves. These individuals may feel more comfortable and able to talk openly about their struggles with a colleague who is at a similar developmental level and who they anticipate is experiencing similar challenges around self-doubt.
- Shame: As mentioned above, professional supervision will tend to have a power imbalance. Interestingly many practitioners believe that supervision is primarily about bringing the "mistakes" we have made (although we see it as an opportunity to bring your successes too). This requires a certain degree of comfort with our own vulnerability. This is more likely to be achieved where the perception is that both parties will bring their blind spots. A professional supervision relationship may feel unequal given only the supervisee is called upon to expose their vulnerabilities.
- Convenience: The number of qualified supervisors available continues to grow and so too does the number of coaches and mentors across the globe. In addition there is the question of "just in time" support. Therefore, when something occurs in our work that warrants immediate exploration and

reflection, a peer is often a simple logistical choice of who is available, when and where.
- Confidentiality: In some markets, coaching and mentoring are niche activities and the competition is high for the work available. Seeking professional supervision from someone outside of their own organization could be commercially risky, due to the nature of their business. For example, practitioners in Brazil infer that it would be a challenge to believe that con-fidentiality would be honored if they do not know the supervisor personally. Under these circumstances practitioners elect for peer supervision within their own consultancies instead.
- Sense-checking: Most professional supervision relationships tend to be session based, organized to a particular rhythm and in advance. However, sometimes a practitioner needs help to articulate what is bothering them. In these cases, an informal conversation can be a handy method for sifting out what will naturally fall into place and what represents a bigger question, compared to what warrants a professional supervision session.
- Study and/or skills-enhancement: Both during training and upon completion of training, peer groups are often formed to foster a safe place to advance their development. These alumni groups often fulfill the three purposes of supervision. For example they often continue to practice particular techniques (developmental); they might share their struggles and successes of building their coaching practice (restorative); and they are likely to chew over questions of how they apply the ethical code in the real world (normative).

The rewards of routinely engaging with peer supervision

From the individual practitioner perspective, we see peer supervision as a fundamental part of becoming a reflective practitioner and we explore this more in Chapter 2. Additionally, when we consider our global communities of practice, peer supervision can serve to accelerate both their professional development and membership growth. A primary inspiration for this book is the experience of the ICF NZ Northern Branch, as illustrated by the comment below. We hope this book serves to inspire other communities of practice around the globe to do likewise.

> During my three year term as president, I've been thrilled to see the positive impact that peer supervision is having in NZ. It feels we have established credibility, professionalism and appreciation within our coaching community. Having peer supervision is essential and highly beneficial for enhancing coaches' practice. This has been further endorsed through recent feedback highlighting that some coaches

> are now joining ICF with the main drive and purpose to get access to a peer supervision group.
>
> Alyson Keller, Immediate Past President ICF NZN

Some words of caution

Within the *Standards Australia Handbook*, "Coaching in Organisations," some interesting points are raised about the benefits and limitations of peer supervision. See Table 1.2 below.

The point made about the experience level of the practitioners concerned in the *Standards Australia Handbook* is echoed by Bachkirova *et al.* (2011, p. 232), who suggests that those involved in peer supervision should be experienced coaches and should not be used for novices as this could create a false sense of security. However, we do not entirely agree. The issue has less to do with experience levels and more to do with the rigor with which peers approach their supervision together. It is our precise intention with this book to offer that rigor in an accessible way to ensure that when peer supervision is carried out, it is carried out well. Nonetheless, within Europe the default assumption among organizations purchasing executive coaching services is that professional supervision would be expected. Therefore those engaging only in peer supervision need to be aware that certain stakeholder groups will see this form of supervision as less prestigious.

There are definitely some pitfalls associated when working as peers in supervision – and we can anticipate most of them. Indeed we devote an entire chapter (Chapter 8) to this topic and offer you a "heads up" on what they are and how to manage them.

Table 1.2 Excerpt from *Standards Australia Handbook*

Benefits of peer supervision	In peer supervision, two or more coaches seek to assist each other in reflecting on their practice including both case specific and coach specific reflection. The broad aims of peer supervision are similar to those found in one to one supervision. However, peer supervision is most effective when coaches are able to bring a variety of perspectives to the supervision. Hence it is more suited to experienced coaches than coaches starting out in their careers.
Limits of peer supervision	When the experience of the participating coaches is limited, the quality of peer supervision can be poor. Even when experienced coaches are involved, peer supervision needs to be well structured and disciplined to be effective. Peer supervision can suffer from extraneous commercial considerations and a reticence to discuss personal issues among one's peers.

Source: Standards Australia (2011), p. 63.

Both these references seem to infer that peer supervision will be carried out in isolation. Conversely, we hope this book will help practitioners understand the exponential benefit they will derive when they find the combination of peer supervision and professional supervision that works for their particular practice.

Final thoughts

Peers have for decades supported each other in their development of skills and understanding, especially in counseling and teaching. Coaching supervision has not grown at the same rate as the increase in coaching and mentoring. Therefore as Bachkirova *et al.* (2011, p. 230) said: "Peer or peer–group supervision is becoming a popular mode of supervision in coaching communities. This is a sign of the increasing awareness of coaches of the value and importance of continuing professional development."

In our definition, we suggest that it is the reciprocal nature of the peer supervision relationship that helps creates a constructive learning environment. We maintain the quality of peer supervision is dependent on the rigor of the individuals involved. The purpose of this book is not to provide practitioners with a comprehensive education enabling them to deliver professional supervision or to replace professional supervision training. We are also not excluding the possibility of both peer and professional supervision as complimentary CPD options. Our hope is to predominantly offer guidance on how to work effectively and rigorously as peers in the absence of a deep underpinning knowledge of coaching supervision.

Key learning points

1 Peer supervision in a coaching or mentoring context is a self-managed learning environment where supervision approaches are used to discuss issues and whose resolution is of mutual benefit to the practitioners, their clients and the wider context.
2 Peers should be considered equals and their relationship is of a reciprocal nature. This, and the fact that no money is exchanged, differentiates peer supervision from professional supervision.
3 Professional supervision is unidirectional, paid and provided by someone purposely selected to work with the entire client system. Currently there are no specific industry standards for compulsory coaching supervision training, and we recommend a certain number of supervision training hours to provide the appropriate kind of support.

4   Peer supervision should be carried out with rigor, including regular reviews in order to be successful. A combination of peer and professional supervision can be advisable to cover a broader range of issues.

References

Bachkirova, T., Stevens, P. and Willis, P. (2005) *Coaching Supervision*. Oxford: Oxford Brookes Coaching & Mentoring Society.

Bachkirova, T., Jackson, P. and Clutterbuck, D. (2011) Peer supervision for coaching and mentoring. In: T. Bachkirova, P. Jackson and D. Clutterbuck (eds), *Coaching & Mentoring Supervision: Theory and practice*. Maidenhead, UK: McGraw-Hill, Ch. 18.

Bellersen, M. and Kohlmann, I. (2016) *Intervision. Dialogue methods in Action Learning*. [online] www.vakmedianetshop.nl/wp-content/uploads/2016/06/Intervision_Preview.pdf [accessed 8 September 2017].

Coaching at Work (2015) To give is to receive. *Coaching at Work*, 10(2), pp. 47–49.

Epprecht, C. (2011) "Intervision": A group-based peer-supervision project by EMCC Switzerland. In: T. Bachkirova, P. Jackson and D. Clutterbuck (eds), *Coaching & Mentoring Supervision: Theory and practice*. Maidenhead, UK: McGraw-Hill, Ch. 22.

French, M. (1985) *Beyond Power: On women, men and morals*. London: Jonathan Cape.

Hawkins, P. and Smith, N. (2006) *Coaching, Mentoring and Organizational Consultancy: Supervision and development*. Maidenhead, UK: Open University Press.

Hodge, A. (2016) The value of coaching supervision as a development process: Contribution to continued professional and personal wellbeing for executive coaches. *The International Journal of Evidence Based Coaching and Mentoring*, 14(2), pp. 87–106.

Inskipp, F. and Proctor, B. (1993) *The Art, Craft & Tasks of Counseling Supervision, Part 1: Making the most of supervision*. Twickenham, UK: Cascade.

Kline, N. (1999) *Time to Think: Listening to ignite the human mind*. London: Ward Lock.

Lawrence, P. and Whyte, A. (2014). What is coaching supervision and is it important? *Coaching: An International Journal of Theory, Research and Practice*. 7(1), pp. 1–6.

Lucas, M. (2015) *What's so Super about Supervision?* Association for Coaching: Member to Member Guide.

OCM *Mentoring supervision: What is it and why should organizations invest?* [online] www.theocm.co.uk/case-studies/mentoring-supervision-what-it-and-why-should-organisations-invest [accessed 19 September 2017].

Proctor, B. (1986) Supervision: A co-operative exercise in accountability. In M. Marken and M. Payne (eds), *Enabling and Ensuring*. Leicester, UK: Leicester National Youth Bureau and Council for Education and Training in Youth and Community Work.

Proctor, G. (2002). *The Dynamics of Power in Counseling and Psychotherapy: Ethics, politics and practice* (6th edn). Ross-on-Wye, UK: PCCS.

St John Brooks, K. (2014) *Internal Coaching: The inside story*. London: Karnac.

Standards Australia (2011) *HB 332–2011 Coaching in Organizations*. Sydney, Australia: SAI Global.

Understanding reflective practice

2

Definition: For practitioners where reflective practice is part of accreditation or who are from a helping profession background such as counseling, the concept of reflective practice is familiar (and in some circles may draw a collective yawn). For those who are unfamiliar with the concept, the *Oxford Dictionary* describes reflective practice as "the process of retrospectively examining one's own professional performance in order to clarify the reasons for one's actions and decisions, and to learn from them." We define reflective practice as "the ability to step away from your work and identify patterns, habits, strengths and limitations in your work and/or within the system you work in and is the foundation of supervision."

What we mean by reflective practice

The bulk of this book focuses on what peer supervision is and how you navigate the complexities to do peer supervision well. However, this chapter is unique because it focuses on the symbiosis of reflective practice with supervision, as peer supervision is an activity that should not be seen in isolation – it is part of a much bigger landscape of reflective practice. Of course reflective practice does not exist in isolation either. In fact we suggest that sharing your reflective practice with others can provide a meaningful and engaging way to better understand yourself and your preferences. We believe through both reflective practice and supervision, you will develop your own internal compass, which can guide you to increasing mastery over time.

Carrol and Gilbert (2011) referred to reflection as gaining a new and perhaps different perspective after having stepped back from one's coaching. The benefit of reflective practice is to "have the capability to reflect critically and systematically on the work-self interface . . . fostering a personal awareness and resilience" (Gillmer and Marckus, 2003, p. 23). In our opinion, this ongoing commitment to self-understanding and the impact to the way in which we work is what creates mastery.

There is a tension between the professional bodies regarding how reflective practice is perceived. In the European bodies, it is embraced as part of adult learning. In the more global bodies there is hesitancy that reflective practice could draw the practitioner into a more psychological or therapeutic endeavor. Staying clear of the potential politics this can invoke, we offer our personal experience of how reflective practice can be a generative experience. We notice that practitioners who engage in continuous improvement through reflective practice and supervision, have an ambition to work towards mastery and to have a bit of fun along the way too!

In this spirit, this chapter explores how to make reflective practice a foundational cornerstone of your consistent development. We start this chapter by considering what it means to be a masterful practitioner. We then introduce you to the three Cs (Competency, Capability and Capacity, Broussine (1998)) and draw your attention to how peer and professional supervision can support you to develop your capacity. However, an essential ingredient to supervision of any kind is the practitioner's ability to engage in reflection both independently and with others. We share with you how you might develop mindful reflection, from reviewing what has happened through to adjusting how you are in the moment with your client. We hope this chapter helps you design an approach to reflective practice that works for you and which resources you as you navigate your path to mastery.

What does it mean to be a masterful practitioner?

Becoming a masterful practitioner may feel daunting, especially if you're new to the industry. It can be tricky because industry standards, practices and modes are not uniform. The way in which we work is eclectic and complex, and as diverse as the people who engage in the work. In general, the professional bodies define master coaching as the demonstration of a consistent application of skills, a minimum number of coaching client hours and training over time. Using a competency-based approach is easier to define and teach core skills and to measure progress. However, each professional body has its own competency framework and most universities worldwide do not subscribe to the narrow professional bodies' standards and believe the *"reliance on competency frameworks oversimplifies coaching practice and expertise."* (Bachkirova and Lawton Smith, 2015, p. 128).

One of the first attempts to amalgamate industry standards was the Standards Australia HB 332–2011: Coaching in Organizations (2011). An industry first, a committee of thirty-five organizations involved in educating, purchasing and delivering organizational coaching outlined the necessary processes for reflective practice and quality assurance. To meet the needs of clients in a complex world, "the discipline of reflection upon, and application of, experience and knowledge that gives coaching its potency" (Standards Australia, p. 47).

In 2016, the Association for Coaching (AC), International Coach Federation (ICF) UK and the European Mentoring and Coaching Council (EMCC) UK formed a joint position in their article "Becoming a Professional Coach: The Development Path": "Following training it is essential for individuals to continue to develop their competence through practical experience, further learning (Continuous Professional Development (CPD)) and reflective practice. These are the elements required to become accredited or credentialed by one of our independent professional bodies" (AC, ICF and EMCC, 2016).

Although this may be a pragmatic way to evidence proficiency, in our opinion, the underpinning quality of what makes coaching masterful seems to be missing. This simplistic metric misses out on the essence of mastery, the quality that somehow the session seems suspended in time; the client and coach seem in synch with each other in an unspoken partnership and the unspoken partnership where together they co-create the conversation. In our opinion, this pinnacle of coaching practice requires the coach to be fully present in the partnership. Although skills training, accreditation or credentialing are imperative for initial development, we believe that to have consistent resourcefulness it may take many years and types of development and the ability to reflect objectively on yourself and your work. So how do you start?

Mastery: The three Cs

Instead of relying exclusively on the professional body's requirements, we have found the three Cs pathways particularly useful to examine your development in more detail. Mike Broussine (1998) originally authored this concept for management development. It has since been referred to and built on by many current authors in the coaching and mentoring fields. Before we go into how this might apply to Coaching and Mentoring, let us look at a more universal example, "Learning to Drive" to illustrate how the three Cs might work.

Competency – knowing the road rules, passing your test and receiving your license
Capability – demonstrating the skill and having the confidence to drive solo on known and unknown routes in a range of conditions accident free

Capacity – having the wisdom to know how long you can personally be behind the wheel before you need to take a rest to keep safe.

Now let's look at how the three Cs might show up in coaching and mentoring.

Competency is having both basic knowledge and ability to complete the job at hand. Universally the professional bodies measure "what good looks like" using a competency-based framework (albeit different competencies!). In other words, do you have the necessary skills to be a competent practitioner? Developing competency can come in the form of training, skills-based workshops, co-coaching and/or feedback on skills application.

Capability measures the ability of the practitioner to consistently apply the skills of coaching, adapt to what is needed in the moment and stay solidly grounded in the relational space co-created between themselves and their client. Developing capability is best achieved through tailored individual support – for example with a mentor, Mentor Coach, co-coaching or in supervision with peers and a qualified supervisor.

Capacity is the emotional intelligence to nimbly move between the functional and the relational of what is required in the moment to co-create the outcomes desired with their clients. Having capacity leads to enhanced coaching presence and fluidity, as evidenced by the master coaching qualifications by the professional bodies. While defining and measuring capacity may be a bit challenging, the route to developing it comes from reflecting deeply and honestly about our work and ourselves. Useful activities to develop capacity are ongoing reflective practice, mindfulness, as well as peer and professional supervision.

The quest for learning can be exhilarating and options endless, though the result can be reactive – signing up for an exciting-sounding conference, the next level of course or joining a peer group predominately because the invitation has been extended, rather than being well considered. Instead what we recommend is deliberate consideration to competency, capability and capacity aspects as part of your development plan. Of course, some of these choices may be beneficial while others, which sound great, may not be the best use of your time or money. So how can you be more targeted in your approach to your professional development? Here we offer some suggestions about how learning opportunities might slot in under the three Cs headings mentioned above (see Table 2.1).

As the table illustrates, there are many more routes to develop competency and capability, which are important for skills development, whereas developing capacity requires ongoing individual reflective practice. Developing our Competency, Capability and Capacity and reaching the summit of mastery requires both a sense of direction and dedication. At times independent reflection can be tough going – you can see something, but you also know that there is more that you can't quite see. We believe that the quest toward mastery is best done with others who can extend our insights, foster new ways of thinking and

Table 2.1 Mapping CPD to the three Cs framework

	Competency	Capability	Capacity
Formal training, qualifications and/or certifications	✗		
Continuing education and skills enhancement	✗	Potentially	
Research, peer literature review and teaching	✗		
Business coaching and/or mentoring	✗	✗	
Individual, group and/or co-coaching or mentoring	✗	✗	Potentially
Mentor coaching (for an ICF credentialing) and supervision for accreditation	✗	✗	Potentially
Peer supervision and reflective practice	✗	✗	Potentially
Professional supervision and reflective practice	✗	✗	✗

applaud our efforts along the way. It is for this reason that we engage with supervision as part of reflective practice. We agree with Carrol and Gilbert that "supervision is a form of conversation that facilitates learning." Supervision provides:

- A forum for reflection
- A forum for accountability
- A focus on experiential learning
- The enhanced understanding of ourselves in the context of our work.

(Adapted from Carrol and Gilbert, 2005)

Both peer supervision and professional supervision help you build your competency, capability and capacity. By bringing material where you have your own insights to a wider audience, typically greater insight is achieved.

Including peer supervision in your reflective practice

Given its "power to reflect on practice together, and peers share vulnerability and support in equal measure" (Chapter 1), peer supervision could potentially provide you with the opportunity to develop all three Cs and enhance your reflective practice. Because of the reciprocal and experiential nature of peer supervision, finding the right people and being clear about what you want from your time investment is also important. Determining whether individual or group forums are a better learning environment for your reflection is the next step.

Including professional supervision in your reflective practice

As we defined in Chapter 1, *professional supervision* is a reflective learning environment where the supervisor is hired by the practitioner(s) and is specifically qualified to look at the entire system in which the work is being undertaken. Although the reflective space is co-created, the professional supervisor is purposefully of service to the supervisee, their clients and the wider system. What is significant is that the supervisor's intention is to develop the practitioner's competence, capability and capacity to become a reflective practitioner of their own work. We suggest having professional supervision as part of your ongoing development because the professional supervisor is purposefully qualified to develop the practitioner's competence, capability and capacity to become a reflective practitioner of their own work. Choosing a professional supervisor to deepen your reflective practice is important, and we suggest reading Chapter 9 for more information.

Reflective practice is our individual responsibility and it may be enhanced through others; however, we are not passive recipients of supervision. Becoming a reflective practitioner maximizes the value of peer and professional supervision.

Becoming a reflective practitioner

Developing "the ability to step away from your work and identify patterns, habits, strengths and limitations in your work and/or within the system you work in" we believe can be achieved by engaging in reflective practice and is paramount to any form of supervision. Yet how do you become a reflective practitioner?

The work of Schön (1983) is helpful in this regard. He distinguishes between "reflection on action" and "reflection in action." The first is where we look back on what has happened and is what is most commonly understood by the term "reflection." There are many ways of reflecting on action – typically all variations of journaling and we list them below. Reflection in action is harder to achieve. The latter is where you are working with two streams of attention simultaneously, when you reflect and evaluate what is happening as it is happening with sufficient fluidity that you can re-calibrate what you are doing in the moment. Reflection in action is, in our opinion, not possible until you are practiced at reflecting on action. Only when you know your habits and patterns, triggers and responses will you have sufficient awareness to adjust your work in the moment. So let's start by looking at how you might develop your reflection on action.

Developing "reflection on action"

As a practitioner, you probably are already doing reflective practice – even if you don't call it this. After the client session, you think about what worked and what didn't, you think about options for next time and practice your new idea next time around. One way of developing this skill is to follow the model outlined by Gibbs (1988).

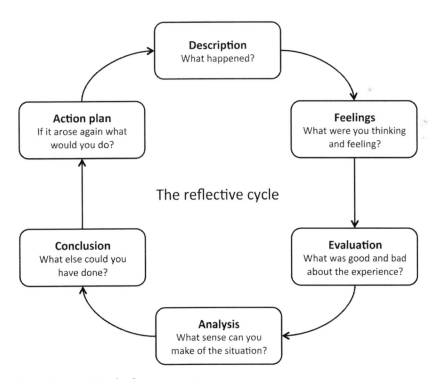

Figure 2.1 Model of reflective practice

Gibbs, 1988

Creating a reflective habit

Finding ways of embedding this reflective cycle in the way you work is a solid first step to developing your reflective habit. This can be tougher than expected. For example, we might intend to reflect immediately after each client session, we might even allocate specific time for it. However, when the session over-runs, when an important piece of work takes priority or we simply need more time to digest what happened – the window for reflection dissipates. With persistence you will come to find time slots that work for you more often than not. For example, one of us uses her train journey at the end of the day to reflect on recent client sessions. Another carves out time to walk with the specific purpose of noticing patterns within her entire client portfolio. Once you regularly find space to reflect, you can start work on deepening your reflections.

Independent reflection

The most common way in which people capture their reflections is through note taking and journaling. Often professional bodies have guidelines about what could be captured in notes and/or may be useful to reflect upon for accreditation, which may be a place to start. Sample questions include:

- What was the session about?
- How well did we work together?
- What interventions were used (models, techniques, competencies, tools, etc.)?
- How did I establish the session outcome and keep the client focused on it?
- What worked?
- Didn't work?
- What do I want to explore next time?

These questions focus upon the practitioner, client and/or intervention. They are often useful in the earlier stages of development, individual recording and/or for preparation for co-coaching and peer supervision sessions. Please see Appendices for forms and further examples.

Reflecting on what's happening in the session

Once you are more familiar with your work, the interventions you used successfully and frequently are ready for expansion; you are ready to ask questions that delve more into the psychology behind what is showing up in the session. Some examples include:

- What am I thinking about while the client is speaking?
- What emotions come up for me when I think about the client?
- What assumptions am I making about them? Their situation? The others in their environment (boss, co-workers, children, partner/spouse, etc.)?
- What might aid or prevent me from doing great work with this client?
- What are the client's values and beliefs, which I think drive their behavior?
- How does the client feel about their circumstances, choices and/or changes they're going through?
- What patterns and/or blockers am I noticing in this engagement?

Reflecting on the interactions and the wider system

Once you've become a more experienced practitioner, your reflection can extend to include what is happening in the dynamic between us, the dynamic between the client and others, the system in which we're working. This is what Peter Bluckert termed psychological mindedness, which encompasses the practitioner's "capacity to reflect on themselves, others, and the relationship between" (Bluckert, 2006, p. 87). Questions for consideration (Cooper, 2017):

- What's the dynamic between us? What's the dynamic between the client sponsor and me? The client sponsor and the client?
- What's the impact of the system on the client?
- What political, social, familial, cultural and/or environmental impacts exist that may have a bearing on the client and/or the system? How does the client and/or their environment affect me?
- What feelings, thoughts and/or assumptions do I have about the client and their environment?
- Who are the key stakeholders in this environment? What is the interaction between them and the client? With others?
- What is my intuition saying?
- How do I notice myself differently in this system compared to others?

Alternative reflective techniques

Remember, written reflective techniques are much more varied than simply journaling your thoughts. For example your written work does not need to be done in a narrative style – you could use mind-mapping techniques for this purpose. If you are an auditory learner then try speaking into a device and bring your reflections to your peer supervision meetings. Similarly if you are an extroverted thinker, this may appeal, or perhaps pair up with another coach and "tell them" what's going through your mind (there is no need for them to comment). Some people prefer to walk and think about their work as part of their reflective practice. Others may choose to put clients, their clients key stakeholders, their issues and/or goals on post-it notes and move them around on a piece of paper or white board. The creative aspects are endless!

Experiential writing

Some people find simply picking up a pencil or, in the case of one of our authors – colored pens – hand writing their experience of themselves helps their reflective process. As a passionate advocate of experiential writing, Jackee Holder suggests that reflective writing interrupts the rational and logical thinking, sometimes taking us to unexpected places. Her "Labyrinth" writing tool (Holder, 2013) is a useful way to approach gaining more insights. She suggests using two copies of her "Labyrinth" template: One labeled "writing in" and the other labeled "writing out" (see Appendix 2.5).

1. You begin the process with the 'writing in' template starting at the entrance to the maze and writing along the pathways with all of the details about the issue to reflect upon, including your thoughts about writing about the issue itself as well as your feelings. Write to get as far as you can along the paths to the center. When you have exhausted your writing, take your pencil and trace a line to the center of the maze.
2. Now take another copy of the "Labyrinth" labeled "writing out," but this time start at the center and write your thoughts and solutions in the pathways. When you have exhausted your thinking, take a pencil and draw a line to the entrance.
3. Stand back and look at what you have got. What new awareness have you gained from your reflection?

This process of thinking combined with writing about your issue will expand your options and offer you new and perhaps hidden solutions. The act of writing releases unconscious thoughts. Completing the process with a pencil line can give us the satisfaction of finishing something and the ability to move on. The second round starting with the end in mind helps us to focus on completion and uses solution focused thinking. Together, employing two different approaches to the same issue yields different results.

Committing to ongoing reflection on action is a generative process. The ideas above are by no means exhaustive. Whatever technique you use, you will tend to uncover more information about what was happening in the moment than you were aware of at the time. This gives you more choices. When you next face a similar situation you are primed with more options than before. Importantly when you reflect routinely on your practice you begin to see themes and patterns. For example, what is most likely to cause resistance in you? What is most likely to draw you away from a non-directive mode?

Reflecting with others

Using co-coaching and/or peer mentoring

As examined in Chapter 1, co-coaching is a peer action learning activity that often happens in triads with a coach, client and observer for the purpose of feedback. Strictly speaking co-coaching is not defined as reflective practice. For many practitioners however, it is the first exposure to reflecting with others. The rotation of roles allows us a unique collegiate environment in which to review our work with others. Typically it will focus on the development of a particular technique or when used for credentialing purposes for feedback against the core competencies.

A common way of structuring the feedback is to ask the coach to evaluate what they did well and what they would like to do better. The client then offers how they experienced the work of the coach and lastly the observer brings in additional perspectives perhaps responding to what has already been raised along with any new information. Where group members are skilled at giving feedback, sharing specific examples of strengths and/or development areas, you may find this also grows your ability to reflect on action. However, if you only receive feedback that you're a "good coach" and/or the group is unable to see alternative ways of working, then engaging a professional coach mentor or supervisor may be a better option.

While co-coaching is of value, it is different from the peer supervision approach outlined in this book. Before you can make good use of peer or professional supervision you need to take control of what you want to use the supervision for. This will take some preparation, which typically starts with independent reflection. Many people prefer to write their reflections in advance of a supervision meeting and as identified above you have many different approaches to choose from. However, the importance of the approach isn't as important as the quality of the exploration. A common frustration as we travel towards mastery is that we routinely don't know what we don't know! This is where

	Known to self	Not known to self
Known to others	1. Arena	2. Blind spot
Not known to others	2. Façade	4. Unknown

Figure 2.2 Johari window

Modified from Luft and Ingham (1955)

reflecting with others can accelerate our independent reflection by identifying blind spots, patterns of behavior and strengths that can be enhanced.

Using the Johari window for reflective practice

So how do you determine what those strengths and development areas are? If you are familiar with the Johari window (Luft and Ingham, 1955) in Figure 2.2, it provides a useful framework to consider how you might grow the range of your reflective practice.

With the Johari window, the overall goal is to increase the size of quadrant 1: Arena. Information that rests in the Arena is both known to yourself and to others, and so is available for discussion. Logically, the bigger the Arena the more data you have to work with and the more masterful you become in both your reflective practice and in your client work.

Helpfully, by reflecting on your work during peer and professional supervision, others may see things that we do not. This gives us information that may have previously been located in quadrant 2: Blind spot. It is through the safety of supervision and recognizing the value of feedback from others that information moves out of the Blind Spot and into the Arena. When we receive feedback and it matches our self-perception it affirms our sense of self. We are likely to integrate it into our current understanding of how we work. Our understanding becomes richer and more nuanced as a result. Where feedback differs either in whole or in part, it brings an invitation to reflect on those differences. We are at liberty to decide what we take on board and what we will put to one side perhaps for future consideration. As our supervision relationships evolve, the braver we become to reflect more deeply about ourselves. We develop courage to share more about the parts of our self, which initially we had kept hidden. This enables the information in quadrant 3: Façade to move into the Arena and it becomes discussable. The more we share, the more we receive feedback. Additionally, this is a two-way process. The more skilled and courageous peers become at giving feedback, they too grow from the experience and so everyone involved in the process can flourish.

As its name implies, there is an illusive nature to quadrant 4: Unknown. It relates to information that lies outside of our conscious awareness, perhaps a "super blind spot." Consequently, information that resides here does not often appear in either individual reflective practice or peer supervision. However, we do sometimes get glimpses into it through professional supervision. For example, parallel process or transference and countertransference experienced through working with our clients may also hold information about ourselves. Working with a qualified supervisor in professional supervision can help you receive useful and new information to understand how you might move information out of the Unknown into Quadrant 1: Arena.

Developing "reflection in action"

As mentioned above, reflection in action is a natural progression from reflection on action. By following the guidance so far we would hope that you have developed an increased awareness of your habits and preferences, your triggers and responses, as well as what is still ongoing personal development for you, and which may influence your client work. The next step is to develop your awareness in the moment, and the practice of mindfulness is useful in this regard.

Using mindfulness

Mindfulness can help assist you in raising your awareness of what is going on for you in your internal processes. The practice grew out of the work done by Jon Kabat-Zinn, in developing mindfulness-based stress reduction programs (Kabat-Zinn, 1990). It is a way of being, and helps us recognize what is going on in the moment. Singh (2010) offers the following definition: "Mindfulness is a moment-to-moment awareness. It is cultivated by purposefully paying attention to things we ordinarily never give a moment's thought to. It is a systematic approach to developing new kinds of control and wisdom in our lives, based on our inner capacities for relaxation, paying attention, awareness and insight." Mindfulness practice can enhance all aspects of your life. If you are interested to know more, the book *Mindfulness* (Williams and Penman, 2014) gives a step-by-step eight-week process.

Working in the moment

When you are practiced at mindfulness you will have an understanding of how your default presence manifests. For example: How do you show up in your client work when you have good capacity and are poised to do your best work? When you add to that a catalogue of prior learning, you have at your disposal information about what might signal that you are moving away from your default presence. Over time you learn how to pay attention to the client dialogue and to pay attention to your shifting sense of self. Initially that experience is unlikely to be fully understood in the session. It is, however, great material to bring to supervision for further exploration.

With experience, mindful reflection provides information that offers you more choices in the moment. When you understand what you are experiencing more fully, you are more likely to have the confidence to articulate your experience during the session and in a way that is in service of your client. Finally when you are able to do this fluidly, seamlessly using mindful reflection to fine-tune your actions, we believe you are working at a level of mastery. The EMCC defines this as follows:

> *Reflects and has conscious access to their client interactions and coaching.*
> EMCC Competency Framework 2015,
> Understanding Self at Master Level

The parallels here with our practitioner work are that we will only achieve mastery if we reflect on and share our growing experience and learn from them. Dedication to this continuous improvement process generates greater resourcefulness the next time something similar happens. The culmination of experience, stemming from the constant iteration of action, reflection (individual, peer and professional supervision) and learning leading to different action, is the kind of reflective practice that leads toward mastery. However, this masterful reflection on action is not an indication that your reflective practice development days are over. Quite the contrary! As we become more masterful we are likely to take on more complex and challenging assignments and so the continuous cycle of learning continues.

Final thoughts

Through this chapter we hope that we have helped you think broadly about your journey towards mastery. Coaching competency and capability plus a catalogue of hours is often the measure of success used by the professional bodies. However, in our experience, it is the various forms of reflective practice that help you develop your artistry and your unique signature as a practitioner. Working in an unregulated market means neither peer nor professional supervision will be required. Reflective practice is not therefore about ticking a box. It is about facilitating a deeper understanding of how we each work. More than that it builds your competency, capability and capacity in equal measure, which will sustain your career for the longer term. We hope this chapter has brought the notion of reflective practice to life – it involves independent reflection and includes peer and professional supervision. When you notice you are able to work fluidly and re-calibrate your work in the moment, you will know you have reached the pinnacle of mindful reflectiveness. Together this forms part of a considered CPD strategy illustrating the professionalism we all need to be at the top of our game. Over time, it will benefit you as a practitioner, on your journey towards mastery and importantly it puts you in the strongest place possible to empower your clients to do likewise.

Key learning points

1 Supervision and reflective practice, an ongoing commitment to self-understanding, both develop an internal personal compass that guides to increasing mastery.
2 Pathways to examine your personal development and reach the summit of mastery are the three Cs:
    - Competency: The skill to be a competent practitioner, developed through training etc.
    - Capability: The ability to apply and adapt those skills, achieved through individual support
    - Capacity: The emotional intelligence to move between the functional and relational requirements of a coaching engagement, developed through reflective practice and/or supervision.
3 Reflective practice is our individual responsibility and maximizes the value of peer and professional supervision. Done routinely, it helps to identify themes and patterns of behavior.
4 Schön (1983) distinguishes between reflection on and in action. Reflection on action is when we look in hindsight at what has happened and why, often through various forms of note taking, journaling, experiential writing, co-coaching, supervision or via tools like the Johari Window. The more complex reflection in action is a natural progression from reflection on action where we reflect and adjust our behavior in the moment it is happening. Reflection in action can be enhanced through mindfulness as it raises awareness to inner processes.

References

AC (2016) Developing your Coaching through Reflective Practice [pdf]. Available from: http://c.ymcdn.com/sites/associationforcoaching.site-ym.com/resource/resmgr/Articles_&_Handy_Guides/Coaches/Handy_Guides/ac_member_to_member_-__refle.pdf [accessed 1 September 2017].

AC and EMCC (2016) Global Code of Ethics for Coaches and Mentors [pdf]. Available from: https://actoonline.org/wp-content/uploads/2016/10/Global-Code-of-Ethics_2016.pdf [accessed 1 May 2017].

AC, ICF and EMCC (2016) Becoming a Professional Coach: The Development Path [pdf]. Available from: www.coachfederation.org.uk/wp-content/uploads/2015/07/The-Development-Path.pdf [accessed 12 August 2017].

Bachkirova, T. and Lawton Smith, C. (2015) From competencies to capabilities in the assessment and accreditation of coaches. *International Journal of Evidence Based Coaching and Mentoring*, 13(2), p. 123.

Bluckert, P. (2006) *Psychological Dimensions of Executive Coaching*. Berkshire, UK: Open University.

Broussine, M. (1998) *The Society of Local Authority Chief Executives and Senior Managers (SOLACE): A scheme for continuous learning for SOLACE members*. Bristol, UK: University of the West of England.

Carrol, M. and Gilbert, M.C. (2011) *On Being a Supervisee: Creating learning partnerships* (2nd edn). Kew, Australia: PsychOz.

Cooper, L. (2017) Developing your coaching through reflective practice. *Association for Coaching: Member to Member*, CS1/052015, pp. 1–3.

EMCC (2015) EMCC competence Framework v2 [pdf]. Available from: www.emccouncil.org/webimages/EU/EIA/emcc-competence-framework-v2.pdf [accessed 20 August 2017].

Gibbs, G. (1988) *Learning by Doing*. Oxford: Oxford Polytechnic.

Gillmer, B. and Marckus, R. (2003) Personal professional development in clinical psychology training: Surveying reflective practice. *Clinical Psychology*, 27, pp. 20–23.

Holder, J. (2013) *49 Ways to Write Yourself Well: The science and wisdom of writing and journaling*. Brighton, UK: Stepbeach Press.

Kabat-Zinn, J. (1990) *Full Catastrophe Living: Using the wisdom of your body & mind to face stress, pain & illness*. New York: Delacorte.

Luft, J. and Ingham, H. (1955) The Johari window: A graphic model of interpersonal awareness. *Proceedings of the Western Training Laboratory in Group Development*. Los Angeles: University of California.

Oxford Dictionary [Online]. Available from: www.oxforddictionaries.com [accessed 16 August 2017].

Schön, D. (1983) *The Reflective Practitioner: How professionals think in action*. London: Temple Smith.

Singh, N.N. (2010) Mindfulness: A finger pointing to the Moon 1:1 [Online]. Available from: https://doi.org/10.1007/s12671-010-0009-2 [accessed 12 August 2017].

Standards Australia (2011) *HB 332–2011: Coaching in Organisations*. Sydney: SAI Global.

Williams, J. and Cowley, P. (2004) Reflective Practice Form. Mid Devon Working Group Approved DMT.

Williams, M. and Penman, D. (2014) *Mindfulness: A practical guide to finding peace in a frantic world*. London: Piatkus.

Appendix 2.1

*Reflective practice form**

REFLECTIVE PRACTICE

Date of Session:

Date of Reflection:

Consider all these questions in whatever order suits you. Answer those that are relevant and support your learning.

What was the event?

What was I expecting to happen?

What actually happened?

What have I learned?

What is significant about this learning for me?

How will this learning change my practice?

What were my feelings about what happened?

What went well?

What didn't go so well?

What were the feelings of the other(s) involved, either known or imagined?

What evidence supports and/or conflicts with my feelings?

How will I apply what I've experienced and learned?

* Adapted from Williams, J. and Cowley, P. (2004) Reflective Practice Form: Mid Devon Working Group Approved DMT.

Reference

Turner, T. (2014) Reflective learning form [pdf]. Available from: www.developingcoaching. com.au/wp-content/uploads/Reflective-learning-form.pdf [accessed 7 September 2017].

Appendix 2.2

Coaching session review form

COACHING SESSION REVIEW FORM

Client:	Session Date:	Session No:
HIGHLIGHTS		LOWLIGHTS
LEARNING		COMMITMENT FOR FUTURE

Figure 2.3 Coaching session review form

Reference

Lucas, M. (2006) Coaching session review form [pdf]. Available from: www.greenfields consultancy.co.uk/gf/wp-content/uploads/2018/01/COACHING-SESSION-REVIEW-FORM.pdf [accessed 24 January 2018].

Appendix 2.3

*Lyrical reflection guide**

When we write "properly" – there are numerous conventions about how to structure a sentence. Sometimes this can interrupt our explorations and move us into more rational expression. Here are three approaches that break with that convention and encourage you to express yourself more freely:

1. Create a poem: First of all remember poems do not have to rhyme, although it is OK if they do! Typically they are written as a series of thoughts. Some of those thoughts may be a short phrase containing a single idea; others may be much longer than a typical sentence and contain many ideas. It doesn't matter! It is also OK for the content to move about – there doesn't have to be continuity or a logical presentation of information. Have fun with it – there's no right or wrong here.
2. Create the lyrics for a song: This is very similar to creating a poem; however, for those people who are quite auditory it might help to consider what "genre" of music would fit the situation best. Is this a heavy metal performance? Or perhaps it's hip-hop rap? Jazz? Pop? What captures your imagination? Most music will have a distinctive beat – when you have that sense of rhythm start to create your lyrics. As with the poem, there is little need to attend to the structure of the lyrics.
3. Create an alpha-poem: This is like creating your own mnemonic. Start by identifying a word that will act as your "muse" – for example you could use the word "REFLECTION." Write that word in a column down the left hand side of a page. Then take each letter as a prompt for writing something that feels true for you about the situation you are working with. For example you might start as follows:
   R – really struggling to know what to write in order to get a deeper level of understanding about what was going on
   E – everyone else seems to get it, they are busy writing something, why can't I?
   F – feeling like I'm different and that's getting in the way, this isn't about me it's about my client
   L – looking back at what happened in the coaching or mentoring session, I notice I am drawn to . . .

And so on . . . It's up to you how long you continue in this manner – for example if you reach the last letter and you feel there is still more to be said, you could go back to the first letter and do another iteration. Or you could pick another word and start again. It's important not to force this – if you run out of inspiration you can stop mid-word if you want to! Sometimes the alpha poem is enough to get you out of the starting blocks and then you might use a different method in order to reflect more fully.

* Influenced by Holder, J. (2017) Reflective practice and journaling for coaches and coach supervisors [web presentation]. Global Supervisors' Network [delivered 6 October 2017].

Reference

Lucas, M. (2017) Lyrical reflection guide [pdf]. Available from: www.greenfieldsconsultancy.co.uk/gf/wp-content/uploads/2018/01/lyrical-reflection-guide.pdf [accessed 24 January 2018].

Appendix 2.4

Reflecting through metaphor

"Desert island fantasy"

This approach can be useful when you prefer more creative and visual ways of working or are simply looking to inject some novelty into your reflection.

A favorite metaphor is to imagine yourself and the client on a desert island and tell the story through drawing out the situation using the desert island as your "muse." When you think you may have finished, pause and consider if there are any other elements (people, things, blockers, enablers) that could be added to the picture.

It's important to just relax and have fun with this technique, try not to over-think it. Our hope is that this more creative approach will pick up on subtleties that are missed when we use our traditional rational and logical approach.

In order to broaden your thinking, you could move the picture around so that you look at what you have created from different perspectives.

Where you gain some additional insight through using the mechanism, consider how best to capture this. It could be that it would be useful to write this in words – alternatively you might want to build that insight into the picture itself.

If the idea of a desert island doesn't appeal, you could replace this with any situation that enables you to create a "scene." So for example, you could start with a stage or a movie set, or you could choose a sport analogy – just experiment and see what works for you.

Reference

Lucas, M. (2016) Reflecting through metaphor [pdf]. Available from: www.greenfieldsconsultancy.co.uk/gf/wp-content/uploads/2018/01/reflecting-through-metaphor.pdf [accessed 24 January 2018].

Appendix 2.5 *Writing the labyrinth*

Holder, J. (2013)

Figure 2.4 Writing in

Figure 2.5 Writing out

One to one peer supervision   3

Definition: One to one peer supervision is a collaborative learning environment created between one coach, mentor or other professional (practitioner) and one other.

What we mean by one to one peer supervision

For the purposes of this book, we are referring to a one to one relationship between two practitioners, neither of whom is trained as a peer supervisor. Together they explore their work in a thought-provoking way both for their own benefit and for the benefit of their client and the wider system.

Often the "currency" for the exchange is that of time – with each practitioner offering the other an equivalent amount of support. The learning environment is characterized by its collegiate nature. The format and the frequency with which peers work will be contracted to suit their particular requirements.

Peer supervision may be carried out face to face, over the telephone or via other virtual media. The chosen medium will be influenced by individual preferences, urgency for the need for supervision and the duo's combined availability.

In this chapter we will consider the benefits and limitations of one to one supervision; we will walk you through how you might go about setting up a one to one peer supervision relationship (including some hints on how you might find someone to work with). We then offer a structure for your peer supervision meetings along with some techniques you could use to explore your client work together. In order to keep your one to one peer supervision productive we offer a way of reviewing, sustaining and closing out your peer relationships. We finish the chapter with a reminder of what risks might emerge through engaging in one to one peer supervision and point you to more detail in Chapter 8.

Table 3.1 Benefits and limitations of one to one peer supervision

One to one peer supervision

Benefits:
- Clear which individual is responsible for "holding the space" each time
- Clear who is "the client" and that they are responsible for deciding how to use the time
- Dedicated time for personal reflection, typically encouraging a depth of exploration
- With experience it may become possible to deliberately chart patterns within your peer's thinking and to notice development over time
- Can be more easily arranged on an "ad hoc" basis should an urgent need for supervision arise

Limitations:
- The facilitator may not be able to offer a breadth of perspectives as they may have a preferred philosophy or approach
- The intensity of an individual relationship may lead to a mutual dependence which if not managed could become unhealthy
- Without outside support or feedback unhelpful patterns could go unnoticed
- The experience may be unbalanced if one of the peers lacks technical expertise, the ability to give feedback or to work with interpersonal dynamics
- The peer supervision process may be seen as eliminating the need for other forms of peer or professional supervision

What are the pros and cons of one to one peer supervision? Clutterbuck, Whitaker and Lucas (2016) offer a comparison of one to one and group supervision with a professional supervisor (see p. 24). Table 3.1 borrows from this and considers the differences when supervision is carried out between peers.

Section 1: Forming a one to one peer supervision relationship

When considering embarking on a one to one and reciprocal peer supervision relationship there are two different starting positions. The first is where you already know the person, but you don't yet have a peer supervision relationship with them. The second is where you need to seek out someone specifically to create a peer supervision relationship. In order to get any one to one peer supervision relationship off to a good start, we would recommend pursuing the following approach to help you set up the relationship for success.

Step 1: Reach out

Approach another practitioner to assess their interest in forming a peer supervision relationship.

> **DISCUSSION POINTS:**
>
> - What kind of supervision arrangements do you have in place at the moment? How well are they working for you?
> - Have you ever engaged in peer supervision? How did you find it worked for you?
> - What kind of qualities are you looking for in a peer supervisor?
> - I'm keen to explore setting up a peer supervision relationship, would you be interested? Or do you know anyone else who is looking to do the same?

Step 2: Connect

Once you have found someone who is interested in partnering with you, find time to have a proper getting to know you meeting (either in person or virtually).

> **DISCUSSION POINTS:**
>
> - How long have you been working in this field, what kind of training have you had?
> - How many clients do you work with at any one time? What does this mean for how often you would want peer supervision?
> - What kind of topics do you imagine bringing to peer supervision?
> - What professional bodies are you a member of? How does their code of ethics influence your practice?

Step 3: Experience working together

Organize a couple of diary slots to have two practice sessions, so that each of you has the chance to work as both the facilitator and the peer supervisee.

> **DISCUSSION POINTS:**
>
> - Would you prefer to work face to face or virtually? What will we do for these practice sessions? How long will the sessions be?
> - Does it make sense to share any information before we work together? For example, it might be worth exchanging our biographies or looking at each other's LinkedIn profiles.
> - Agreeing a date for reviewing the practice sessions. Ideally this should not be immediately after a practice session – we will need time to reflect on the experience.
> - Would it be helpful to record/video the sessions in order to have a reference point for the review discussion?

Step 4: Pause to review

Carry out the review of your practice peer supervision sessions.

> **DISCUSSION POINTS:**
>
> - What did I learn through the practice session that will impact on my client work?
> - What did we learn about the reciprocal nature of peer supervision – what worked well? What didn't work so well?
> - How is our relationship developing? What's our sense of trust? What's our sense of how easy it would be to manage differences of opinion or conflict? How open and honest do we feel we can be right now?

Step 5 (a): Prepare for your contracting conversation

This step assumes there was enough commonality for both people to want to continue the relationship. Agree what materials might be useful to share with each other – for example greater detail on your approach, swapping of psychometric information, any standard documentation you use in the normal course of doing business. Set up another meeting to discuss these materials.

> **DISCUSSION POINTS:**
>
> - Agreeing confidentiality and that we will not circulate this information elsewhere.
> - What do we notice that is similar or different in our approaches? What might this mean for our peer supervision relationship?
> - What are we hoping that peer supervision will help us achieve in our practice in the next year (this can be both about professional and commercial development)?

Step 5 (b): Additional experience of working together

This can be useful where you are feeling like there are some significant differences in your approach or you are starting to get overwhelmed by all the information you are sharing with each other. Rather than ploughing on with the contracting process, pause and have another practice session to see whether that helps cement the potential value in the relationship . . . or not.

Step 6: Creating an initial one to one peer supervision Contract

By this point both parties are as certain as they can be that the peer relationship will be of mutual benefit. Hawkins and Smith (2006, pp. 154–155) propose five key areas to cover in your peer supervision Contract and we have used this structure (see below). You will probably find that in the process of working together to get to this stage you will already have answers to some of these matters.

Agreeing practicalities

Deciding how often to meet

When starting out with a new peer supervision relationship it can be difficult to know how often you should meet. We would recommend you start by meeting monthly and monitor whether the intensity feels appropriate for you both. However, as a minimum we would recommend that you meet quarterly, otherwise the level of connectivity drops and you may find that topics that felt like good issues for discussion when they occurred fade by the time you talk.

Deciding on the duration of each session

Our recommendation would be that each of you has an hour as the facilitator. Monitor whether this session length feels appropriate and adjust it accordingly. However, in terms of a minimum, we would suggest no less than thirty minutes otherwise there may be insufficient time to fully explore the issue. In terms of a maximum, we would suggest no longer than two hours – there comes a point of mental fatigue when you are likely to become less productive.

Deciding where we will meet

Many people prefer to work on a face to face basis – however, finding a suitable location can be difficult. Any location needs to be free from distractions and ideally a confidential space – so coffee shops are, in our view, less than ideal. To maintain a sense of equality, alternating between each other's offices can work. However, some people experience a home ground advantage (they feel more comfortable in their own space) or disadvantage (they are prone to interruptions). Despite the cost it can therefore be beneficial to find a "paid for" venue that is convenient for both parties.

Given the complexities outlined above, working on the phone or Skype can be a useful alternative! There is no cost and each person can control the space that they want to work from. Working remotely will need an agreed etiquette. For example, managing the practicalities of background noise or being overheard, and you will need to have a contingency plan if technology fails. Where remote working is your choice, if geography allows, meeting once a year on a face to face basis can help develop your sense of connection.

Agreeing boundaries

Deciding on the content of the peer supervision discussion

Based on our experience, it helps to keep the primary source of discussion in peer supervision to client cases. For example you could explore:

(a) What client work has gone well
(b) What am I feeling stuck with
(c) What would be helpful to prepare for?
(d) What do I notice I would prefer not to bring!

This list deliberately excludes commercial questions. Questions about how you get more clients, how much you should charge are better addressed through sourcing another practitioner to support you. We encourage this distinction to ensure that the primary motivation for the peer supervision is to improve how you work in service of the client. By starting the relationship in this way you develop a sense for the energy in the relationship between you when you are

Table 3.2 Clues in the dialogue that territory other than peer supervision is being covered

Clues in the dialogue	Most likely territory
What's your experience of . . . ?	Coach mentor
What do you think of this . . . ?	Professional sounding board
I'm sorry to be taking up so much time on this; I just can't seem to get past . . .	Counselor
Is it just me, or . . . ?	Critical friend
There's something niggling me about what happened in my last session with X . . .	Peer supervisor

clearly operating in peer supervision. This makes it more noticeable, should you stray into different territory.

Deciding what is out of scope for the peer supervision discussion

Just as for a professional relationship, there will be times when you are not the best person to continue the work. Table 3.2 above offers some clues that might arise in the dialogue which suggest that you might need to close out the discussion and suggest referral to another practitioner.

This highlights that each individual will need to establish alternative support mechanisms so that appropriate boundaries are respected and managed proactively.

Deciding what other supervision arrangements are/will be put in place

Some practitioners like to have a mix of supervision arrangements and so one or both of you may also have other peer supervision partners and/or receive supervision from a professional supervisor. In our view this is an individual choice so could be quite different for each person in the partnership. However, it is important that the peers work transparently about what they are choosing to take where. In Chapter 9, we offer some ideas on how accessing the services of a qualified supervisor could bring value to your peer partnership.

Agreeing the working alliance

Deciding on how confidentiality will be managed

While you will probably quickly agree that you expect to work in a confidential manner, this is such a well-used phrase that we may not always stop to think what it actually means. We would encourage you to see confidentiality as being the responsibility of both the giver and the receiver of the information. The receiver commits not to pass the information on, and this is our normal focus. The giver also has a duty of care to consider what they share, because in reality they cannot guarantee that confidentiality will be observed.

> **DISCUSSION POINTS:**
>
> - What does each of us understand by the word "confidential"?
> - Under what circumstances would we breach confidentiality?
> - What will we do if we suspect the other person has breached confidentiality – either between us or the confidentiality of a client?

Deciding on the level of preparation required
There are two schools of thought about preparation. One would suggest that preparation is essential in order to get the most out of the supervision session. The other would suggest that working with whatever emerges is most fruitful.

Due to the importance of equity in a peer supervision relationship, we feel it is prudent to agree what level of preparation is expected prior to the session. At the very least we would expect both parties to come to the session having identified "something" that they want to explore. At the other extreme they might have engaged in self-supervision, which has then raised further questions that they cannot answer alone. Ideally the level of preparation will be in synch in the partnership; otherwise the sense of investment in the relationship will get out of balance. If one peer likes to prepare and the other does not, then perhaps agree to do things "out of preference" on an alternate basis and see what difference this makes to your peer supervision experience.

For those who would like to explore how to prepare, we have outlined a number of methods in Chapter 2.

Deciding on the focus for our peer supervision relationship
You may have already started this discussion (see Step 5 above); however, it can be useful to formalize what outputs will help you monitor your progress. You could have some simple aims, which relate to the peer supervision relationship itself for example:

- I want to look forward to having the session.
- I want to receive one piece of feedback that gives me considerable "food for thought."

You might also have some aims for the impact that the supervision is having on your clients:

- I want to take away at least one new technique from each session.
- I want to see a gradual increase in the complexity of the work I am delivering.

Just as you might expect a client to establish their program goals as you start working with them, you could apply the same principles to your peer supervision program. Appendix 2.1 offers you a basic template for capturing your individual goals and you will see that it encourages you to review this on a regular basis.

Deciding what we want to share about our practice
You may have already started this discussion (see Steps 2 and 3 above) and this may be sufficient.

However, where you are working with a peer who has had a different training to you, it is often helpful to take this one step further. Some training programs provide you with a model of coaching or mentoring to use, while others require you to articulate your own model or approach. Sharing this level of information is not only an opportunity for good CPD; it will help place your peer's practice in context. It is quite possible that your peer is familiar with a technique that you have never encountered (and vice versa). For the relationship to work well, you need to feel free to ask the "dumb" question without fear of embarrassment. Recognizing the differences in each other's professional landscape will help you keep a curious and non-judgmental stance.

Agreeing the session format
For one to one peer supervision to work well, careful thought has to be given to how time will be structured. We cover this in greater detail in Section 2: Facilitating the peer supervision session.

Agreeing organizational and professional context

Deciding what code of ethics we will operate with
Again you may have started this discussion already (see Step 2 above). In our view it is not particularly important that you both observe the same code (all of the professional bodies' codes cover similar ground). However, we see peer supervision as a professional encounter and so it is important that you know which code each of you will refer to when you are exploring areas of ambiguity in your practice. Also if the worst happens, you will need to know what the appropriate complaints procedure is! We discuss Ethics in more detail in Chapter 7.

Deciding what other stakeholders have an interest in our work
This is most relevant for internal practitioners. Where the peer supervision work is being sanctioned by the organization, it will be important to understand what kinds of conflicts of interest could arise and how they would be handled.

> **DISCUSSION POINTS:**
>
> - Is it OK to bring to supervision an issue that relates to a client from my private practice rather than an internal client?
> - If we bring to supervision client information that would require escalation in a different context (e.g. an issue of gross misconduct or of suspected bullying), what would we do?
> - If we feel that one or the other of us is less competent than the organization would expect, do we have a duty to share this with the person responsible for this service in the organization?
> - Where we are noticing themes and patterns in our client work beyond the contracted goals (e.g. indications of workplace stress rather than absence of individual time management skills), who should we share this with?

It is less obvious how this might affect independent coaches. However, wherever there are other shared relationships, such as working for the same associate company or volunteering for the same charity, then challenges similar to those facing internal coaches could occur.

Deciding on professional indemnity insurance
Across the globe there are different expectations around whether or not practitioners should have (or indeed are allowed to have!) professional indemnity insurance in place. This is complicated, as in some regions practitioners will have difficulty procuring this type of insurance. Therefore be clear about what insurance each of you have and/or is available. Critically, if you are working across country boundaries check to see that both of your countries are covered with any insurance you do have.

Co-creating a written one to one peer supervision Contract

In Appendix 3.2 we offer a template Contract that covers most of these items and which you could co-create at the outset. As you can see, this could lead to quite a long discussion! It may therefore be prudent to chunk it up over a number of sessions. Moreover, the items mentioned above will only inform your initial Contract. Over time there are many more nuances that it will be useful to explore and agree. We have dedicated Chapter 5 to these additional items – and would recommend that you fully experience working under your initial Contract before you attempt to broaden your Contract.

So far, our guidance starts from the position of having someone to engage with. However, in the second situation that we outlined, the initial challenge is how you locate someone who may be willing to engage in peer supervision. We look at this next.

How to find a peer to work with when you do not have an existing relationship to build on

If you need to find a peer to work with, a good place to start is to leverage the communities of the professional bodies, most of whom have a range of forums where you can meet others, either in person or virtually. For example:

LinkedIn Groups: Once you are a member of a professional body, you are typically able to join their LinkedIn group and post requests to connect with other members. If you choose this option, we suggest that you are clear about what you are looking to give and receive, for example.

> **EXAMPLE POST:**
>
> Hi! I am a practicing coach, I finished my coach training (PG Diploma level) two years ago and I currently have about ten coaching clients in my practice. I also deliver leadership training. I would like to set up a reciprocal peer supervision relationship with a coach who has a similar level of training and coaching experience. I would like to meet between four and eight times a year – I am happy to work over Skype, and I am based in Hong Kong (GMT + 8 hours). If you are interested please get in touch here.

CPD events

This is a good opportunity to network with colleagues who have similar interests to you. The only thing you need to remember is a supply of business cards and a reminder not to be shy to ask your colleagues for theirs. Mention that you are looking to set up a peer supervision relationship and engage them in a dialogue to see whether they have considered doing the same. Where you seem to have

Training programs

This is where a lot of peer relationships start, often as a means of keeping in touch once the training has finished. If you didn't do it at the time, it's probably not too late. Many training providers have alumni events or LinkedIn groups where you can reconnect. Where there was an agreement to share contact details among the cohort, you could always contact your training provider and request contact details again.

Co-coaching communities

Members come together on a regular basis to practice coaching. Often a member of the forum will offer some input based on their own training or a recent piece of CPD. This provides the inspiration for the event, and then those present divide into twos or threes and take turns in practicing something related to the input. It's important to remember that co-coaching is a peer relationship (coaching the coach), which is different from peer supervision. However, it is an obvious next step for members who have an interest in peer supervision to partner up with someone else in that community. The Association for Coaching in the UK commonly offers this approach, and many other networks will run similar activities.

Book clubs

With many more books to read than there is time available, a book club can be a good way of keeping abreast of the literature without having to read every book from cover to cover. If you can locate a book club then this has the advantage that those attending are probably committed to their professional development and, through discussion, you are likely to get a sense of those who operate from a similar or different philosophical base to yourself. Over time you are likely to find the right moment either to make a general request of the group or to approach one of the individuals directly to see if they would be interested in setting up a peer supervision relationship with you.

Section 2: Facilitating one to one peer supervision

Roles and responsibilities

In one to one peer supervision there are only two roles to hold, and it is important that they do not become blurred:

Facilitator: Their responsibility is to
- Hold the space for an agreed period of time on behalf of their peer
- Listen carefully to their peer and ask questions to clarify the client case
- Invite their peer to choose a technique that will best support their learning and their client's growth
- Focus the discussion around the chosen technique
- Focus on their peer's learning and not distract their peer's attention e.g. by exploring their own learning on connected issues during the peer's time slot
- Actively manage time boundaries.

Peer: Their responsibility is to
- Come to session having engaged in the appropriate amount of preparation (as outlined in the Contract)
- Present their case as clearly as possible
- Protect the confidentiality of their client
- Where possible, form a question or focus for what they hope to explore or achieve through the peer supervision
- Be mindful of time boundaries.

Meeting structure

Over time each pairing will develop their own style of working. If you are not sure how to get started, we would recommend operating within this simple structure, based on a two-hour session. When you share a session, it is important to share the time equally to protect the sense of balance in your partnership.

1. Check in (10 minutes) – what's been happening in each of our worlds?
2. Arrivals (5 minutes) – what needs to be said/done to ensure we are ready to work – a short mindfulness exercise can be invaluable here.
3. Logistics (5 minutes) – who will go first today, confirm the finish time and confirm the "switch over" time and set an alarm accordingly.
4. Client Case Reviews (35–40 minutes each) – we offer some techniques for facilitating the discussion in Appendix 2.3.
5. Independent Reflection time (5 minutes) – pause the discussion and consider what the learning has been from the whole session. Remember, learning for your own practice may come from both the experience of receiving and of giving peer supervision.
6. Learning review discussion (15 minutes) – this should consider two key questions:
    (a) What am I learning that will influence my practice?
    (b) What are we learning about how we work together?

7   Close out (5 minutes) – a quick discussion to help move your energy away from the reflective space you have been in, and connect with an appropriate energy for what will come next in your day.

If you are new to reciprocal working, then we would recommend that you organize separate sessions initially (just modify the structure above accordingly). This will help to keep the different roles you play separate and clean. For example, imagine working together for two hours, and spending the first hour working through a challenge with a client who had evoked an emotional reaction in you. How easy would it be to put that to one side, switch roles and give your peer great attention?

Over time as you become used to reciprocal working it may be easier to switch roles effectively within a single appointment. Nonetheless it can be helpful to mark the switch in some way. If working face to face, take a quick comfort break or switch chairs as this helps to change the dynamic. If you are working on the phone then dial out and dial in again. If one peer initiates contact each time, it is a good way of signaling which role you are adopting.

Peer supervision techniques

While there are many techniques that professional supervisors will use, not all of them are appropriate for peer supervision relationships. In Appendix 3.3 we offer four techniques that could be used in one to one peer supervision relationships as they encourage facilitation of your peer's thinking, more so than offering guidance and advice. In Appendix 4.4 we offer four techniques that we would recommend for use in peer group supervision. With a little thought these could also be applied in a one to one setting.

Of course you may simply prefer to have a free-ranging discussion; however, these kinds of discussions can often turn into opinion giving and "why don't you . . ." Our suggestion is to be alert for these sorts of risks.

Section 3: Maintaining and sustaining your peer supervision relationship

Once your one to one peer supervision relationship is up and running, you will begin to find your groove in the way you work together. This is a good sign that your rapport is building and that you are getting a sense of how this type of reflective practice can work for you. Staying consciously competent is key here. To help achieve this we recommend a regular process review. A good discipline is to engage with a process review after each of you has completed three sessions each way and then continue to do so as a regular feature of your relationship. It can be useful to discuss the same question as mentioned in Step 4 above.

> **DISCUSSION POINTS:**
>
> - What did I learn through our peer supervision sessions that will impact on my coaching practice? (Note: This could be when you are in either the role of the facilitator or the peer.)
> - What did we learn about the reciprocal nature of peer supervision – what worked well? What didn't work so well?
> - How is our relationship developing? What's our sense of trust? What's our sense of how easy it would be to manage differences of opinion or conflict? How open and honest do we feel we can be right now?

In addition to these regular reviews, it can be helpful to have an annual review to help you take stock of the benefits you are gaining from the relationship. To do this fully, some individual reflection and data gathering is helpful. For example, useful pieces of individual preparation are:

- What were my aspirations for my development as a practitioner in the past year – and to what extent have I achieved them? (See template for Coach Development Plan in Appendix 8.4.)
- What client cases did I bring to peer supervision – do I seem to be bringing the same type of topics or am I bringing increasingly complex matters?
- What do I say about my approach to working with clients? Does it still feel relevant for how I work?
- What competency framework informs my work (see box below)? How would I rate my current level of practitioner behavior?

> Links to professional body competency frameworks:
>
> Association for Coaching: www.associationforcoaching.com/media/uploads/accreditation-documentation01/Coach_Competency_Framework_AC_.pdf [accessed March 2017]
>
> EMCC: www.emccouncil.org/webimages/EU/EIA/emcc-competence-framework-v2.pdf [accessed March 2017]
>
> ICF: https://coachfederation.org/files/FileDownloads/CoreCompetencies.pdf [accessed March 2017]

With this information as your individual backdrop you are then ready to engage with an annual review discussion.

> **DISCUSSION POINTS:**
>
> - What of our individual preparation would be useful to share?
> - On a scale of 1–10, what value am I receiving and what value am I giving from this relationship? If there is a disconnect between giving and receiving, why is that so? What do I need to do for it to be different?
> - How will we know if this relationship has run its course? And if we didn't work together, how would our work be supervised?
> - Would it be a positive choice for each of us to continue to work together?

Having a discipline of regular reviews is a useful way of checking that the relationship is still serving both parties. Sometimes a relationship may feel constructive but be in danger of becoming a bit predictable. At this point it may be useful to think of how you might inject some novelty into your work together. Some quick ways of doing this include:

1. Identify a number of articles or books that are of interest to one or both of you and divide up who will read what. In future sessions you could support each other as you would normally and then proactively question how the new topic might offer different insight to the discussion.
2. Experiment with new supervision approaches – we identify some techniques in this section; you could also convert some of the techniques normally used for groups (see Chapter 4).
3. Invite another practitioner to observe you working together and seek feedback on what seems to be working well and what you could consider doing differently – they might also have some practical tools and techniques that they use in their own supervision that they could share with you.
4. Engage a professional supervisor to have a conversation with both of you together. Professional supervisors will of course do this in their own particular way. However, you might expect them to ask some of the following questions:
    - What are you enjoying about the peer supervision relationship?
    - What is it that feels predictable?
    - What would be different if it felt less predictable?
    - What is not being said that could be said now?
    - What do you need from me (professional supervisor) to help you move forward?

Section 4: Managing endings

This could happen in a number of circumstances, and we identify three common situations here:

1. The natural close – for example you may have contracted for a finite number of sessions, recognizing that this is a helpful way to manage the potential for dependence.
2. The premature close – for example some external and unforeseen circumstances mean that the relationship is no longer tenable.
3. The uncertain close – one or both parties disengage from the relationship.

Depending on the type of closure and whether it is a mutual or unilateral decision, will determine whether having a final review discussion is more or less possible. Useful points to discuss are outlined below. Importantly if the closure was unilateral and you are unable to do this with your peer, it is still useful to have this conversation with yourself.

> **DISCUSSION POINTS:**
>
> - What have we learned about ourselves through being in this peer relationship?
> - What have we learned about our professional practice through being in this peer relationship?
> - What have we learned about working in a peer supervision relationship that will influence future peer supervision relationships?

Final thoughts

Our intention in this chapter was to help you develop an approach to your individual one to one peer supervision relationships that helps you get the most from them. However, whether you are working with someone you already know, or working with someone new, a number of risks could nonetheless emerge. How these risks might manifest themselves along with how you could navigate those risks is identified in Chapter 8. It is important to remember that even the best one to one peer supervision may need to be supplemented by professional supervision, and we offer some indications of when that might be useful in Chapter 9. Finally, while we hope our guidance is useful to get you started, one to one peer supervision will work best when both of you are working as your authentic selves. So, we'd encourage your creativity too – take a look at what we suggest, play with it and experiment with it and make it your own.

Key learning points

1. One to one peer supervision occurs between practitioners in a collegiate, non-hierarchical learning environment. It occurs without a professionally trained supervisor.
2. There are a wealth of forums and communities which you can access to find a peer for one-on-one supervision.
3. Before committing to supervision, form a trusting relationship through practice sessions and spending time getting to know each other.
4. Even in reciprocal peer supervision it is essential to establish a contract, identify which code(s) of ethics will be observed and define your aims for the supervision.
5. Be transparent about other supervision arrangements you have in place, and how these will complement the peer supervision.
6. Your experience as practitioners will provide you with the skills to establish a successful peer supervision relationship. Peer relationships can, however, be tricky and therefore you need to be vigilant about managing risks like collusion and developmental stagnation.
7. Effective peer supervision involves agreeing responsibilities, choosing a supervision technique and applying an agreed meeting format and structure.
8. Use regular and annual reviews to monitor the strength and effectiveness of the peer supervision relationship and process.
9. Keep your supervision sessions fresh and interesting by using a variety of techniques and inviting input from other professional colleagues.

References

Association for Coaching: www.associationforcoaching.com/media/uploads/accreditation-documentation01/Coach_Competency_Framework_AC_.pdf [accessed March 2017].

Clutterbuck, D., Whitaker, C. and Lucas, M. (2016) *Coaching Supervision: A practical guide for peer supervisees*. Abingdon, UK: Routledge.

EMCC: www.emccouncil.org/webimages/EU/EIA/emcc-competence-framework-v2.pdf [accessed March 2017].

Hawkins, P. and Smith, N. (2006) *Coaching, Mentoring and Organizational Consultancy: Supervision and development*. Maidenhead, UK: Open University.

ICF: https://coachfederation.org/files/FileDownloads/CoreCompetencies.pdf [accessed March 2017].

Kline, N. (1999) *Time to Think: Listening to ignite the human mind*. London: Cassell.

Appendix 3.1

Personal peer supervision goals template

Table 3.3 Template for personal peer supervision goals

Name:	
Time Period:	

PERSONAL GOALS
(i.e. What impact do you want the peer supervision to have on your self-awareness?)

PROFESSIONAL GOALS
(i.e. What impact do you want the peer supervision to have on your practice?)

	What does success look like?	What support do you need?	How did you do? (complete at the end)
Objectives relating to self-awareness			
•			
•			
•			
Objectives relating to chosen competency framework			
•			
•			
•			
Objectives relating to theories and models			
•			
•			
•			
ANNUAL REVIEW			
What have been the most significant personal insights?			
How has this benefited your coaching practice?			
How do you want to develop further?			

Appendix 3.2

One to one peer supervision Contract template

This Peer Supervision Contract was created on DATE between NAME 1 in their capacity of Coach/Mentor at INSERT ORGANIZATION and NAME 2 in their capacity of Coach/Mentor at INSERT ORGANIZATION.

Our Contact numbers are:
INSERT 1
INSERT 2

We will keep this Contract updated every X months starting from DATE; we will have a full review in MONTH/YEAR.

1 Practicalities
(a) Session frequency: We will meet every X weeks/months.
(b) Session duration: We will each have XX minutes receiving peer supervision.
(c) Venue: We will meet at LOCATION OR through TECHNOLOGY PLATFORM.
(d) Session notice: If we need to reschedule our session we will give a minimum of XX hours' notice.

2 Boundaries
(a) We will focus on our client work and be mindful when another practitioner would better serve our peer.
    An example of a useful topic for our peer supervision would be:

    An example of a topic that we would take elsewhere would be:

(b) Currently we have the other supervision activities in place

NAME 1	NAME 2

3 Working Alliance

We commit to working in the spirit of confidentiality and have agreed that we will . . .
We commit to preparing for our sessions and have agreed that we will . . .
We will structure our session in the following way: • Check in (XX minutes) • Arrival (XX minutes) • Logistics (XX minutes) • Client case reviews (XX minutes) • Reflection time (XX minutes) • Learning review (XX minutes) • Close out (XX minutes)

4 Organizational and professional context

(a) We agree to abide by the following Codes of Conduct:

   Name 1: INSERT HYPERLINK TO RELEVANT CODE

   Name 2: INSERT HYPERLINK TO RELEVANT CODE

(b) We believe the following stakeholders may need to be informed about our work together under some specific circumstances.

Stakeholder	Specific circumstances

Our signatures below reflects our commitment to honoring the above terms throughout our peer supervision relationship.

Signature 1   Dated:

Signature 2   Dated:

Appendix 3.3

Four example techniques for facilitating client case reviews

Technique one: Embracing independent thinking

This approach borrows from the Thinking Environment methodology developed by Kline (1999). We believe it can be particularly useful in peer supervision as it recognizes the power of individuals thinking for themselves and minimizes the temptation we often have as peers to be overly helpful! Note: This approach is not a substitute for full Thinking Environment training as it only captures a small part of the process.

- Step 1: Begin the peer supervision session by positioning the work, ask the question "in the context of our peer supervision work, what would you like to think about today?"
- Step 2: Allow your peer to free wheel, sharing their thoughts and ideas without any interruption, without reflecting back and without paraphrasing. Just ensure you give them good attention by listening to their story.
- Step 3: When you are absolutely sure they have nothing more to say, stay quiet and wait to see if you could be wrong!
- Step 4: When invited to ask another question or to "help" in some way – simply invite them to "tell me some more about that . . ."
- Step 5: About 5 minutes prior to the end of their time slot – if they have not yet noticed the time, gently remind them of how much time they have left.
- Step 6: Ask your peer if there is anything they want to write down and wait for them to do so.
- Step 7: Offer a short appreciation to each other, a simple "thank you" for sharing their thoughts/listening so well, may be sufficient.

Technique two: Keeping it real

This approach is often used in groups, and is also useful in a one to one peer relationship. Its primary value is around the sense of connectivity that it generates between individuals, which can be particularly useful when the peer supervisee is feeling "alone" with the matter in hand.

- Step 1: Before you invite your peer to tell their story, the pair reminds themselves on how a shared experience might occur. It is important to remember that the shared experience does not have to be a direct replica of the situation – for example we may have a shared experience for one of the following reasons:

- o You may have had a situation with a client where one of the elements was similar.
- o You may have had a very different situation with a client but the feelings it evoked in you seem to be similar to the feelings it is evoking in your peer.
- o You may have imagined this kind of situation occurring and considered what reaction it would generate in you and what you might feel inclined to do in those circumstances.
- o There may be something in the story which resonates with you for some apparently unconnected reason.
- o There may be an absence of conection with you which may in itself be an interesting experience to explore further.
- Step 2: The peer supervisee tells their story ideally for no more than 20 per cent of their time slot and the facilitator listens without interruption considering what experiences it is evoking in them.
- Step 3: The facilitator shares what experiences it has reminded them of. Where there are a number of experiences it can be helpful to give just the headlines of each experience and allow your peer to decide what they would like to hear more about. What is important about this stage is that the facilitator shares their experience as it occurred for them and takes a "warts and all" approach. It doesn't really matter if the situation was resolved to everyone's satisfaction or not – life has a habit of being imperfect and messy! So this technique embraces that, encouraging the facilitator to share their own reality in as much detail as they can. As the facilitator, consider what you did, how you felt, what you reflected on at the time, what you celebrated and what you regretted and how you are feeling about it now. Again this should not take up more than 20 per cent of your peer's time slot.
- Step 4: Ask your peer to consider what is connecting for them in the shared experience. This step is what is likely to generate most of the discussion as you compare experiences and you should allocate most of the time to this. A great question for the facilitator to ask is, "So where has that taken you to?" This allows your peer to take what feels most relevant to them and recognizes that some more processing may be necessary. Occasionally it might also be appropriate to ask, "What do you think you will do now?"
- Step 5: Check that your peer is OK to close their part of the work now. As with other approaches listed here, you may want to check whether it would be helpful to write anything down or to offer a short appreciation of each other.

Technique three: Using metaphor

This technique is great for tapping into our more creative brains and as the facilitator it helps ensure we are focused on our peer's map of the world, not our own.

- Step 1: Decide upon a metaphor that could be useful. A common suggestion is to use the analogy of a desert island and to consider if your peer and their client were stranded there, how would it be?
- Step 2: Typically the peer supervisee would then physically draw this out. Remember this is for your peer's benefit, so it really doesn't matter if the facilitator can see what has been drawn!
- Step 3: Ask some exploratory questions of your peer, for example:
    o How easy or difficult was that for you?
    o What do you notice now that you didn't notice before?
    o What stands out most in the picture you have created?
    o Might there be anything missing from your picture?
    o How do you feel about this situation now?
    o What's your sense of what you need to do next?
- Step 4: Check that your peer is OK to close their part of the work now. As with other approaches listed here, you may want to check whether it would be helpful to write anything down or to offer a short appreciation of each other.

Some hints and tips when using this technique:

The primary skills you need to use in this technique are listening, reflecting back, paraphrasing and summarizing. This technique does not require the sharing of experience and opinion.

If you can see the picture created, it can be tempting to ask questions based on your own interpretation! However, it is typically more helpful to work cleanly. So for example – rather than say "I notice that the client is a long way away from you – what does that mean?" you could say, "What do you notice about the space between you and the client?"

Although the desert island is commonly used, you can use almost anything to facilitate the exploration. For example, you could frame the situation as a play, a theme park, a movie or even a piece of music or opera. The intention is to have some fun with the exploration so that you can stimulate your creative brain and see additional nuances that were previously outside of your conscious awareness.

Technique four: The seven-eyed model

This technique can be useful when you have been working together for some time, when you both understand the model itself and when you have at least 30 minutes for the peer supervision discussion. Note: A full explanation of the model is provided in Appendix 3.4.

- Step 1: Invite the peer supervisee to draw out the model on a piece of paper – see Figure 3.1 below for an example of how you might do this. As the facilitator you might notice any differences in your own interpretation as they do this – reserve these observations for the review section of your meeting.

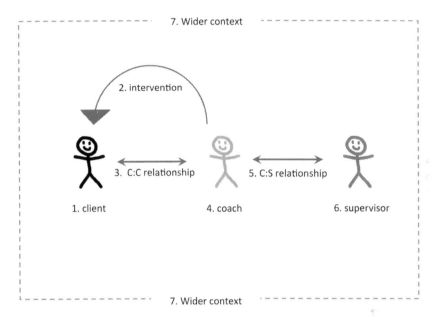

Figure 3.1 A schematic of the seven-eyed model
Lucas (2010); adapted from Hawkins and Smith (2006)

- Step 2: Ask your peer to tell the story of their client situation and as they do so, identify which eye of the model each part of the story might be connected to. An alternative here is to work through sequentially each eye in turn.
- Step 3: Reflect on what has been captured, for example was there much more to say about some of the eyes compared to others? Depending on what you have contracted for in the relationship, it may be possible as the facilitator to offer your own insights. This can be particularly useful where one of the eyes seems to be ignored. It could of course be that this eye was not relevant in this situation; on the other hand it could be that you have identified a blind spot for your peer and they might welcome your input.
- Step 4: Check that your peer is OK to close their part of the work now. As with other approaches listed here, you may want to check whether it would be helpful to write anything down or to offer a short appreciation of each other.

Appendix 3.4

An explanation of the Hawkins and Smith (2006) seven-eyed model

For an explanation from the original authors take a look at pp. 157–176 of the Hawkins and Smith (2006) book. Alternatively you could read an interpretation of the model in the context of the peer supervisee in the book by Clutterbuck, Whitaker and Lucas (2016), pp. 80–86.

However, here we produce our own version of the model below along with a quick explanation of what each of the seven eyes considers. Bear in mind that our coaching conversations are hugely complex and dynamic, and each of these eyes simply provides a different lens with which to review our work. In reality more than one aspect may be useful at any one point in time, and indeed some aspects may not be relevant at all.

Eye 1: The client system

Here we recognize that our client does not live in a vacuum. While we may be working on their here and now and moving into the future, they will also bring their history with them. This lens also reminds us to consider the huge range of individual differences. So we need to be aware of how things like the client's personality, culture and values might impact on their presenting issue.

Eye 2: The intervention

Here we review what question we asked, what tool we used and what model or theory informs our work. Remember that it's difficult to see this eye in isolation as our choice of tool may well depend on our own (the coach) preferences and the level of relationship we currently have with our client.

Eye 3: The client–coach relationship

Here we consider the level of rapport that exists between our client and ourselves. It is generally our assessment of the relationship that helps us determine how challenging we feel we can be with our client and to assess what the client might be ready for. It can also be an indicator of how the client manages their relationships more generally, for example if we are finding it hard to get to know them, would others experience them in the same way?

Eye 4: The coach's processes

Just like Eye 1, the coach does not live in a vacuum either! And so this lens encourages us to heighten our own self-awareness so that we can make a conscious choice of how to be with the client. When we can do this we can be more confident that our responses are based on our client's needs, rather than our own.

One to one peer supervision 73

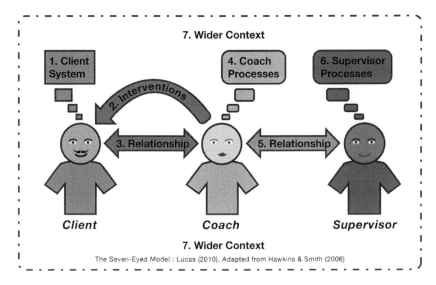

Figure 3.2 A schematic of the seven-eyed model
Lucas (2010); adapted from Hawkins and Smith (2006)

Eye 5: The coach: Peer supervisor relationship

Here we consider the strength of the relationship between the coach and their peer supervisor – which could of course be yourself (if you are reflecting independently) or a colleague (if you are engaging in peer supervision). Just like Eye 3 – the strength of this relationship will determine how safe you feel to reflect. In addition this is where we have the opportunity to pick up on a parallel process in action. So for example if your client lacks confidence and constantly asks you for advice, when you bring that client to supervision you may also present with a lack of confidence and seek reassurance from your peer supervisor.

Eye 6: The peer supervisor's processes

As with Eyes 1 and 4 – the peer supervisor does not exist in a bubble! With a qualified peer supervisor you might expect them to have done a significant amount of work on themselves so that they can work cleanly with you. In addition, once they know you well, they are in a good position to pick up on nuances in how you are reflecting on your work with the potential of spotting the parallel process that we mentioned in Eye 5. In addition, with your permission, they may offer to share some of their "here and now" experiences as this could offer additional insights as to what is occurring in the relational dynamic.

Eye 7: The wider context

Here we look at what might be influencing the client beyond what they are stating is the presenting issue. This can be really useful in an organizational context, as we need to consider how the organizational culture, business security, change initiatives might be impacting on the client. This is also about remembering that whatever the issue for coaching, we are working with the whole person. So even when working with a career goal it is diligent to consider any knock-on impact to the client's family system. Similarly, when working with a personal issue it is also appropriate to consider whether this is leaking into their work life. This eye reminds us that any coaching topic is unlikely to be an isolated matter.

Reference

Hawkins, P. and Smith, N. (2006) *Coaching, Mentoring and Organisational Consultancy: Supervision and development.* Maidenhead, UK: Open University.

Group peer supervision 4

Definition: Group peer supervision is a collaborative learning environment created between a number of coaches, mentors or other professionals (practitioners).

What we mean by group peer supervision

For the purposes of this book, we are referring to a group relationship between practitioners, none of whom is trained as a supervisor. Together they explore their work in a thought-provoking way both for their own benefit and for the benefit of their clients and the wider system.

Often the "currency" for the exchange is that of time – with each practitioner offering the others an equivalent amount of support. The learning environment is characterized by its collegiate nature. The format and the frequency with which the peer's work will be contracted to suit their particular requirements.

Peer supervision may be carried out face to face, over the telephone or via other virtual media. The chosen medium will be influenced by the member's preferences, urgency for the need for supervision and availability.

As it implies, working with peers is offering time and support to group members in a non-hierarchal manner. There may be a timekeeper and/or facilitator who manages the group process, however they are not the overall group leader and this role is often rotated. No money changes hands for this development.

Peer group supervision is different from professional group supervision in that it does not have a qualified supervisor who is specifically paid to attend to the group dynamics, processes and/or client needs on behalf of the group. Given this construct, the group agreements and Contract need to be tightly managed and maintained for groups to flourish (see example in Appendix 4.1), which we will discuss later in this chapter and in Chapter 5.

When making a decision to form or join a peer supervision group, we suggest weighing up the benefits and limitations of working in a group (compared to one to one) to see whether it best fits your goals. Although some cross overs from one to one exist in group peer supervision, Table 4.1 offers some ideas to consider:

Table 4.1 Benefits and limitations of group peer supervision

Benefits:	Limitations:
• Being part of a peer supervision group can be a positive mechanism, feeling part of a wider coaching community and enhancing your capability • Others' contributions can broaden reflections over and above what might occur in a meeting • Peers can build upon processes and/or methodologies they learned in coach-specific training, especially if they've studied together previously • The group tends to generate a greater variety of input. As neuroscience research is showing, novelty can enhance learning • Peers who know each other may have high levels of understanding and support for each other's developmental stage and needs, which could be shared among members • Offers a wider perspective on challenges an individual faces • Group dynamics, if handled well, can accelerate learning • Clear that the meeting facilitator is responsible for "holding the space" on behalf of the group • Peers can organize supervision meetings at their own convenience and suitable venues • There are minimal costs to participating in a peer supervision group, as money does not change hands	• Meeting time shared with other group members, thus less overall time for exploration of any one individual's issue • Peers may fall into the potential trap of the meeting becoming a peer coaching or mentoring process rather than a peer supervision process • Peers may avoid challenging each other when it is necessary to do so, especially if competition and/or collusion exists within the group • Group dynamics if not handled well can impede learning. (This is such an important part of ensuring effective peer supervision that we provide more detail in Chapter 8) • Peers may compare themselves to others in the group, leading to feelings of incompetence, shame or conversely arrogance and "one-upmanship" • More experienced peers can become exasperated at the "waste of time" when less experienced members ask naïve questions • The logistics of managing appointments can often be problematic • Peers may lack elements of necessary experience and expertise to provide robust supervision, feedback and/or work with group process • The peer supervision process may be seen as eliminating the need for one to one professional supervision

Both peer and professional supervision can be useful continuous professional development throughout your career. To better understand when you may benefit from individual peer supervision or additional professional supervision, please see Chapters 3, 8 and 9.

Understanding your attraction to joining a peer supervision group is an important first step to getting clear as to both your reasons and the potential limitations you may experience in the group. If you're clear that peer group supervision is something you'd like to experience, read on.

Section 1: Forming a peer supervision group

Step 1: Reach out

Many people find working with groups supportive and generative. To get started, we offer a few options here.

Short-term trial

If you've never been a part of group supervision before, consider signing up for a short-term peer supervision group. Professional bodies, universities and/or coach training organizations may have opportunities for their students to form groups during or after their courses. Often these are limited to fewer than six meetings.

Before joining, discover what the focus and/or outcome of the defined period of time is and any particulars such as credential, accreditation and/or level of training. Once the group completes, and if you're working well together, the group may want to continue. If so, re-contract and agree a new group contract. If not, consider alternatives to other group or individual peer or professional supervision.

Joining an established group

If you know of someone in a group, ask them whether the group is looking for new members and if they are, do you fit. Assess for yourself perhaps using some of the questions under Step 2: Discussion points.

Forming a new peer supervision group

This can be the most challenging and rewarding pathway, so be prepared to put some time and energy into this option. Perhaps begin by asking other practitioners if they're currently in supervision and/or would like to join a group. If you don't have enough interest from your immediate circle of peers, consider extending your reach through social media, your local association, universities and/or training organizations by posting an advertisement with the details and any initial first steps. A few things to consider and discuss before beginning include:

Group size
The size of the group needs to be large enough to still have a functioning meeting if some practitioners are unable to attend a particular meeting. Balanced against the fact that if the group is too large, then feedback on cases could become overwhelming and/or members may not be able to present their work regularly. If it is too small, group members may not feel they're getting enough value and/or if someone is absent, the experience may not feel like a group. Agreeing how often members want to present and how long they want to spend on a case may determine size. We recommend the optimum size of the group is between five to seven practitioners, to allow for the group to function if members are missing for a meeting.

Frequency and length of meetings
Regular supervision supports practitioners in attending to the breadth, depth and intensity of their work portfolio. Monthly appears to be the norm. Depending on group size, how many people share a case and how long the group spends on a particular case will influence how often and how long the meetings would last.

Geography
People who prefer to work face to face will want a group where they don't have to travel far, so consider choosing a location that best fits group members.

Composition
Determining who could form a productive group is important. It can be useful to seek a group across different professional bodies, various cultural backgrounds, genders and/or diverse training to gain wider perspective. There are no specific guidelines as any number of combinations may work for a particular group. Agreeing the purpose of the group and focus areas will help to optimize who might best benefit.

We go into more depth in determining meeting frequency later in this chapter. Once you've established a few members who are interested, we suggest continuing the process outlined below.

Step 2: Connect

Whatever the group composition, it is important for members to feel included so that the group has the best opportunity for cohesion and risk-taking. Who can join and what background they bring to the group's construction is up to group members and the agreed group purpose and/or focus. Agree among the group what the appropriate criteria for membership are, and continue to revisit what works and doesn't work over time.

> **DISCUSSION POINTS:**
>
> To start the discovery process:
> - How long have you been coaching or mentoring?
> - What background and training do you have?
> - How many clients do you work with at any one time?
> - What professional bodies are you a member of?
> - How does their Code of Ethics influence your practice?
>
> If you're joining an existing group:
> - Ask the above questions to highlight: What is the group make up?
> - Ask questions to understand the group focus, meeting times, expectations, costs, etc.
> - How committed have group members been in attending meetings?
> - What transitions have been made in the group?
> - What kinds of topics have previously been brought to peer supervision?
> - What options do you have if you don't wish to continue?
> - Do you have any conflicts of interest that prevent you from joining?

Group membership and these discussion questions may need to be revisited as the group forms, adds additional members and works together. We will discuss this later in this chapter. Although the steps below are similar to one to one, we have altered them for peer groups. We suggest using this section of the book if you are proceeding together.

Step 3: Experience working together

This step assumes there was enough commonality for members to consider forming a group or adding a new member(s). It now becomes important to take time to better understand the group, who is in it, how you fit in and/or how you can work together. This step is not a peer supervision meeting. Instead we suggest having a meeting to get to know each other a bit more and share greater details on your coaching or mentoring approach, background, professional associations and/or things that are important to you to work with your peers. It may also be useful to revisit the questions in Step 2 as an entire group, as often they will be done individually with various group members. Other discussion topics may include:

> **DISCUSSION POINTS:**
>
> If a new group is to be formed:
> - Why did you choose group supervision?
> - What is important to you working within a group?
> - What kind of topics do you imagine bringing to supervision?
> - What are you hoping that peer supervision will help you achieve in your coaching practice in the next year (this can be both about professional and commercial development)?
> - How often and where might we meet?
>
> And . . . before joining an established group:
> - What are the other's backgrounds?
> - Why did they choose group supervision?
> - What topics have been brought previously to meetings?
> - What's important to the group that they're focusing on?

Despite the fact the content of this initial meeting is focused more on sharing more pragmatic getting to know each other elements, rather than supervision per se, the way in which the group interacts with each other is important to notice. How do they engage with each other? If some members over or under share, how does the group take this into account in this very first meeting? More details about groups can be found in Chapter 8.

Step 4: Pause to review

Whether it is during the first group meeting or at separate meetings afterwards, each member reflects on his/her experience of this initial meeting. Hearing how each person experienced the group leads to a better understanding of how the group worked and can offer useful insights to how it will work together in the future.

> **DISCUSSION POINTS:**
>
> - What did we learn about working together?
> - What did we learn about the reciprocal nature of peer supervision: What worked well? What didn't work so well?

- How is our relationship developing? What's our sense of trust? What's our sense of how easy it would be to manage differences of opinion or conflict? How open and honest do we feel we can be right now?
- How confident are you about confidentiality and that others will not circulate information elsewhere?
- What do we notice that is similar or different in our approaches? What might this mean for our peer supervision relationship?

Remember that this was intended to be an information gathering experience. Despite everyone's best intention, the group may work for some and not for others. Gauging interest and commitment to take the next step to building a cohesive peer supervision group is the final step before contracting.

Step 5: Creating your initial group supervision Contract

By this stage, many of us are ready to start the work of supervision. However, our recommendation is to resist the temptation and take the time to properly establish the group Contract. In our opinion, it is important that members take the time to establish exactly how they want the group to work, to agree the commitment they are making and together ensure the group maintains its supervision focus. We recommend these areas that are discussed and agreed before any supervision begins to save potential pitfalls and difficulties in the future. The areas below are a starting place, and they are organized according to Hawkins and Smith (2006) into five areas for the Contract. Please note this need not determine in which order you discuss them with your group. For more detailed topics to include in your Contract, and how to develop the skill of contracting, please see both Appendix 4.1 at the end of this chapter and Chapter 5.

Contract Area 1: Agreeing practicalities

Attendance protocol
In our experience, peer group supervision works best when all group members commit to attending every meeting and limit missing meetings except for extreme circumstances. The group may want to determine what they believe is acceptable non-attendance and any consequences of non-attendance. Some groups have a donation to charity for missed meetings, while some allow for a total number of missed or attended as part of their agreement.

Entry and exit of practitioners

To maintain a highly functioning peer supervision group, it will be important that the group manages entry and exit carefully. The group may want to consider a process they use when a coach or mentor exits the group to ensure minimum disruption to group dynamics. It will be important to limit the number of opportunities for new entrants to join the group as the new members will need to have the time to discuss and agree or amend the group agreements, and undertake a similar joining process as other members. It may be useful for the group to agree to only accept new members at a set time and ensure that other members have veto rights to members whom they don't think would fit the group.

> **DISCUSSION POINT: Managing individual migration**
>
> - Do members have to give notice of leaving? If so, how much time is needed?
> - If people are consistently absent, at what point are they no longer considered part of the group?
> - Does the leaving member need to give a reason for leaving? If so, who do they communicate with and how?

Group size and frequency of meetings

Typically this will already have been established in getting to this stage. If not, then please see above Step 1: Forming a new peer supervision group.

Contract Area 2: Agreeing boundaries

Deciding on the content of the peer supervision discussion

Based on our experience, it helps to keep the primary source of discussion in peer supervision to client cases. For example you could explore:

(a) What client work has gone well
(b) What am I feeling stuck with
(c) What would be helpful to prepare for
(d) What I notice I would prefer not to bring.

This list deliberately excludes commercial questions. Questions about how you get more clients, or how much you should charge are better addressed through sourcing another coach to support you. We encourage this distinction to ensure that the primary motivation for the supervision is to improve how you work in service of the client. By starting the relationship in this way you develop a sense for the energy in the relationship between you when you are clearly operating in peer supervision. This makes it more noticeable, should you stray into different territory.

Deciding what is out of scope for the peer supervision discussion

Just as for a professional relationship, there will be times when you are not the best person to continue the work. Table 4.2 below offers some clues that might arise in the dialogue which suggest that you might need to close out the discussion and suggest referral to another practitioner.

Table 4.2 Clues in the dialogue that territory other than peer supervision is being covered

Clues in the dialogue	Most likely territory
What's your experience of . . . ?	Coach mentor
What do you think of this . . . ?	Professional sounding board
I'm sorry to be taking up so much time on this, I just can't seem to get past . . .	Counselor
Is it just me, or . . . ?	Critical friend
There's something niggling me about what happened in my last coaching or mentoring session with X . . .	Peer observer

This highlights that each individual will need to establish alternative support mechanisms so that appropriate boundaries are respected and managed proactively.

Professional supervision support

Working as a group can sometimes bring up issues that may be beyond the group's expertise and/or comfort. For specific issues such as difficulties with ethics and/or if the group cannot effectively manage group process, we recommend having a professional supervisor who oversees and/or can be available for escalation (please see Chapter 9 for more information). Agreeing what areas may be useful to bring to professional supervision and what kind of background this professional supervisor has, may be starting points. We suggest having a couple of nominated members to research and vet a few potential professional supervisors for the group's review and set a deadline to agree when this role will be filled before he/she is needed. If issues arise, we offer a suggested process for escalation as well as other areas of ethical considerations in Chapter 7.

Contract Area 3: Agreeing the working alliance

Confidentiality

This may be a topic that members take for granted because none of us would knowingly breach confidentiality. As a result, this area can be overlooked. However, we suggest reviewing these initial gray areas, which may provide clarity before commencing peer group supervision.

> **DISCUSSION POINTS:**
>
> - What do we mean by confidentiality?
> - What specific information do we agree will not be circulated elsewhere?
> - What happens when one of us hears something outside of peer supervision that we suspect someone in the group shared?

The tone here is more from curiosity, as many times the "breach" is an oversight and/or unconscious behavior of the member who unwittingly shared something they didn't think had the degree of importance to another. Consequently, agreeing to review and revisit these sorts of issues can be important as the group relationship progresses.

Roles and responsibilities

Before commencing peer group supervision, we suggest practitioners agree how they will organize themselves during the group meetings. Being clear about roles, responsibilities and commitments creates psychological safety and underpins the success of the group dynamic. For more information about group dynamics and other pitfalls, please see Chapter 8.

Reflective practice

Being able to distance yourself from your work to identify patterns, habits, strengths and limitations in your work and/or within the system in which you work is the foundation of supervision. Understanding group members' commitment to reflective practice and/or the way in which members think about their work may inform how the group works together during a supervision meeting.

> **DISCUSSION POINT: Reflective practice exploration**
>
> - What is involved in each member's reflective process?
> - How often and/or what method do members reflect?
> - Are the processes uniform throughout all group members or different?
> - What details do group members share about their self-awareness in presenting their cases?

Results

A clearly identified and measured purpose and focus of the group helps members stay on track and to continually improve the group process. The box below offers some questions for discussion to help clarify the group's aims and objectives.

> **DISCUSSION POINT: Group aims and objectives**
>
> - What are we trying to achieve? Are we trying to increase self-awareness, develop skills, look at process, recharge our energies, etc.?
> - Are we trying to better understand or extend learning groups from university or professional training? If so, how is this continuing or extending our knowledge or skills application?
> - Do we want to include social interaction and/or talking about generating more business? How do we strike a balance between client case conversation and other useful discussions?
> - How do we know if we're receiving value? How do we measure our own growth?
> - When and/or how often do we review our needs and objectives?
> - What options do we have if we are not achieving our outcomes?

Measuring outcomes and group progress contributes to group cohesion and growth as well as checking members' satisfaction with the group interactions. In Chapter 5 we offer some hints and tips on how to "call it" when issues and/or content go off-track and how to renegotiate the focus and/or group requirements. In addition, holding regular reviews about group needs can help ensure that all members receive value.

Contract Area 4: Agreeing the meeting format

For groups to work well, careful thought has to be given to how time is structured and by whom. We cover this in greater detail below in Section 2.

Tracking how time is shared:

In one to one peer supervision relationships (Chapter 3) it is important to track the equality in the relationship.

In group supervision relationships, it may be difficult to track the individual time taken but it is important that you track who takes the role of the presenting peer and who takes the role of the facilitator each time. Just as with one to one peer supervision relationships, it is important that over time there is equity in the amount of time each person receives peer supervision and the amount of responsibility each person takes.

Typically a presenting peer will get less time per case than they would if they were receiving one to one supervision. We would recommend that each person receive no less than 15 minutes peer supervision. That may sound really short, but it is surprising how much can be achieved in even a short time frame. The use of techniques that structure the group's input are often used in these circumstances (see Appendix 4.4). There are a range of other techniques such as role plays and constellations. If any unusual group dynamics arise as a result, we suggest openly talking about them or bringing in a qualified supervisor for a meeting.

Contract Area 5: Agreeing organizational and professional context

Ethics and ethical code

If you are part of a professional body, it may be useful to consider what ethical code of standards the group may be using and/or to compare the various codes if members belong to different bodies.

We recognize that this is a large topic, and ethics is covered in more depth in Chapter 7.

The way we do things

The group initially may want to do some high-level thinking about some basic ethical considerations for peer supervision groups.

> **DISCUSSION POINTS:**
>
> - What happens when practitioners representing different commercial entities bring a case from the same client organization?
> - What happens when a group member brings a case that involves another member, boss or direct report?
> - What happens when group members feel awkward about bringing uncomfortable issues?
> - What happens when members feel awkward about the issue that another member has brought?
> - What happens if a group member presents a case where it is clearly unethical (such as having an intimate relationship with their client or taking a bribe)?
> - Who facilitates the group process when ethical issues divide the group?
> - When is professional supervision an appropriate way forward?

Deciding on professional indemnity insurance
Across the globe there are different expectations around whether or not practitioners are required to have professional indemnity insurance in place. This is complicated, as in some regions practitioners will have difficulty procuring this type of insurance. We recommend sharing what insurance each of you have and/or is available. Critically, if you are working across country boundaries check to see that the countries in which you deliver the work either require insurance or are covered by your policy.

Co-creating the written peer group supervision Contract
Regardless of how the group forms, having a detailed Contract to start off with can make the experience far more enriching once peer supervision actually occurs. It may be useful to review other sections of the book, such as Chapters 3 and 5, to have additional tips for understanding what may be required to form and/or join a peer supervision group.

Once the group has agreed all of these areas it will be useful to develop a Contract that all group members sign (see Appendix 4.1). Again, this is a commitment to being a member of a professional group of practitioners focused on each other's development and maintaining the professional standards of coaching and mentoring.

Section 2: Facilitating the peer group meeting

Meeting preparation

As we've already mentioned, we believe reflective practice is the foundation of supervision. We suggest each group member engage in some form of ongoing reflective practice throughout the peer supervision period. This approach fosters each member's learning and provides content to the peer supervision meeting. Many people think of reflective practice as journaling. Although this type of reflective practice may be useful for some people, there are many other ways to reflect on your work – see Chapter 2. The group may wish to agree on a standard reflective practice method or case presentation format as a result of the reflection. Below we offer one way of preparing.

Before the meeting, regardless of whether or not you plan to present a case, set aside at least 30 minutes to prepare for the meeting. Using the group's or your own agreed reflective practice, read through your learning journal, listen to your recordings, etc. and consider the following questions to prepare.

- What's working or not working currently?
- What consistent patterns or trends have I noticed in my work that I'd like to share?
- Is there a client case which is challenging and which I'd like to get a broader understanding about?
- What tools, theories, interventions, processes do I use ineffectively and/or are dependent upon?
- What specifics from my reflections would be most beneficial for me to share with the peer group?
- What do I notice I am avoiding bringing to the group?

These are only guidelines and with any reflective practice, each member will need to adjust according to their own individual needs, including appropriate boundaries, given their level of trust with the group and their sense of the group's ability to support their requirements.

Roles and responsibilities

In our experience, having defined roles and responsibilities increases certainty and is an important process as it helps to signpost the formality of the arrangement. It is critical to share these roles equally regardless of personal preference or experience. Managed well, it not only ensures equity but enhances psychological safety.

Facilitator or moderator

At each meeting agree who will be the facilitator or moderator. They will be responsible for:

- Guiding the meeting
- Inviting everyone to participate and share their learning
- Ensuring the supervision process is contracted and adhered to
- Ensuring the group principles are being upheld
- Listening carefully to the case being presented and asking questions to clarify understanding
- Empowering the presenting peer to choose a process to best support his/her learning and their client's growth
- Ensuring the peers remain true to the process chosen to explore the case
- Identifying any potential areas of conflict and facilitating resolution using the agreed group principles.

Time keeper

In addition to the facilitator or moderator, a member who can:

- Support the group to set and stick to agreed time limits through the meeting
- Give updates on time during meetings, if necessary
- Ensure the meeting finishes at the agreed time
- Manage latecomers.

Centering or arrival role

This role may:

- Invite members to clear the space, their thoughts and/or sharing to bring the group fully into the meeting
- Facilitate a short round of meditation or calming techniques such as breathing or centering techniques to provide cohesion and focus for members.

Presenting peer

In each meeting there will be an agreed number of members who bring a case for discussion. The group can decide whether this happens on the day or they can agree to roster members for each meeting to ensure each person has regular supervision opportunities. The presenting peer(s) takes responsibility for:

- Engaging in reflective practice, showing appropriate vulnerability in presenting their self-awareness and what's happening in the client engagement in presenting their case.

- Presenting their case as clearly and succinctly as possible, which protects the confidentiality of their client and/or the organization the presenting peer works in.
- Ensuring all key information is presented for the peer members.
- Formulating a key question or focus to guide the meeting.

Group members

Group members who are not acting in the role of facilitator or moderator or presenting peer have the responsibility to equally:

- Listen carefully as the case is presented, using their skills as a professional, not as a friend or colleague.
- Consider the case through the supervision lens.
- Offer his/her ideas and opinions openly and non-judgmentally from a systems or supervisory context.
- Offer his/her opinions and/or advice as suggestions or observations, without attachment, on the need to be right or for validation from the group.

If a peer inadvertently steps out of their supervision lens (for example, giving advice or opinion as an expert), it is best practice to name this in the moment. If the peer has not taken responsibility for the behavior, it is incumbent on either the other group members or the facilitator or moderator to work with the behavior as part of the overall group work. This could be done as part of the regular reviews – see Chapter 5 for more information on how to do this. If the group consistently has difficulty with behaviors that are unhelpful to the group's growth, we recommend professional supervision for either the entire group or the individual.

Meeting structure

Once meeting length is determined, each group can organize appropriate steps with time estimates to achieve their commitments and agree responsibilities for each, ensuring each step is considered in the meeting process. Here is a basic meeting structure to begin contracting, based on a 90-minute meeting. Please see Appendix 4.3 for a more complete version.

1. Welcome: 3–5 minutes
2. Getting fully present: 3–5 minutes
3. Peer supervision technique or case presentation: Based on number of total remaining minutes agreed (of the 90 minutes)

4   Getting complete: 3–5 minutes
5   Meeting finish: 1 minute.

Potential meeting issues

Be wary of any "traps" or "games" and/or group dynamics that can creep into a peer supervision forum. Over reliance on more experienced members and/or more vocal individuals can easily tip the peer supervision group into a mentoring space and limit growth. These can be especially tricky in organizations where peers work closely together on a regular basis and/or groups with different levels of coaching experience. In the book *Supervision in the Helping Professions* (Hawkins and Shohet, 2000, pp. 192–193) reference Gaie Houston's group dynamics (1985):

- Competing to be the most potent or best and suggests be on alert to "Mine is better than yours . . ." language and comparisons of each other, clients and/or experience levels.
- Reinforcing how bad a situation is for a member and looking out for "Ain't it awful?" mentality and group members feeling helpless.
- Giving false praise or colluding by making inferences and/or comments such as "We are so wonderful."
- Focusing on the problem, difficult and/or less experienced person "Hunt the patient" (someone who is broken or needs healing) rather than looking for opportunities for growth.

Be on alert to ensure everyone has opportunities to share their insights. The facilitator can take an active role in this, though it is the responsibility of all group members. When any group dynamics arise, surface them openly and discuss options to address them as part of the supervision group. It will be good practice for you as a practitioner and raise the group awareness. If the group cannot shift the dynamic and/or wants to learn how to shift them quickly, invite a professional supervisor from outside the group to work through them. We discuss these potential issues in more detail in Chapter 9.

Here are some guidelines that may keep individual members within a group on equal terms:

- All group members commit to their own individual reflective practice.
- All members get equal time allotment for case presentation and/or sharing throughout the group Contract (for example, a year). These can be logged into a spreadsheet maintained by the timekeeper.
- The presenting peer determines which technique they would find most beneficial for the case they are sharing.

- During a technique, it is important that peers keep their contributions laser like and succinct – the focus is on the presenting peer and broadening the scope of his/her perspective, avoiding personal judgment.

Finally, we recommend avoiding personal judgments and/or negative critical assessment either in the meeting or afterward.

Meeting techniques

(Note: The word "technique" is being used specifically to differentiate from overall group process).

Meeting techniques help create time and space for reflection and encourage discussion through the supervision lens. Consequently, peer observers share their thoughts, feelings and experiences during the technique with the sole purpose of presenting information that encourages the presenting peer to reflect and think more deeply. (For more details please see Appendix 4.4, Group Techniques A–D.)

- Group Technique A: Questions to deepen the reflection and expand the presenting peer's thinking
- Group Technique B: Broadening the presenting peer's capability
- Group Technique C: Rehearsal
- Group Technique D: Deepening self-reflection as a practitioner.

The real benefit to the group will be in the discussion and sharing of how they can use the techniques to deepen their own learning, modifying them over time to suit their individual needs. In each of the following techniques it is the presenting peer's responsibility to accept or reject any of the contributions.

Section 3: Maintaining and sustaining your peer group

Reviewing a peer supervision group

Regular group supervision process discussion

Even if your group is established, a regularly agreed timeframe to review how the group process itself is working is another element to ensure group growth and satisfaction. In the early stages of group formation, we recommend the first review be completed after you have completed three meetings. The discussion points below are the same as in Chapter 3.

DISCUSSION POINTS:

Regular process review, each group member shares:
- What did I learn through our peer supervision meetings that will impact on my practice? (Note: This could be when you are in either the role of presenting peer or peer observer)
- What have we learned so far about the nature of group peer supervision? What worked well? What didn't work so well?
- How is our group developing? What's our sense of trust? What's our sense of how easy it would be to manage differences of opinion or conflict? How open and honest do we feel we can be right now?
- Does anything in our group agreement need to be re-contracted?

Quarterly review discussion
Every three months, include a 15–20-minute assessment around how well the chosen techniques are working. It is an opportunity to personalize the existing techniques, to research new ones in order to support the needs of the group and their work. This is different from the peer supervision group review described in Section 1, Step 4, as it is to see whether the selected techniques could be improved and/or changed. However, the group can also allocate additional time to share their experiences on the role they play in the group, either formal (e.g. timekeeper) or informal (e.g. provider of useful questions). This will act as both in the moment reflective practice for the member and to perhaps offer useful learning for others who will take on the role in future.

Annual review discussion
Ideally around the anniversary of when you started working together, spending an entire group meeting reviewing the inter-workings of the group can build cohesion and new energy for both individual members and the group. Doing some pre-thinking and each group member coming prepared for this unique meeting, sets everyone up for success.

DISCUSSION POINTS:

Annual review preparation:
- How did I hope I would develop as a practitioner in the past year – and to what extent have I achieved this?

- What client cases did I bring to peer supervision?
- What competency framework informs my work? And how am I developing against it?
- What do I say about my coaching or mentoring approach? Does it still feel relevant for how I work?

Annual review discussion:
- What of my individual preparation is helpful to share?
- On a scale of 1–10 what value am I getting and giving from the peer supervision? If there is a difference between members' values, why is that so? What do I need for it to be different?
- How will we know if this group has run its course? If we didn't continue to work together, how would our work be supervised?
- Would it be a positive choice for each of us to continue to work together?

Ongoing learning and development

An important aspect of development of a peer supervision group is their commitment to ongoing learning and development. Each group will want to give consideration to how it might continue to grow the individual and group supervision knowledge. Some ideas for consideration include:

- Book review: Each group member taking turns to read a book or article on supervision and share their learning with the group.
- Video review: The group watch a short video on supervision, e.g. from a professional body's websites, conferences, peers outside the group (with permission) and discuss what it means for their group.
- Have a professional supervisor attend a peer supervision meeting on a quarterly basis to give feedback on the peer supervision processes they observed or run the meeting.

Many of these sorts of activities may also attract continuing education points for credential or accreditation. Please check your professional body's websites for further details.

Section 4: Managing endings

Although peer supervision may be an important development opportunity, sometimes life or other development possibilities take precedent. Sometimes one practitioner needs to take a break or isn't a fit for the group. Sometimes the group itself has run its natural course and it is time to disband. It is in these circumstances that taking time to close out the relationship and celebrate your time together can ease the conclusion.

> **DISCUSSION POINTS:**
>
> - What have we learned about ourselves through being in this peer group?
> - What have we learned about our coaching or mentoring practice through being in this peer group?
> - What have we learned about working in a peer supervision group that will influence future peer supervision relationships?
> - What have I given the group and what has the group given me?

Final thoughts

Peer group supervision is convenient, cost effective and can be developmentally enhancing to members. Individual reflective practice is at the heart of the group foundation. Being open to bumps along the path while the group develops, committing to the group and its agreements and processes, as well as your own needs will in our experience produce the best result. Group dynamics can both help and hinder learning and we explore this more fully in Chapter 8. When there are consistent limitations in your group, try individual peer supervision (Chapter 3) and/or professional supervision (Chapter 9) to extend your development and satisfaction.

Key learning points

1   Peer group supervision occurs between coaching practitioners in a collegiate, non-hierarchical learning environment. It occurs without a professionally trained supervisor.

2   In setting boundaries for topics of discussion, know when to seek alternative support mechanisms where supervision is not appropriate, or where a professionally trained supervisor is required.
3   Spend time creating a group contract, which includes forming the group, confidentiality, ethics, roles, responsibilities, commitment to the group, creating psychological safety, clarity of purpose, format and structure.
4   Reflective practice between and preparation before meetings enhances the peer learning and enriches the conversations.
5   In addition to assigning the presenting peer and observing peer roles, each member takes on a specific process role.
6   Attention to group dynamics, meeting structure, meeting techniques and reflective practice will support high quality supervision.
7   To strengthen the peer supervision experience, invite members to engage in learning and development focused on expanding their knowledge of supervision processes.
8   Arrange quarterly and annual reviews to assess the group process and individual and collective learning. This generates energy for enhancing future meetings.

References

Hawkins, P. and Shohet, R. (2000) *Supervision in the Helping Professions: An individual, group and organisational approach*. Philadelphia, PA: Open University.

Hawkins, P. and Smith, N. (2006) *Coaching, Mentoring and Organizational Consultancy: Supervision and development*. Maidenhead, UK: Open University.

Houston, G. (1985) Group supervision of groupwork. *Self and Society: European Journal of Humanistic Psychology*, 13(2), pp. 64–66.

Appendix 4.1

Sample peer supervision Contract

Identifying what to put into a group Contract can be an iterative process. Below is a suggested starting place. Please feel free to modify and/or add to this sample Contract to suit the needs of your peer supervision group.

How we will work together

This is a contract between the following members to engage in peer supervision. We are clear the purpose of this group is peer supervision focused on supporting the ongoing professional development of fellow practitioners and maintaining the professional standards of coaching. By signing this contract we all agree to adhere to the following agreed by the group:

Add the group's agreed criteria here so everyone is clear

This contract shall be renewed annually or at such time as the membership changes. However, this contract can be amended to suit the group at any time.

Name	Contact details	Qualifications and/or training	Professional body credential or accreditation	Memberships/ affiliations and/ or code of ethics

By signing this contract, we agree to the spirit and terms in which the group will work together. We endeavour to uphold the group agreements to the best of our ability.

| Name | Signature | Date |

| Name | Signature | Date |

| Name | Signature | Date |

Figure 4.1 Peer supervision member details for Contract

Appendix 4.2

Establishing a peer supervision group

Below are some sample terms and conditions that may go into a group contractual agreement and can be contracted with group members at regularly scheduled intervals.

Membership joining process
1. To join, members must all have up to date professional body membership.
2. Maximum numbers of the group are X.
3. The prospective new member will be introduced to the group through an existing member (the sponsor) by presenting a biography to the group.
4. If the group agrees, the sponsor will invite the new member to join the group.
5. The sponsor will be responsible for going through the Contract with the new member to acquaint them with the group's processes and policies.

Meeting agreements
1. Meetings will be a mix of face to face and virtual forums.
2. There will be X scheduled meetings per year on Y (e.g. a pre-arranged day and time of each month).
3. Each member endeavors to attend a minimum of _____ total meetings per year face to face and the rest can be virtual.
4. Minimum numbers to hold the peer supervision meeting are X. If fewer, the available peers will decide whether to cancel the meeting or perhaps use the time for article review or other learning.
5. The peer supervision group will have X social event(s) each year and _____ learning reviews each year.

Peer roles and responsibilities

Presenting peer: At the end of the peer supervision meeting, the presenting peer will be the facilitator for the following meeting.

Meeting facilitator: Will circulate a confirming email the week before to ensure there is a quorum. Confirmation email will include date and time, apologies, venue and/or meeting cancellation notifications and any administration for that peer supervision meeting.

Peers: Apologies for absences are to be emailed a minimum of one week in advance of scheduled meeting to the meeting facilitator for that session.

Appendix 4.3

Meeting structure

This short outline includes a few tips for peer supervision groups to get their meetings up and running. Once the group chooses a typical 60- or 90-minute meeting structure, we recommend having the timekeeper review how the group goes against the time at each meeting and continue to modify to suit what the specific group requirements are over time.

1. Welcome: 3–5 minutes
    - Facilitator begins the meeting with a reminder of ground rules and an invitation to build on them.
    - Welcoming of guests or new members if any.
2. Getting fully present: 3–5 minutes
    - An uninterrupted round of sharing or a mindfulness activity where practitioners have the opportunity to share any thoughts, feelings or events which are in their mind and might detract from their participation in the meeting. After an initial quick round of clearing and creating the space, move onto the peer supervision process.
3. Peer supervision technique: Based on number of total remaining minutes agreed (of the 60–90 minutes)
    - If not already agreed, the facilitator supports the group in choosing number of peers and/or topics for the meeting agreed.
    - Note: Guideline is one to three cases, topics and/or networking activities maximum per meeting, depending on how many people in the group and/or how much depth the group wants. This can be part of the group agreement up front.
    - Facilitator supports the group in determining who will present, the order of presentations and/or conversation topics and works with the timekeeper to determine specific meeting requirements.
    - Case presentation(s)
        o Guidelines: The peer takes 5–7 minutes to present their case.
        o The peer identifies their chosen group technique.
        o The facilitator ensures the technique is followed and calls out any unhelpful group dynamics or individual behaviors.
        o The timekeeper shares time stamps and/or maintains time agreements.
        o Once that case is complete repeat, if needed, using the above process.

4   Getting complete: 3–5 minutes
    - During this segment, those who have presented a case have the opportunity to share anything they might need to say to complete their involvement in the meeting; these might be an awareness they have gained, a quick acknowledgement or some thoughts or feelings.
5   Meeting finish: 1 minute
    - Housekeeping: Agree particulars for next meeting, if required.
    - *Important!* Avoid reopening discussions about the peer supervision meeting, including speaking further about the merits of the case and/or meeting outcomes.

Appendix 4.4

Group techniques A–D

The following techniques have been developed and tested in a number of peer supervision groups in Australasia.

Group technique A: Questions to deepen the reflection and expand the peer's thinking

Aim: To provide the presenting peer with a range of reflective questions that will deepen the peer's self-awareness and the impact this has. This process provides the peer with a wide range of potential ways they might be limiting and/or enhancing the situation that they have described.

Time allocation: 35–50 minutes, depending on group size and agreements. Agree time and facilitator or moderator manages accordingly.

Summary of steps in the technique:

1   Presenting peer outlines the case they are bringing for supervision, including their personal insights.
2   Round of clarifying questions.
3   Round of probing questions (questions for insight).
4   Presenting peer shares initial new insights with group.
5   Peer observers share initial learning from meeting.

Step by step guidance

Overall: The presenting peer shares any pertinent details for the case they are bringing for supervision, including their personal insights from their reflective practice. Details about the client, organization and/or others in the system must be presented confidentially, as part of the group agreement. Personal boundaries about self-reflection are both set by the presenting peer and respected by the group.

Step 1 (5–10 minutes): Case presentation by presenting peer

(a) Speaks about her/his case in general terms, though particularly highlighting what is happening for her/him in relation to the case. Self-awareness and reflections about their personal reactions, limitations, blockers and/or sense of importance are possible areas to share.
(b) Suggests a potential area they may want specific feedback or observations on, potentially offering any new observations from this meeting's opening segment that may aid their learning.

Step 2 (5–10 minutes): Reflection and clarification

Peers can ask any clarifying questions needed to clearly understand the case being presented, facilitated by the group moderator. *Clarifying questions* are short and are looking to establish facts.

(a) Brief – 3 minutes – for independent silent case reflection and defining key questions.
(b) Round of clarifying questions. The presenting peer responds with short answers to fill out any details, rather than to "defend" their position and/or why they made the choice.

The purpose of the clarifying question is to:

- Extend the group's relevant understanding of the case
- Check accuracy of information that was already shared
- Add to details which support the presenting peer's stated outcome.

Clarifying questions are NOT:

- Why questions
- Questions that only satisfy your personal curiosity, hunch or to showcase your expertise
- Probing questions.

Examples of clarifying questions:

- What interventions, resources or tools were used?
- Did I hear you say . . . ?
- What criteria or methodology or framework was used to . . . ?
- Did I paraphrase or summarize what I think you've said correctly?
- What is the relationship between you and the client sponsor?

Step 3 (10–15 minutes): Peer supervision round

A round of pithy awareness-building questions to draw out what is going on for the presenting peer and expand their self-awareness within the case. Presenting peer can answer as many or few questions as they like, time allowing.

In this step peers can ask probing questions to encourage the presenting peer to think more deeply about:

- Assumptions about their role, the engagement
- The client's or client sponsor's expectations
- Their relationship with others in the system
- What perspective they bring to the case presented
- What impact they have on the client
- Understanding the relationships between various people in the system, which could also include the presenting peer.

Tip: Ensure there is a gap between questions, so the presenting peer has the opportunity to consider each question. The presenting peer is not expected to respond to each question that is asked. Indeed the facilitator or moderator may remind the presenting peer to consider each question rather than to respond to it.

Examples of probing questions:

- What is the relationship between you and the client?
- What is the relationship between the client and . . . ?
- What was the impact of using the tool or intervention or model?
- Why do you think this is the case?
- What do you think would happen if . . . ?
- What would you do differently next time?

Step 4 (15 minutes): Closing the meeting

The moderator asks for final reflections from the presenting peer. Each member is also asked for a final reflection or take-away to reflect upon that they can take to their own practice to close out the meeting. Note: This is not an opportunity to summarize the learning they think the presenting peer has achieved.

Group technique B: Broadening the presenting peer's capability

Aim: To provide the presenting peer with a range of alternatives in which to work with a client.

Time allocation: 20–50 minutes, depending on group size and agreements. Agree time and facilitator or moderator manages accordingly.

Process steps:

Step 1 (5–20 minutes)
Presenting peer

1   Outlines the case they are bringing for supervision.
2   Poses the questions they've been mulling over in their reflective practice.
3   Suggests anything they might want as a result of the group supervision.
4   Closes out the meeting.

To gather any missing factual information, the group moderator may facilitate peers asking clarifying questions.

Step 2 (5–10 minutes)
Peers discuss and think out loud about aspects of the case and possible alternatives for the presenting peer to consider and reflect on. This could include other possible interventions, theories and/or ways to strengthen the presenting peer's skills as a coach. Peers offer these alternatives as suggestions and/or observations rather than from an expert opinion and to avoid "teaching."

Step 3 (5–10 minutes)
Once the discussion is complete, the presenting peer responds by sharing what she/he is going to take away from the discussion and practice.

Step 4 (5–10 minutes)
All members add the learning that they can take to their own practice to close out the meeting. This is not an opportunity to summarize the learning they think the presenting peer has achieved.

Group technique C: Rehearsal

Aim: To give the presenting peer an opportunity to practice in a safe environment with peers to address an issue with a client in a future conversation, practice a new technique or tool and/or give difficult feedback.

Time allocation: 45–75 minutes, depending on group size and agreements. Agree time. Timekeeper keeps time and facilitator runs group process.

Summary of steps in the technique:

1   Presenting peer shares case and meeting focus.
2   Member reflection and individuals share their insights.
3   Peers share suggestions and presenting peer chooses one to practice.
4   Group role play.
5   Sharing insights learned to close out the meeting.

Technique steps:

Step 1 (5–20 minutes)
Presenting peer shares

1   The scenario that she/he wishes to address with the client.
2   Any specifics that illustrate the client, the scenario, the organization, the tool/intervention.
3   His/her self-awareness, e.g. feeling confident or stuck.
4   What he/she wants the peers to notice during the rehearsal.

To gather any missing factual information, the group moderator may facilitate peers asking clarifying questions.

Step 2 (2–5 minutes)
Peers independently take a few moments to reflect and formulate what they might do in the same scenario. Rather than forming hypothesis of what's going on in the case or giving "this is what I would do . . ." advice, the opportunity for peers is to offer suggestions such as creating an opening statement to start the rehearsal: For example, "I've been thinking about your feedback and wondered if you have as well . . ." or question that they think would be useful for the issue, e.g.: "How have you and your boss been getting along recently?"

Step 3 (5 minutes)

1   Each peer offers one suggestion.
2   Once all the peers have given their opening statement or questions, the presenting peer considers all contributions and chooses one of the suggestions to spend an agreed period of time practicing.

Step 4 (15–30 minutes)
Peers can play the role of the client and/or others within the client organization, family system, etc. to support the presenting peer in an experiential learning process.

Step 5 (15 minutes)
To close out the meeting, all members add their individual learning from their experience which they can take to their own practice. Again, the focus is on their learning, not the presenting peer or others.

Group technique D: Deeping self-reflection as a practitioner

Aim: To enhance group cohesion, build on current reflective practice for both the presenting peer and other group members.

Note: This technique is recommended for more established groups and senior practitioners. This technique works best when members prepare before the meeting. To avoid members falling into the role of expert or "teaching," the facilitator takes an active role, ensuring interruptions or other individual points of view are kept to a minimum and is quite strict on this technique, which rotates each meeting.

Time allocation: 40–65 minutes, depending on group size and agreements.

Summary of steps in the technique:

1 Each member shares one observation about his/her development as a peer group member.
2 Peer group discussion or supervision about impact to group.
3 Peers share initial learning from meeting.

Technique steps:

Step 1 (10–15 minutes)
Each member shares one observation about his/her development as a peer group member. Being vulnerable and sharing what has been difficult, what has become easier over time and/or when you're triggered during group process may be examples of useful data points for discussion. It can also be helpful to note any themes and/or new awareness's that are emerging as a result of his/her independent reflective practice and from the group supervision. An example might be: "I have learned that my tendency within the group is to wait to share last. I notice this pattern also comes up for me with powerful male clients." No one needs to respond or normalize this observation. The moderator may say thank you, if useful.

Step 2 (20–35 minutes)
Once everyone has shared their personal insight, the group then discusses how these individual reflections as a whole inform the way the group is working together currently. Using the example above, conversation may be about: What patterns has the group developed as a result of someone consistently sharing last? What options does the group have to break this pattern? How do I as a peer member interpret this behavior as impacting on me?

Step 3 (10–15 minutes): Final round
Each individual shares what they are willing to try out as a result of their new awareness of their behavior in the peer supervision group.

Simplifying Contracts and contracting   5

Definition: Contracting is the process of agreeing boundaries and is a dialogue that establishes and then sustains the relationship. Contracting is important at the beginning of a relationship to set out the initial terms of engagement, i.e. it creates the "Contract" (an agreement that clarifies mutual expectations and obligations). Additionally, it is a critical set of skills that are used throughout the relationship, which enables all parties to voice and explore issues when things become unclear or difficult.

What we mean by contracting

We hope this definition clarifies that here we will be talking about two different things, which are highly interrelated. As a result this chapter is organized into two sections: The first looks at how you create the Contract (noun) for your peer supervision work. The second section looks at the skills of contracting (verb). We believe that both of these are needed for successful peer supervision.

The chapters on one to one and on group peer supervision include guidance on the essential elements of your Contract. However, once you are up and running, typically you will discover greater granularity to these elements. In Section 1, we include a number of additional items for discussion, which provoke you to develop a more expansive Contract to work with.

In Section 2 we focus on the skills of contracting, a much overlooked area of expertise. We place it second because only when you have the Contract in place, do you have a formal reference point for your contracting dialogue. While the Contract may be a physical document, it is the contracting dialogue that keeps it alive. We would encourage you to revisit your Contract on a regular basis (we call this re-contracting) to ensure you are deriving the most value from your peer supervision relationships. We offer some examples that might hint that a re-contracting discussion would be useful and which could prompt greater detail or clarification to your original Contract. Once you have developed your contracting skills through regular re-contracting you will be in a position to engage in "spot" contracting. This demonstrates the skills of contracting in its fullest sense. It is done in the moment as you become aware of nuances, which have the potential to undermine the efficacy of the peer supervision relationship. We offer some practical examples of how this might work in practice. We also provide our thoughts on what personal characteristics contribute to developing these good contracting skills.

Section 1: Developing the peer supervision Contract

Your personal preferences and the culture that you work within will determine how formal or informal you want your Contract to be. It can be tempting to feel that if you have had a good discussion about how you want to work and you have developed a sense of trust between you, that the Contract does not need to be documented. However, we would encourage you to have some kind of physical record. This could be a typed-up document that all parties sign up to, a photo of a flip chart that was created together or perhaps the contracting conversation is recorded. This can then act as a reference point when something arises that has the potential to cause tensions in the partnership or group.

According to Hawkins and Smith (2006), they would propose five key areas to cover in your peer supervision Contract. Observing these five areas, we have created Table 5.1 to illustrate what decisions, as a minimum, need to be made to create your initial Contract.

Chapters 3 and 4 give more detailed guidance context to one to one and group peer supervision Contract content, and reflect these five broad areas.

Additional considerations for your Contract

According to Hay (2007), there are three main elements which require consideration when contracting with peers. These are described as procedural, professional and psychological. We would add a fourth element, labeled political, as we discovered this could be important when peers are allied to the same organization (whether an employer, a third party or a training organization).

When you create an initial Contract you will probably have touched upon each of these four elements of the Contract. However, realistically it is not possible to cover every eventuality before you start. Peer relationships are particularly complex, and the longer you work together the greater the likelihood

Table 5.1 Five areas for contracting and decisions to be made for a peer supervision Contract

Area identified by Hawkins and Smith (2006)	Decisions to be made in order to form initial Contract for peer supervision
Practicalities	How often will we meet and for how long? Where will we meet? How will we manage cancellation or rescheduling?
Boundaries	What kind of topics will we bring to peer supervision? What kind of topics would we not bring to peer supervision (and where would we take them instead?) What professional supervision arrangements do we want to put in place?
Working alliance	How will we manage confidentiality? What level of preparation will we commit to? What are our hopes and fears for our peer supervision relationship? What do we need to know about each other's practice before we start peer supervision?

Meeting format	How will we structure the time during the meeting?
	What techniques will we work with?
	In a group:
	  How will we share the role of facilitator?
	  How will we share the role of peer supervisee?

Organization and professional context	What Code of Ethics will we operate with? What other stakeholders have an interest in our work and how will we keep connected with them?

Hawkins and Smith (2006)

that something will shift in the relationship that has yet to be contracted for. Indeed some contracting issues will not even manifest themselves until you have begun to work at a deeper level.

So once you are up and running there may be more contracting discussions to undertake. Using Hay's three contracting elements, we offer some key questions for discussion with your peer(s). We also identify how, in answering these questions you will be able to manage wider issues. The list is not exhaustive, neither is it a checklist to follow. We hope, however it prompts you to explore whether or not these issues might be present in your peer supervision relationship and if they are, then we highlight why it will be important to surface and manage them and expand your Contract accordingly.

Our intention is to help you set up your peer supervision relationship so that

- It is robust and professional.
- It has a sense of equity and collaboration.

- All parties are clear about who is responsible for what.
- There is transparency around how any difficulties will be managed.
- Your contracting skills become well developed.

Contracting element 1: Procedural matters (Tables 5.2, 5.3, 5.4)

Procedural matters concern the logistics and practicalities of setting up and maintaining your peer supervision relationship. Typically it is these practical considerations that are most naturally included in a Contract. The essential items will have been covered within your initial contracting discussion, and we provide the relevant guidance on these within Chapters 3 and 4. However, there is often a difference between what we agree in principle and what happens in practice. In Table 5.2, Table 5.3 and Table 5.4 below we identify a number of common practical matters that are likely to arise and which may benefit from further discussion.

Table 5.2 Practical matters to discuss: Frequency

Question for discussion	Issues it will help manage
How far ahead will we plan the meetings?	Individuals have different time management preferences. There is also a difference between cultures and their conventions of time keeping. In discussing this it may highlight how people will manage their competing priorities. For example you may have agreed to give 48 hours' notice of cancellation, but then you feel conflicted when a client wants to use the time slot allocated to peer supervision. How easy it is for you to honor the peer supervision agreement? Exploring this helps a discussion about how flexible the planned schedule will be.
How do we manage "emergency" needs?	When working on a one to one basis it is important to understand when your peer is willing to be available to support you and what both of your expectations are.
	When working on a group basis offering support on a pre-agreed or rotated basis is advisable. Without this, a dependency upon more experienced individuals can emerge and/or sub-groups may start to form.

Table 5.3 Practical matters to discuss: Time management

Question for discussion	Issues it will help manage
How strict will we be about start and finish times?	Different personalities and cultures vary in their perspective on punctuality. Resentment is likely to build if someone routinely arrives late or leaves early or if the

continued

Table 5.3 *continued*

Question for discussion	Issues it will help manage
	meeting often over-runs. Flushing out "what will we do if . . . ?" helps you establish workable boundaries.
How will we track how the meeting time is used?	Tracking how you manage your time can help you to avoid inequities creeping in. For example you may be thinking why NAME always goes first/last. Or how come NAME always uses up more than their share of the airtime. If you have data on this it is easier to discuss than working with perceptions and can benefit both one to one and groups.
Under what circumstances does someone "lose" a meeting?	Although all parties might welcome some flexibility, there may come a point when recurrent requests to reschedule or frequent "no-shows" feel unacceptable to the other peer(s). This discussion will uncover what kind of "penalties" would be deemed acceptable should elements of the Contract not be observed.
How will we manage lateness?	To avoid disrupting the flow of a meeting, determine some time parameters. How else will you know if it's OK to leave the venue, start work on something else or wait a little longer in the hope that your peer arrives?
	If this is not agreed in advance, decisions to exclude the peer from the meeting may seem punitive or conversely inclusion might be interpreted as collusion that the time boundary is not important.

Table 5.4 Practical matters to discuss: Location

Question for discussion	Issues it will help manage
How appropriate is our location?	An agreed venue could unwittingly create inequity. For example – someone might offer the use of their office, but then find that they have to put extra time into preparing or tidying the room after the meeting. Difficulties can also arise when working online. Not everyone experiences stable internet connection and glitches in the quality of communication may mean that some people have a less complete peer supervision experience than the other(s).
	Unless these sources of inequity are discussed they have the potential to impact on the perceived value of the peer supervision encounter.
How will we manage credit control?	When a venue incurs a cost, one person may offer to pay the bill and others will reimburse them. Although the amount may be relatively small, should someone

continued

Table 5.4 *continued*

Question for discussion	Issues it will help manage
	default on the reimbursement it can create embarrassment and ill feeling. Agreeing how this will be managed, in advance, makes it easier to raise an issue.

Contracting element 2: Professional matters (Tables 5.5, 5.6)

Peer coaching supervision is an interesting discipline as it has overtones of many other helping relationships. For example: Coaching the coach, mentoring, critical friend, trusted advisor, counselor and professional sounding board . . . to name just a few. The professional elements of contracting consider the content of what is discussed within peer supervision to ensure they sit in the most appropriate domain.

Table 5.5 Practical matters to discuss: Boundaries

Question for discussion	Issues it will help manage
What was the "tone" of our conversation?	Peer coaching supervision can overlap with other "helping" conversations. How can you know the difference? Consider how others might perceive the discussion. Could they have seen this as a mentoring, a coach the coach or a counseling meeting? Taking this evaluative perspective will help you stay true to your original peer supervision Contract. Noticing the patterns can help you decide when the Contract needs re-contracting or when a referral to other practitioners is most appropriate.
What will we do if we feel out of our depth?	It is a common experience to be surprised at what direction a peer supervision conversation takes. You might start with something apparently simple and through dialogue uncover a personal developmental issue. The surprise can affect the planned route. As a result, someone might need additional time and/or to access additional support. If this situation is not explored there may be pressure to continue the conversation as planned – and yet if powerful emotions are present, an alternative course of action may be more prudent.
Are we sure we are working in service of our clients?	Peer discussions can often shift away from their original focus into the adjacent issues of running a business or sharing new learning. Although these discussions have value for the practitioners, the needs of their clients may be overshadowed. Checking for evidence as to how you have applied your reflections from your peer supervision discussion is a good test of how well you are serving your

continued

Table 5.5 *continued*

Question for discussion	Issues it will help manage
	clients and if necessary, restructure your meetings to specifically discuss client work.
What will we do if we feel someone is working unethically (either with their clients or within the peer supervision relationship)?	This is probably the most dreaded situation not just for facilitators but for professional supervisors too. To help you, we offer a process for escalation (Appendix 5.1). Just having the conversation about this process will be a useful exercise; it will tend to make ethical issues more discussable and will prepare you for any real difficulties that may emerge.

Table 5.6 Practical matters to discuss: Confidentiality

Question for discussion	Issues it will help manage
What do we do if we realize there is a breach of client confidentiality?	Unfortunately no one has an erase button. In the event that confidentiality is broken, you cannot "un-know" what you now know. Therefore it can be helpful to establish under what circumstances the breach should be communicated to the client, when it can be managed within the peer supervision relationship and when advice from a professional supervisor should be sought.
Is it OK if I share with my partner (a personal relationship) what we have discussed in peer supervision? Does it make a difference if they are a coach too?	Discussion of this will trace people's understanding of private vs. confidential conversations. It will help establish common perspective on whether sharing unattributed information constitutes a breach in confidentiality. It also clarifies which other professionals the confidentiality extends to. Typically this leads to amuch tighter and conscious management of client and peer information.
What is our communication etiquette if we take to peer supervision outside of this peer relationship?	Practitioners will often have more than one source of supervision. Where an issue has already been processed before peer supervision, it can help to make that explicit. Without this the peer(s) are likely to feel something is missing in the narrative. Similarly, where you have processed the outcome of peer supervision in another supervision setting, sharing this at the next meeting is advisable. In both instances this is relevant information when you are assessing the usefulness of your peer supervision arrangement.

Contracting element 3: Psychological matters (Tables 5.7, 5.8, 5.9)

Although we are all professional practitioners, we are first and foremost human beings. When we enter into a peer supervision relationship we don't just bring our professional selves, we bring a whole bundle of history, good and bad experiences, vulnerabilities, ego, assumptions and belief systems. For any supervision to work well, individuals need to have a sense of psychological safety. Any one of these influences has the potential to contaminate the effectiveness of the peer supervision work. The questions in the tables below will give you a platform for raising potentially sensitive issues in a constructive manner.

Table 5.7 Practical matters to discuss: Openness and trust

Question for discussion	Issues it will help manage
When do we notice that we are editing what we say?	In peer supervision we need to create a space where we feel safe enough to be vulnerable. Establishing this space is not a formula and the sense of safety often ebbs and flows depending on what is being brought to peer supervision and how the peer(s) react. Through noticing what we are editing in our narratives, it gives us clues about what else might need to be made transparent and contracted for.
How is our previous experience of supervision impacting on this peer supervision relationship?	Because it takes time to build openness and trust we will tend to approach a new peer supervision relationship based on our experience of prior and similar relationships. Where that prior experience was positive, you might find yourself being prematurely open compared to your peer(s). Where that prior experience was negative you may find yourself holding back in comparison to your peer(s). If this prior history is not understood, erroneous conclusions could be drawn about your engagement in the current relationship.

Table 5.8 Practical matters to discuss: Managing feedback

Question for discussion	Issues it will help manage
How are we experiencing the level of support and challenge given and received?	It is easy to make assumptions that others share our understanding of what appropriate levels of support and challenge look like. If we play safe, the relationship becomes too cozy; if we are too bold, we may make it more difficult to be vulnerable. By giving attention to how support and challenge are being experienced, it helps everyone refine the skill of giving feedback.
What are the areas for which you will find feedback most useful?	We have noticed that many practitioners hungry for developing their work will invite all manner of feedback from their peers. However, because there is so much to attend to in the supervision dialogue, it can be more helpful to narrow down what you would value feedback upon. This places greater responsibility on you to choose your development focus, and increases account ability for working with the feedback that you have requested.

continued

Table 5.8 continued

Question for discussion	Issues it will help manage
What's your experience of giving and receiving of feedback?	Without this focus feedback can feel quite scattered and may indeed be overwhelming to manage. Peer supervision is a rich opportunity for the giving and receiving of feedback – however not everyone will come with the skills to do this effectively. Feedback handled poorly (either giving or receiving) can cause individuals to withdraw from developmental work. Proactively giving feedback on how the feedback message was managed (along with any suggestions of what might have worked more effectively) will build the skill set of all involved.

Table 5.9 Practical matters to discuss: Managing peer comparisons

Question for discussion	Issues it will help manage
What experience does each of us have of working with peers?	Our peer supervision relationships will not exist in a vacuum. We will each have some history that could influence how we feel about working with our contemporaries. If someone has prior experience of working in peer supervision, proactively sharing their lessons learned creates more equity than constantly turning to them to ask, "What should we do now?" Similarly, if someone has had a negative experience of working with peer(s), e.g. bullying, this is also helpful to know. It could help explain an individual's reticence to trust, it prompts all parties to be consciously competent about their contributions and also allows challenges to be made if unhelpful relationship patterns emerge.
What kinds of things make us feel inferior or superior?	Discussing this kind of question will test the level of trust that exists. However, this is precisely the kind of information that is useful to know as it allows you to spot potentially unhealthy dynamics. When something occurs that feels out of place it may be an indication of an issue that lies just outside of our conscious awareness. With an understanding of each individual's triggers, you can engage in a fuller discussion and explore some hypotheses about what might be going on in the relationship dynamics. This can be rich territory for developing increased self-awareness.
How will we honor diversity in our approaches?	Practitioners are likely to work in their own unique way. Occasionally, a peer will describe a way of working that feels odd to us. It is therefore important to have some working. What might seem incongruent with our own way of working may be entirely congruent with theirs.

continued

Simplifying Contracts and contracting 115

Table 5.9 *continued*

Question for discussion	Issues it will help manage
	When this wider context is understood, it is easier to hold open our curiosity. We are more likely to make enquiries about what prompted someone to work in the way they did, than make suggestions about what might have worked better from our own perspective.

Contracting element 4: Political matters (Tables 5.10, 5.11)

These elements occur when differences between peers are subtle or sensitive, and where most people would not naturally surface them for discussion we have called this political matters. What are the politics around here what are the often unspoken rules or norms? Political matters can be easy to make assumptions about or perhaps reflect an unconscious bias at the individual or systemic level. These can be particularly prevalent for internal coaches who also have a regular job in the organization – hierarchy, dual relationships, role boundaries and shared history may all serve to complicate the peer supervision relationship. Through working transparently, identifying what political issues could be in play and agreeing how they will be managed, the relationship dynamics can be kept healthy.

Table 5.10 Practical matters to discuss: Power imbalances

Question for discussion	Issues it will help manage
What is the range of experience among us?	Peers are often reluctant to be explicit about the precise nature of their experience. This could be masking all manner of agendas, from "I don't want to be seen as a know-it-all" to "I can't admit to how few clients I have" or simply a desire to fit in with the others. However unwittingly, this may cause a degree of posturing because at some level most people do want others to honor our experience (or lack of). By sharing quite explicitly, our client hours, typical clients, our experience of supervision, peers can actively use the diversity of experience in the relationship. A novice practitioner can be valued for their fresh perspective; a more seasoned practitioner can be valued for the nuances they have uncovered along their way.
When could our context have a ripple effect on our working relationship?	This is most useful for internal coaches as there are many opportunities for dual relationships to emerge. For example – when one of you has responsibility for matching the other with a client or perhaps you attended the same development program. However,

continued

Table 5.10 *continued*

Question for discussion	Issues it will help manage
	it could also occur with independents, especially if you work for the same associate company or belong to a coaching community. It could be that there are no adverse consequences of the wider context. However, in discussing the issue it raises awareness of the potential for it to happen and will encourage peers to be proactive in spotting the unforeseen consequences of their other relationships.

Table 5.11 Practical matters to discuss: Unconscious bias

Question for discussion	Issues it will help manage
What evidence do we have that we truly work with perspectives that we don't initially connect with?	Humans have a tendency for "confirmation bias," i.e. only paying attention to those ideas that support our existing views. Plaister-Ten's (2013) cultural kaleidoscope model provides a model to look at culture through multiple lenses. This will help you identify which elements of your personal make up offer the greatest diversity of thinking for each other. Importantly, this is about more than discussion – it's about encouraging experimentation in your practice. Therefore sharing what you might do differently and precisely how you would be different, offers a guided opportunity to experience how your practice could be without your in-built bias.
How will we know if the right time to discuss a particular issue is appropriate?	Practitioners often bring to supervision something that has recently occurred. However, it is highly possible that the emotions that the issue is evoking will cloud the ability to be objective. There might be some merit in allowing a peer to vent. However, arrival techniques (where the issue is acknowledged, but parked) would enable the peer to select the supervision issue, which is pertinent in the context of their whole practice.
Where do we feel most confident and strong? How might this cause you to stumble?	When we feel competent, experienced or knowledgeable about what we might do next with a client (yours or someone else's) we will experience a sense of confidence and certainty, which is highly likely to be misplaced! It is actually very difficult to predict the future with any sense of reliability or accuracy. It can therefore be useful to deliberately consider "What would we definitely not do?" and then play with what positive consequences could possibly occur if we did.

continued

Table 5.11 *continued*

Question for discussion	Issues it will help manage
	This often has the effect of introducing humor to the perspectives helping practitioners extend their repertoire beyond the tried and tested.
Does it feel like collaboration or competition?	All of us are in the same market and as humans we naturally compare with each other. How comfortable will you be about sharing your contacts and/or business successes? If you perceive others are doing better than you, how does that affect the power dynamics? Comparison can lead you to feel a range of emotions: Envy, superiority or inferiority, for example. Discussing these things openly can help to mitigate negative impacts on relationships.

Section 2: Developing the skills of contracting

What we have discovered in our own experience of working with peers is that when we start out, we tend to show up with our best behavior. We have a positive mindset and we want the relationship to work and approach the contracting discussion constructively. However, then life happens! We discover that what we thought was possible is more tricky than we imagined. We start to relax occasionally about the ground rules agreed. We start to notice nuance in our peers' behavior or attitudes, which causes an emotional response in us, and similarly we notice that our peers are being impacted by how we are showing up. What happens next is critical for the survival of a healthy peer supervision relationship. Will you call it out? Or will you suppress your reaction for fear of handling the conversation awkwardly and causing conflict? If you have surfaced the tension and handled the resulting discussion well, the likelihood is that the skills you used were contracting skills.

As a practitioner engaging in peer supervision, the primary tool you have for managing all of the complexities you are likely to encounter is how (not just what) you contract for the relationship. The process of contracting can:

- Help both the individuals and the group to understand more fully the terms and conditions already agreed in working together
- Provide an opportunity to review and assess in the moment what is working and what is not working, in order to establish a pathway forward
- Give a lens in which to view and dismantle unconscious bias
- Break power dynamics
- Help make the un-discussable, discussable.

118 Simplifying Contracts and contracting

Peer supervision is a co-created endeavor and yet each person needs to take individual responsibility for the health of the relationship. As Hay (2007) said, "Contracting is both an essential skill and also a way of working with another person that invites and encourages them to stay in the here-and-now and take responsibility for their own actions." With this in mind we believe it helpful to consider the goals of peer supervision within the frame of the "Shared Outcome Model" described by Turner (2014). See Figure 5.1 below.

This model highlights that in order to reach a shared outcome there needs to be a shared understanding of who has Accountability and Responsibility for how the peer supervision relationship will be managed. These "above the line" behaviors help the relationship thrive. We experience Curiosity, Compassion, Courage and Mindfulness. Conversely when "below the line" fear-based behaviors of Blame, Denial, Excuses and/or Avoidance emerge, the health of the peer supervision relationship is jeopardized.

So how does this work in practice? What we like about the Hay quote above is the reminder that managing a potential dent to the relationship is best done when it happens. Working in the moment does however take courage and skill! When you first create the Contract it is likely that you will not cover all of the issues that may arise throughout the peer supervision engagement. Therefore

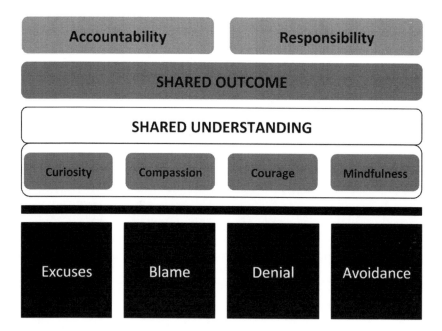

Figure 5.1 The shared outcome model
Turner (2014)

contracting for regular re-contracting is a helpful principle and will help you hone your contracting skills. Periodic re-contracting meetings encourage each person to reflect on three things:

1 What is working well for them?
2 What is not working as well?
3 What with hindsight would benefit from further clarification?

Table 5.12 gives some examples of when it might be time to revisit an element of the Contract and have a contracting discussion about it. These examples are not exhaustive, but give a flavor of the subtleties involved in peer supervision conversations about contracting.

With the re-contracting meetings planned in advance there is time to prepare for them. It is good practice to identify what patterns or themes you have noticed emerging in the relationship and then to consider how best to communicate what you have observed. In order to stay with the "above the line" feedback, your choice of language is important. Some practical tips are to stay curious, identify specific examples that helped to raise your awareness of the matter and to take personal responsibility for your own emotional reactions and the impact they have on you.

Table 5.13 below gives some examples to illustrate how you might convert below the line feedback to above the line feedback.

As the peer supervision relationship matures and your contracting skills deepen, we would encourage you to take your skills one step further and to engage in "spot contracting." Here you do not wait for the next official opportunity to review how the relationship is working – you surface the sense of disconnect in the moment taking the "above the line" perspective.

Remember there are cultural differences in communications styles and with increasing globalization the need to surface these differences and discuss how they might show up is important, spotting them when they happen and then exploring this difference can help.

To engage in spot contracting, you need to keep your shared outcome in mind, be clear about your perspective, take a deep breath and speak from the heart so that your peer(s) can feel your authenticity. As we outlined in Table 5.13, the choice of language is important so that you don't infer blame or allow excuses. Here are some examples of what that might look like:

- "I noticed that . . ." (e.g. You have arrived late for the last two meetings; I'm wondering whether we need to review our agreed time slot?)
- "May I share some frustration that's rising in me? (e.g. When we contracted, we agreed that we would each put some time into preparing for our meetings. I am honoring that commitment. In the last few meetings it feels

Table 5.12 Clues that a contracting discussion is needed

Element of the Contract	Clues that a contracting discussion might be timely
PRACTICALITIES	
Frequency	• Noticing that either you or a peer have either too much or not enough to bring • Feeling like you have to wait to bring an urgent issue to your next meeting, by which point the moment has passed
Punctuality	• Sitting on an irritation about how punctuality is managed at the start or end of the meeting • Honoring the peer supervision meeting causes you difficulty in other elements of your schedule • One or more of the peers may be more rigid or more relaxed in how much notice is felt to be reasonable when there is a need to cancel or reschedule
Venue	• Feeling like the agreed venue benefits some more than others • Noticing that where money is concerned, different people appear to have different values or behaviors
BOUNDARIES	
Topics	• Noticing differences in the choice of topics you and your peer(s) are bringing for supervision discussion
THE WORKING ALLIANCE	
Scope of the work	• Feeling surprised at how deep or conversely how superficial the supervision discussion was • Not understanding how a peer's contribution fits within the world of supervision
Preparation	• Noticing that a peer struggles to recollect the details of the case they bring • Feeling as though you do more or less preparation than your peer(s)
Confidentiality	• Noticing a hesitation before you share your own vulnerability or perhaps choosing not to share at all • Feeling as though you might know who is being talked about, but not knowing how to tackle that for fear of breaching your own client's confidentiality
MEETING FORMAT	
Duration	• Noticing that the discussion feels either rushed or labored • Feeling like the time is not shared equally
ORGANIZATION and PROFESSIONAL CONTEXT	
Transparency	• Feeling awkward that your peer(s) has additional knowledge about you from other relationships, which might be impacting on the peer supervision relationship or vice versa

Table 5.13 Language differences between below the line and above the line feedback

BELOW THE LINE FEEDBACK	ABOVE THE LINE FEEDBACK
Peer relationship:	
You really irritate me with all your requests to reschedule	I notice that when you ask to reschedule that I experience a real irritation in me. Could we revisit that part of our Contract?
How come NAME always goes last?	I've noticed that NAME often has a preference for going last, I would prefer it if we mixed this up more. What do you think?
Why do you always make me feel so uncomfortable?	I notice that I often feel uncomfortable when you help me explore a case – I would actually find it more helpful if you did XXXX?
Some people seem to have a habit of ignoring our contracted start and finish times and no one's saying anything about it	I notice that in our Contract we agreed to start and finish on time and that it doesn't always happen; my sense is that it might be helpful to revisit that part of our contract?

as though you have come unprepared. This raises a concern for me that we might have different perspectives on our contract.)
- "Would you tell me more about . . ." (e.g. Your intention behind your contribution on the last supervision case, on the receiving end it landed awkwardly?)
- "What was going on for you when . . ." (e.g. We were discussing finding a new venue, I thought I noticed something that looked a bit like frustration in you?)
- "Could I check out what you just said for a moment? XXXX works quite well for me, and I'm curious to know how well it works for you?"

As a practitioner you know using open-ended questions can lead to new possibilities and ways of relating in a constructive "above the line" way. Knowing when and how to "spot contract" gives all parties the opportunity to redefine accountability, responsibility and/or ownership to suit the current reality and get back on track in the peer supervision relationship. By working with difficulties as they arise, it will minimize risk and increase your sense of satisfaction in the engagement.

Developing good contracting skills rests on four inter-related capabilities:

1 Your own self-awareness – an ability to know what your triggers are, what kind of state you are currently in and you are sufficiently resourceful to actively manage your responses to your triggers.

2   Your objectivity – an ability to divorce yourself from your own experience and consider what might be happening for other people in the moment.
3   Your communication style – an ability to bring attention to an issue using non-judgmental language.
4   Your groundedness – an ability to hold the importance of relationship and the importance of task in equal measure in order to develop a shared outcome.

All of these skills are helpful in your client work too. Table 5.14 offers some hints and tips on how you might continue to deepen these skills specifically in the context of your peer supervision relationship.

The skills of contracting will grow the more you use them. It can be helpful to contract with your peer(s) to jointly develop your contracting skills so that you quite deliberately "have a go" at raising issues for discussion. Where you have access to a professional supervisor, they can help accelerate your learning. Not only can they role model contracting skills, they could offer you a space for rehearsing your contracting discussions so that you feel more courageous to raise the concerns you have.

Final thoughts

In this chapter we have discussed many elements that can form your Contract, plus the contracting skills you might need and offered some tips for how you might manage them. However, both client and peer relationships are complex and therefore this list is probably not exhaustive. When we train as coaches we are schooled in the notion that contracting needs to happen "up front." That of course is helpful. However, if you discussed all of the elements above before you

Table 5.14 Hints and tips for developing your peer supervision contracting skills

Self-awareness	Journal your experience of the peer supervision meetings. What do you notice makes a difference to how satisfied you are with the work and the relationship?
Objectivity	Visualize putting yourself in the other persons' shoes or sit in a chair opposite an empty chair to imagine how your peer(s) will perceive you.
Communication style	See Table 5.13 for examples. Reflect on any awkward communications and consider how you would have rephrased them.
Groundedness	Practicing mindfulness so that you can access your more resourceful self in a few seconds.

started working together it would probably be a very long and exhausting meeting! Creating your Contract is critically important as you commence the relationship and it also needs to be revisited frequently and, when you have the contracting skills, addressed in the moment. Your peer supervision Contract needs to be co-created. Where you are working in a group and a member leaves or joins it is a useful protocol to revisit the Contract. It is important that each peer sees him- or herself as equally responsible for its efficacy. We would invite you to select a handful of elements from this chapter that feel most pertinent to each of you – and then to keep a watching brief on how your peer discussions develop. Whenever you experience a moment of hesitation before you offer something to your peer(s) or an irritation over what just happened, this is probably an indication that something in the Contract needs to be further explored.

Key learning points

1. A Contract is a document that contains the terms under which work is agreed. Contracting is a verb and the skill that is needed in order to put together the contract. Both are required for best practice.
2. To avoid misunderstandings or conflicts, even "common sense subjects" (punctuality, etc.) should be included, as they do not go without saying and can cause unnecessary tension.
3. Reviewing the Contract periodically can provide a rich opportunity to review your practice and strengthen your peer relationships.
4. When below the line behaviors surface, spot contract to surface the cause and using above the line behavior to agree a shared outcome.

References

Hawkins, P. and Smith, N. (2006) *Coaching, Mentoring and Organisational Consultancy: Supervision and development*. Maidenhead, UK: Open University.

Hay, J. (2007) *Reflective Practice and Supervision for Coaches*. Maidenhead, UK: McGraw-Hill.

Plaister-Ten, J. (2013) Raising culturally-derived awareness and building culturally appropriate responsibility: The development of the Cross-Cultural Kaleidoscope. *International Journal of Evidence Based Coaching and Mentoring*, 11(2), pp. 53–69.

Turner, T. (2014) *The Importance of Contracting: Using the shared outcomes model* [pdf]. Available from: www.developingcoaching.com.au/wp-content/uploads/Tammy-Turner-Article-Contracting-using-shared-outcomes.pdf [accessed 8 September 2017].

Appendix 5.1

How to escalate an issue when one of the peers feels there has been an ethical breach

1. During the peer discussion one of the parties experiences a level of discomfort.
2. As soon as is practical the individual noticing the discomfort "calls it" and shares their concern with the other person(s).
3. Both parties acknowledge that they appear to have a different view of what "good practice" looks like.
4. Each person explains their perspective on the issue.
5. In the spirit of curiosity the peers consult the Ethical Code of Conduct that you each subscribe to. Each person shares their interpretation of the relevant key points to see what might be causing the difference in perspective.
6. Assuming a common ground cannot be found, the peers agree a period of time for reflection – this may or may not include an invitation to receive professional individual supervision during the intervening period.
7. The peers reconvene and share what new insights have emerged since their original discussion.
8. Members offer their suggestion of what they feel would be an appropriate course of action.
9. Some time is spent exploring each suggestion to see how the other would feel as a result.
10. Where there is still a lack of alignment, one of the peers should escalate the issue to the chosen professional supervisor to arrange a joint meeting. Ideally this would be the person whose practice is the cause of concern. However, if this person is reluctant to do so the peer with the discomfort could take the initiative, transparently but unilaterally.
11. The chosen professional supervisor facilitates a discussion between all peers in the spirit of curiosity and to ensure the issues are fully explored.
12. Where a way forward can be found, actions are identified and the professional supervisor will check in at an appropriate point to ensure they have been carried through.
13. Where a way forward is not found, members will work transparently agreeing who will contact the individuals' professional membership body, such that they are in a position to deal with it according to their internal processes. Again the professional supervisor will check in at an appropriate point to ensure that the matter has been attended to.

Exploring coaching and mentoring dilemmas   6

We have mentioned in previous chapters how to use peer supervision to support your continuous development as a coach. However, when you are new to supervision, it's not always clear what sort of things you might bring for discussion. Each peer relationship will mature at a different pace, and as individuals we will differ regarding our need for privacy or expression. In this chapter therefore, we provide you with a range of scenarios that have been preprepared. We hope these dilemmas will help you "kick-start" your peer supervision discussions. Each scenario helps to illustrate what content you might bring to peer supervision and it will help you flush out your own experiences for comparison. For each dilemma we offer a range of options of what is "likely" or "less likely" to be an appropriate way forward. Interventions are highly contextual and so we hope this approach will help build your repertoire of possible options. Once you have exhausted using the dilemmas provided, you could even generate some additional dilemmas inspired from your own practice.

What we mean by dilemmas

The scenarios that follow cover a range of genuine coaching and mentoring dilemmas; they have each been produced as one of a set of cards (Whitaker and Lucas, 2014). To aid your understanding, the scenarios are organized into four categories which look at different ethical challenges: Confidentiality, Boundaries, Conflicts of Interest and Dual Relationships.

You will notice that most dilemmas span more than one category, and that's because in "real life" most situations don't fit neatly into one box! For each scenario we offer five multiple-choice options – each of which is likely to be more or less appropriate, depending on the context of the coaching work. To act as a catalyst for your peer discussions, we provide our perspective. However, we would encourage you to discuss the scenarios and the multiple-choice options before looking at our "answers."

Whether they feel appropriate or not may depend on your own experience, value set and coaching or mentoring approach. This is what can be so fascinating for the discussion – most people will have a "gut reaction" to what they would or wouldn't do . . . . so what informs that response? To act as a prompt within the table we repeatedly ask "Your thoughts?" – there really are no "right" or "wrong" answers . . . just what is right for the circumstances and people involved.

We'd encourage you to have a good debate about both perspectives of each option. We recognize that there are probably many more options than the four we have provided you with. Therefore make some time to discuss option "E" each time, as this is where you can develop some more ideas for future circumstances. This will help broaden your perspective and stretch your own thinking once you encounter them.

After each comparison table, we include a learning summary. We hope this serves to bring together some of the guiding principles that influence the appropriateness of each option. If any of the options themselves don't make sense to you, read this learning summary and then take another look. If you are still stuck, then perhaps seek out additional perspective from other practitioners or from a professional supervisor.

To broaden your thinking still further we suggest you perhaps look at all the dilemmas in the other contexts. While your experience might be located in one particular setting, for example working as an independent coach, it may be of interest to look at the other contexts too, for example the dilemmas faced by internal coaches. You are likely to find that although the settings are different, elements of the dilemma will still resonate with your own experience. Of course where that's not the case, this can again be a really fruitful discussion. What is different about this context that shifts your sense of what might be appropriate or less appropriate? Consider whether that kind of situation could ever occur in your context.

The four contexts (these are not exhaustive but cover the majority of situations) that we will use to illustrate the dilemmas are listed below. We have organized them into sections so that you can select which contexts you want to bring into your peer discussions.

1   Independent coaches
2   Internal coaches
3   Line manager as coach
4   Mentors.

Within each context we will provide a short scenario for each of the four categories that provoke potential ethical dilemmas: Confidentiality, Boundaries, Conflicts of Interest and Dual Relationships.

Section 1: Example dilemmas for independent coaches

Ethical category 1: Confidentiality

The scenario here considers the complexity of handling information when working with multiple stakeholders: "Horses for courses"?

You're working with a client to help them develop a more effective leadership style. You become aware that their espoused style conflicts with your own values, and, from your understanding, it would also conflict with the values of the organization.

What could you do?

A   Carry on with assignment and work with their values.
B   Voice your sense of personal dissonance, be prepared to walk away from the coaching assignment if you cannot resolve the differences.
C   Explore with the client what they notice about the organizational landscape.
D   Explore organization values with their sponsor or the human resources contact.
E   Something else.

> **DISCUSSION POINT (SEE TABLE 6.1):**
>
> Which option are you most drawn to? What is influencing your perspective?

Further thoughts

In our experience we see two slightly different "issues" here. The first is how we handle ourselves when faced with a client that sees the world differently from us. Each of us will have a different level of sensitivity regarding whether or not we choose to work with someone who holds a value set that conflicts with our own. So this is about reflection and self-management.

The second issue is the one that speaks mostly to the quandary of how to maintain confidentiality. If your view is that the client's value set is in conflict with the organization's value set, then that might be a useful piece of information

Table 6.1 Independent coaches – confidentiality: Horses for courses?

Option	Likely to be appropriate	Less appropriate
A: Carry on with assignment and work with their values	Where you are confident you can boundary your own perspective and not contaminate the discussion Your thoughts?	Where the difference is so fundamental it would affect your rapport Your thoughts?
B: Voice your sense of personal dissonance, be prepared to walk away from the coaching assignment if you cannot resolve the differences	Where you have a good rapport with your client and this feedback would support their development Your thoughts?	Where the client has a history of rejection and you may be responding to a parallel process (unconscious links between the coach and client) Your thoughts?
C: Explore with the client what they notice about the organizational landscape	Where your client has indicated openness to challenging their perceptions Your thoughts?	Where the client has little interest in "others" and you sense you would get more engagement if you explored his story of how his value set has developed Your thoughts?
D: Explore organization values with their sponsor or the HR contact	Where information about the organization values are already in the public domain and you can get clarification without breaching the confidentiality of the client Your thoughts?	Where there is an express Contract with your client that you will only engage with other stakeholders when they are also present Your thoughts?
E: Something else	Your thoughts?	Your thoughts?

to explore with the client. However that's where the danger lies. How have you come to form this view on the organization's values? Could you bring your views into the discussion without revealing how you had formed that opinion? Interestingly here the potential breach of confidentiality may not be to your client, it could be to other clients or stakeholders that you work with in the same organization.

In this scenario the coach is external to the organization – so while the coach may have an understanding of organizational values they could be mistaken! If the coach wanted to check out their understanding how could they ask another stakeholder while protecting the identity of their client? However, it is always risky and once something is said it cannot be withdrawn and may compromise the sense of trust and confidentiality in the coaching relationships!

If you believe your values are being triggered by a conflict with your clients, this may need further exploration and could be helped by self-reflection with professional supervision.

Ethical category 2: Boundaries

The dilemma here explores what might cause us to stray from professional coaching territory: "Coach or consultant"?

The client repeatedly asks you for advice on what to do. They know you are well informed about the organization and believe you can give a perspective that will help the coaching process and outcomes.

What could you do?

A   Explore why they are asking you for advice.
B   Control the amount of information you provide.
C   Withhold your perspective until they have articulated theirs.
D   Use what you know to inform your coaching questions.
E   Something else.

> **DISCUSSION POINT (SEE TABLE 6.2):**
>
> Which option are you most drawn to? What is influencing your perspective?

Further thoughts
We hope this dilemma illustrates a common paradox about how clients choose their coach. While we know that coaches do not need to have an understanding of the subject matter in order to coach, many clients choose their coach based on something familiar in the coach's background. To respond to this dilemma you need to remember this about the coaching selection process. You may also need to consider where you sit on the spectrum of a "directive" or "non-directive" approach.

We put this dilemma in the category of boundaries to invite you to think about at what point a directive style of coaching ceases to be "coaching" and becomes something else . . . when does it become consultancy or one to one training? In our experience as a coach the challenge here is how to help the clients to expand

Table 6.2 Independent coaches – boundaries: Coach or consultant?

Option	Likely to be appropriate	Less appropriate
A: Explore why they are asking you for advice	Where you think they may not understand or have had experience of coaching before Your thoughts?	Where you have a directive style and have contracted for the sharing of experience Your thoughts?
B: Control the amount of information you provide	Where you think it would be more useful for them to use their network to gain the information Your thoughts?	Where they might interpret this as a lack of your trust in them and dent the rapport you have built Your thoughts?
C: Establish what the client knows and assumes before offering any contextual information	Where you can explain the importance of the client forming their own views therefore enhancing their thinking processes and avoiding a dependence on you Your thoughts?	Where they genuinely do not have sufficient experience or access to information to begin to form a view Your thoughts?
D: Use what you know to inform your coaching questions	Where you hold your experience "lightly" and are careful to ensure they consider multiple options Your thoughts?	Where their questions suggest they need training before they can benefit from coaching Your thoughts?
E: Something else	Your thoughts?	Your thoughts?

their independent thinking and yet sometimes we might need to be pragmatic and share what we know.

This dilemma also happens in other contexts – for example, with mentors their clients may see their knowledge of the profession or industry as an opportunity to gain consultancy advice on their issue.

The thing to watch out for here is generally what is happening to our ego! Sometimes we might enjoy being asked for our opinion and of course often before we became a coach we may have been paid to be "the expert," which can be a hard habit to break! In our experience, it can be helpful not to offer advice too early as this can limit the client's learning and can create dependency on us. Further, even if our advice comes with good intent and saves the client from making a mistake, how do we know that the client would not have gained more from tripping up and learning from the personal experience?

Ethical category 3: Conflicts of interest

The dilemma here recognizes the organizational complexities that could hinder the coaching relationship: "What's the real issue"?

You've been asked to coach someone who is regarded as "talent" in the organization. As you work together it becomes clear that his next career goal is a move outside the company. He asks to focus the coaching on improving his reputation in the market place.

What could you do?

A   Insist on an internal focus for the engagement.
B   See where it goes and offer to help him rehearse difficult conversations internally.
C   Suggest you focus on developing his brand (which could be used internally or externally).
D   Highlight the potential conflict and suggest a three-way meeting with you, the client and coaching sponsor to determine the appropriateness of continuing.
E   Something else.

> **DISCUSSION POINT (SEE TABLE 6.3):**
>
> Which option are you most drawn to? What is influencing your perspective?

Further thoughts
The central feature of this dilemma is the question of "who is the client?" and is a regular feature. Is it the person in front of you in the coaching chair, or is it the person who is paying for the coaching?

When the coaching is sponsored by the organization whether or not we meet the individual budget holder, we need to have an awareness of the organization as a stakeholder or beneficiary of the coaching work, and it is useful for you to put how you will deal with this in your Contract. We find that some organizations do take a mature perspective. They understand that if the company isn't right, right now for the individual then the most appropriate way forward is to support them to make a good decision. If they take the long-term view and support the individual to do what is right for them, they are likely to create an ambassador out there in the market place. Other organizations are more traditional, if they are paying for the coaching, then they want to derive the benefit for it.

132 Exploring coaching and mentoring dilemmas

Table 6.3 Independent coaches – conflicts of interest: What's the real issue?

Option	Likely to be appropriate	Less appropriate
A: Insist on an internal focus for the coaching	When there is clear contracting that the coaching is for internal benefit only Your thoughts?	Where this potential conflict was raised in the Contract and the organization takes a mature stance, recognizing the value of having ambassadors outside the organization Your thoughts?
B: See where it goes and offer to help him rehearse difficult conversations internally	Where the organizational culture is mature and embraces transparency and you both recognize the importance of handling those conversations well Your thoughts?	Where the organization has sponsored the coaching specifically to get him ready for internal promotion Your thoughts?
C: Suggest you focus on developing his brand (which could be used internally or externally)	Where this may help him to develop his potential and open up other internal opportunities Your thoughts?	Where your motivation for the suggestion is to avoid the conversation about how the organization might react to his external focus Your thoughts?
D: Highlight the potential conflict and suggest a three-way conversation with the coaching sponsor to determine the appropriateness of continuing	Where there is an open and collegiate culture, where the client has good personal relations with his boss and the client recognizes that the coach's reputation could be damaged if this issue is not dealt with proactively Your thoughts?	Where the logistics of getting a three-way conversation organized delay the coaching such that the client has no coaching support while needing to make decisions on how to act Your thoughts?
E: Something else?	Your thoughts?	Your thoughts?

It is therefore really important to discover the stance of the organization so that you have a sense of where your "loyalty" needs to lie. This also puts you in a position of choice as to whether or not you agree to take on the assignment. For example, if you have a sense that the individuals and the organizational motivations are at odds with each other, you could decline to get involved. Support the organization to keep the individual and you may diminish the individual's opportunity. Conversely if you support the individual to find work externally, the organization may perceive this as treacherous and they may avoid giving you any more work. As a coach there is therefore a need to clarify the organization's views about the expectation from the coaching. Three-way conversations are good opportunities for everyone to get agreement on how to manage information that arises as part of the coaching process and to work transparently with the issues.

Ethical category 4: Dual relationships

The dilemma here recognizes that practitioners may wear different "hats" over time or indeed at the same time and are therefore party to information from a range of sources. We need to be mindful of the origin of our knowledge and consider the impact and consequences of working with what we know in a different setting: "Who said what?"

You're working with two people from the same team. As you work together you're aware that you are party to information about each client that has come from their colleague. Sometimes you forget how you know things – which client told you what.

What could you do?

A   Carry on with the coaching.
B   Be transparent about your confusion.
C   Vow to make better notes.
D   Organize for another coach to work with one of the clients.
E   Something else.

> **DISCUSSION POINT (SEE TABLE 6.4):**
>
> Which option are you most drawn to? What is influencing your perspective?

Further thoughts

In this particular dilemma, some of the difficulties could have been anticipated as the two individuals sit within the same team and are working with the same coach. This highlights the importance of surfacing this possible tension as part of the contracting discussion. Many organizations are pragmatic and see the efficiency of having the same coach working with two team members – without understanding the inherent complexity of the task for the coach. It can therefore

Table 6.4 Independent coaches – dual relationships: Who said what?

Option	Likely to be appropriate	Less appropriate
A: Carry on with the coaching	When you can hold your own confusion comfortably such that it is not a distraction to the work Your thoughts?	When you feel this conflicts with your values and would be incongruent for you Your thoughts?
B: Be transparent about your confusion	Where this possibility was "anticipated" in the contracting phase and it was agreed to "call it" Your thoughts?	Where the organizational culture would see this confusion as a weakness; and you are not in a position to challenge this culture: For example, you may be doing the work through a third party Your thoughts?
C: Vow to make better notes	Where you are able to do this without reducing the attention you can give your clients and where you have permission to do so Your thoughts?	Where this is a response to your own sense of inadequacy and is seen as an easier option than doing any of the others! Your thoughts?
D: Organize for an alternative coach to work with one of the clients	Where you are uncomfortable with the level of energy required from you to maintain separation of the work Your thoughts?	Where changing the arrangement is likely to reinforce an existing power or political agenda Your thoughts?
E: Something else	Your thoughts?	Your thoughts?

require the coach to take an educative role for the organization around how coaching actually works. When this level of transparency is role modeled early on in the relationship, it helps raise everyone's awareness of the complexity of the situation that they are about to enter into.

Where this difficulty has already been muted it makes it simpler to question the appropriateness of the arrangement when the coach becomes aware that this kind of "contamination" is interfering with the quality of their work. It makes it more likely that the organization will not see the coach as being "incompetent" and if the contracting was done fully, a process will have been agreed to decide who, under these circumstances would stay with the existing coach, and who would be given a new coach. Therefore no one individual would feel victimized if a change of approach was determined.

In addition, what is particularly interesting here is to examine the notion of being non-directive. This requires us to consider what is informing our questions. We might feel we are making an objective enquiry, but when we have been party to additional information how can we be sure that it is truly neutral? Once we know something, we can't "not know" it! Moreover, where the clients are aware that we have other relationships in the organization, even if we have managed to separate out our prior knowledge, they may assume that our questions are being informed by our wider understanding and they may place more significance on the question than was anticipated or warranted.

Section 2: Example dilemmas for internal coaches

Ethical category 1: Confidentiality

The scenario here considers the complexity of handling information when working with multiple stakeholders: "Tip of the iceberg"?

As an internal coach you are noticing some patterns in your work. It seems that a particular division within the organization is frequently referring people for coaching. You are getting the impression that the presenting development issues would be more effectively addressed through line management.

What could you do?

A   Raise it with the head of human resources (HR) or senior manager in that division.
B   Encourage the referring line manager to come for coaching.
C   Encourage your client to identify what support they might need from their line manager and discuss it with them.
D   Discuss with other internal coaches.
E   Something else.

> **DISCUSSION POINT (SEE TABLE 6.5):**
>
> Which option are you most drawn to? What is influencing your perspective?

Table 6.5 Internal coaches – confidentiality: Tip of the iceberg?

Option	Likely to be appropriate	Less appropriate
A: Raise it with the Head of HR or Senior Manager in that division	When you have Contract with all parties to feedback themes and where there is sufficient volume to your work such that those themes will not indirectly identify an individual Your thoughts?	Where there is no agreement to feedback themes or where you are only working one function and so the source of the theme would be known Your thoughts?
B: Encourage the referring line manager to come for coaching	Where you have a separate relationship with the referring line manager, and they could not draw links to the other coaching work you are doing Your thoughts?	Where we need to respect the fact there are internal processes for who receives coaching Your thoughts?
C: Encourage your client to identify what support they might need from their line manager and discuss it with them	Where this will help your client develop the skills and ability to manage upwards, and this is congruent with their original coaching goal Your thoughts?	Where there is no time to work on this as well as the original coaching goal and therefore could be seen as counter-productive Your thoughts?
D: Discuss with other internal coaches	Where there is a designated forum (like peer group supervision) to discuss emerging themes and this has been contracted for Your thoughts?	Where those discussions are "informal" and could be perceived as the internal coaches "gossiping," serving to undermine the professionalism of the pool Your thoughts?
E: Something else	Your thoughts?	Your thoughts?

Further thoughts

We hope these alternatives illustrate breaching confidentiality can happen directly or indirectly. Most of us would not deliberately breach confidentiality; however, when working within an organization much information is already known. Therefore, even when we are sharing non-attributed (anonymized) or information themes it is possible for other people to "join the dots."

Ethical category 2: Boundaries

The dilemma here explores what might feel uncomfortable or unfamiliar to you given your own cultural norms and experiences: "Inappropriate contact or just different cultural practice?"

Following a successful chemistry session, a new client greets you at the first proper session with a big "hello" and kisses you, European style on either cheek. You were expecting a handshake and you are taken aback, but you say nothing.

What could you do?

A   Reflect on your different cultural backgrounds and consider how this might play out in the relationship.
B   Rehearse how you will manage the greeting at the next session.
C   Use the contracting session to explain that your preference is to shake hands.
D   Say nothing and try to forget it.
E   Something else.

> **DISCUSSION POINT (SEE TABLE 6.6):**
>
> Which option are you most drawn to? What is influencing your perspective?

Further thoughts

We hope this dilemma illustrates how difficult it can be to manage ourselves in a culturally flexible manner while being assertive about our personal preferences and boundaries. Although cross cultural teams and global working are increasing, for many of us we will have ingrained cultural norms that we are largely unaware of until we meet individuals from different backgrounds. The potential for misinterpretation and offence abounds. In coaching we need to create a safe space where cultural differences can be discussed without embarrassment and used to inform the coaching work, even when this may not be the explicit coaching goal. As this is potentially sensitive material, it is important to ensure you have a good level of rapport and have prepared yourself in the most appropriate way. At this point you can be reasonably confident that when you surface the matter, you will not be leaking any embarrassment and can engage your client with curiosity and respect.

Table 6.6 Internal coaches – boundaries: Inappropriate contact or just different cultural practice?

Option	Likely to be appropriate	Less appropriate
A: Reflect on your different cultural backgrounds and consider how this might play out in the relationship	Where you work in a culture where this behavior is sometimes acceptable and you are simply prompted to be more alert about how cultural differences might manifest in the work Your thoughts?	Where you are certain that this kind of greeting is a cultural "faux pas" and you believe it would be a useful educational piece to share this sooner rather than later Your thoughts?
B: Rehearse how you will manage the greeting at the next session	Where you don't feel you have sufficient rapport to raise cultural differences and want to do some personal work before raising it with the client Your thoughts?	Where you know that the desire for rehearsal is really an excuse to avoid discussing a sensitive matter, which actually you are well positioned to manage Your thoughts?
C: Use the contracting session to explain that your preference is to shake hands	Where you have good rapport, are comfortable about talking about cultural differences and feel confident that this will have a positive impact on deepening the coaching relationship Your thoughts?	Where you know your reaction is wrapped up in "your stuff" and bringing attention to the different behaviors could divert attention from more central issues Your thoughts?
D: Say nothing and try to forget it	Where the coaching goals are about developing cultural sensitivity Your thoughts?	When you feel personally embarrassed by this kind of greeting and start to dread re-connecting with the client Your thoughts?
E: Something else	Your thoughts?	Your thoughts?

Ethical category 3: Conflicts of interest

The dilemma here is recognizing organizational complexities that could hinder the coaching relationship: "Ready, steady . . . stop?"

A line manager has completed the coaching needs analysis (CNA) form thoroughly, but he continuously fails to respond to requests to meet for a three-way conversation to kick-start the coaching program. The client is keen to start the program without the line manager's active involvement in the three-way conversation.

What could you do?

A   Request a one to one with the manager.
B   Get started with the program without any input from the line manager.
C   Get started with the program and advise the manager that's what you've done.
D   Refer the issue to the manager of the coaching pool.
E   Something else.

> **DISCUSSION POINT (SEE TABLE 6.7):**
>
> Which option are you most drawn to? What is influencing your perspective?

Further thoughts

In this dilemma, we aimed to highlight how easy it is for the internal coach to get drawn into the wider system of the client. This is true for independent coaches too, but the internal coach is already part of the organizational system and so they will need to work harder to be aware of their "normal" environment. Most of us enjoy our coaching work and therefore we are likely to carry an unconscious bias that means we are keen to get started.

However, as we hope to have illustrated in this scenario – what might we be missing if we respond expediently? It is of interest why the line manager has done "part" but not all of the existing process. The pragmatists among us will favor the notion that most processes don't work in their purist of senses, and therefore as long as there is some contribution from the line manager "what can be the harm?" of simply continuing.

Of course, in some contexts the pragmatic approach may be the most appropriate one. However, in order to judge this, it can be useful to put a more skeptical hat on and consider why the line manager is not following through with

Table 6.7 Internal coaches – conflicts of interest: Ready, steady . . . stop?

Option	Likely to be appropriate	Less appropriate
A: Request a one to one with the manager	Where this is a pragmatic response to a genuinely busy schedule Your thoughts?	Where you sense a lack of engagement between the manager and the client and holding the three-way conversation could provide useful information about their dynamics Your thoughts?
B: Get started with the program without any input from the line manager	Where the coaching objectives are largely concerned with the client's internal motivations. You can contract how to involve the line manager as the coaching program continues Your thoughts?	Where you sense there is more going on than meets the eye and the client may want you to hear "their side" first Your thoughts?
C: Get started with the program and advise the manager that's what you've done	Where there is a bigger organizational agenda in play which is connected to the line manager and not the client; further that delaying the start of the program would disproportionately disadvantage the individual client Your thoughts?	Where you believe you would be colluding with the line manager to avoid their formal responsibility Your thoughts?
D: Refer the issue to the manager of the coaching pool	Where there is a forum to raise issues and you believe the situation you are experiencing is a symptom of a wider systemic issue Your thoughts?	Where the organization is high on pragmatism and they have a track record of relying more on the CNA form than the three-way conversation itself Your thoughts?
E: Something else	Your thoughts?	Your thoughts?

their commitment to the engagement. This could give you useful information about what is really going on in the dynamic between the client and their line manager. This same dynamic may be influencing what they have brought as their coaching goal – so ignoring this important piece of information could undermine the coaching program as a whole. If you are able to attend to your natural response as a possible link to your unconscious processes (parallel process), then this is likely to be particularly useful either as a theme for the organization or as a hypothesis when working with the individual. This may also be an opportunity to bring to your peer supervision group to see whether others are experiencing similar issues. If so, there may be a wider cultural imperative that may need to be addressed to engage line managers with their staff.

Ethical category 4: Dual relationships

The dilemma here recognizes the impact and consequences of shared knowledge and of the need to be mindful of the origin of that knowledge: "Can you coach someone you know well?"

You have been matched with a client whom you have known for a long time. Your paths have crossed over the years and you would consider them more of a friend than a colleague.

What could you do?

A   Decline the assignment.
B   Suggest a one-off session to explore the line between colleague and friendship.
C   Suggest they work with another coach.
D   Get on with the assignment.
E   Something else.

> **DISCUSSION POINT (SEE TABLE 6.8):**
>
> Which option are you most drawn to? What is influencing your perspective?

Further thoughts

Here the core of the dilemma is whether you are able to stand back from your familiarity with the person and truly take an independent view. This situation is common for coaches, and therefore it is a very human response to only feel comfortable revealing that to someone with whom you already feel safe and who understands you.

Table 6.8 Internal coaches – dual relationships: Can you coach someone you know well?

Option	Likely to be appropriate	Less appropriate
A: Decline the assignment	When you feel you know too much about them to be objective. Or when you fear that having a coaching relationship could change the nature of your friendship Your thoughts?	Where you already have experience of working effectively with this person in a whole host of different contexts Your thoughts?
B: Suggest a one-off session to explore the line between colleague and friendship	Where you sense this will provide a good illustration of the difficulty of working with a friend and this would help the client understand why you might not be the best person to coach them Your thoughts?	Where the client is likely to "go in deep" to the issue in the first session and it will then increase the level of difficulty in extracting yourself from the coaching relationship Your thoughts?
C: Suggest they work with another coach	Where the client will understand the tension between the two relationships Your thoughts?	Where you know the client has a history of rejection and there is no opportunity for you to personalize the message they will receive Your thoughts?
D: Get on with the assignment	Where you are experienced in managing challenges to your boundaries and are open to the idea that coaching them may or may not be an appropriate way forward Your thoughts?	Where you believe you are immune to collusion Your thoughts?
E: Something else	Your thoughts?	Your thoughts?

However, along with that prior relationship there is the possibility of contamination. For example, are they approaching you because they feel you will understand their point of view? If so, the relationship may be primed for collusion. Alternatively are they attracted to working with you because you have a reputation for challenge? – in which case the relationship may be primed for you assuming an expert role. Either way, dispelling this original positioning and working out what the client genuinely needs could be tricky.

When your prior relationship means that you are emotionally invested in their success or in your relationship, this heightens the challenge. For example, would you feel disappointed in both you and them if they did not realize their true potential? Could their decisions subsequently impact on your objectives or your relationships and network? If so, maintaining objectivity may be difficult at a practical level and moreover it could be ethically difficult. As an internal coach you and your clients will operate in the same system. Most internal coaches are familiar with the challenge of navigating the complexities of multiple relationships. Recognizing the possible conflicts of interest that could arise from the relationship is a critical first step. As a rule of thumb, if you are able to put the issue on the table and have a good discussion about the potential difficulties you will probably be able to develop a joint decision. On the other hand, if you find the prospect of this kind of discussion uncomfortable "in principle," this is probably a good indicator that engaging in the relationship would be inadvisable.

Section 3: Example dilemmas for line manager as coach

Ethical category 1: Confidentiality

The scenario here considers the complexity of handling information when working with multiple stakeholders: "Is a little knowledge a dangerous thing"?

You are coaching a team member to understand their development areas from their performance review. They are struggling to come to terms with a particular comment in their 360-feedback report. You are pretty sure you know who said it because you remember them saying something similar to you in a coaching conversation.

What could you do?

A   Coach them on how to talk to all their contributors and ask for examples of the feedback.
B   Explore with them who they think has made this comment and why.
C   Don't disclose your hunch.
D   Focus the exploration on their strengths and how they can leverage them.
E   Something else.

> **DISCUSSION POINT (SEE TABLE 6.9):**
>
> Which option are you most drawn to? What is influencing your perspective?

Table 6.9 Line manager as coach – confidentiality: Is a little knowledge a dangerous thing?

Option	Likely to be appropriate	Less appropriate
A: Coach them on how to talk to all their contributors and ask for examples of the feedback	Where this is an expected part of the process and could help them develop their skills for asking for feedback Your thoughts?	Where exploring the comments further would delay deriving main learning that the 360 already offers for their development Your thoughts?
B: Explore with them who they think has made this comment and why	Where it's becoming "the elephant in the room" and they seem unable to move forward until their suspicions are voiced Your thoughts?	Where there is already a sense of divisiveness in the team and this could fuel an existing tension Your thoughts?
C: Don't disclose your hunch	Where you are not 100% certain of where the comment came from and even if you were you would regard it as unprofessional to share information without permission Your thoughts?	Where the setting for the 360 is Team Coaching and there is an explicit Contract that the whole team will be open about information that serves the team relationship over and above individual learning Your thoughts?
D: Re-focus the exploration on their strengths and how they can leverage them	Where there is a strengths-based culture and you think it would be more productive to help them build on their strengths Your thoughts?	Where they are keen to discount the feedback, and you sense that it is speaking to a real blind spot Your thoughts?
E: Something else	Your thoughts?	Your thoughts?

Further thoughts

We hope this dilemma highlights the multiple relationships and sources of information that a line manager has to juggle! A great question for the line manager as coach is "how have I come to know that?" Where the line manager is having a dedicated coaching conversation it is more likely to be clear that the information gained is confidential and sat within the boundary of the coaching relationship rather than the line management relationship. However, even if the information was gained informally, the line manager still has to think about the impact of sharing what they know. What will it do to the sense of trust between the line manager and the team as a whole? If this is not managed carefully the line manager as coach could enter into manipulation territory – with people feeding the line manager information in the hope that it will be passed on. Should this happen it would undermine the opportunity for the team to own their issues, putting the line manager into a "rescuer" role.

Ethical category 2: Boundaries

The dilemma here explores what might cause us to stray from professional coaching territory: "When is it too close for comfort"?

You have a graduate on placement in your department and you have taken them "under your wing." In your conversations they share with you that their rental accommodation is less than ideal, contributing to them getting limited sleep which impacts on their concentration at work. You also know they have been asking around to see what other accommodation is available. You have a spare room are wondering if they are aware of your spare room.

What could you do?

A   Suggest they talk to human resources (HR).
B   Offer them the opportunity to use your spare room as a temporary measure.
C   Explore what other options they have, how they can widen their search.
D   Do nothing.
E   Something else.

> **DISCUSSION POINT (SEE TABLE 6.10):**
>
> Which option are you most drawn to? What is influencing your perspective?

Further thoughts

We hope this dilemma highlights the potential consequences of getting too involved with an individual. This is an issue whether looking at the dilemma from the perspective of a coach or as a line manager. Whenever there is potential for a blurring of roles and responsibilities, then it is important to consider what unintended fallout could be possible. It is interesting how a very "human" response could inadvertently cause tensions within the wider team, or indeed in our home-life! Would your partner really want one of your employees living under the same roof – even for a short time? It clarifies why we need to have

Table 6.10 Line manager as coach – boundaries: When is it too close for comfort?

Option	Likely to be appropriate	Less appropriate
A: Suggest they talk to HR	Where you know you have a tendency to want to "problem solve" for them and the range of HR services is well publicized already Your thoughts?	Where HR only have the resources to deal with housing issues for graduates on an "exceptional" basis Your thoughts?
B: Offer them the opportunity to use your spare room as a temporary measure	Where the individual asks directly for your help as a short-term solution and you are comfortable that you could handle any perceptions of "favoritism" within the team Your thoughts?	Where you feel you would need to keep the arrangement "a secret" from the team and/or where you recognize this is more to do with your own "empty nest" than it is to do with the individuals shortage of options Your thoughts?
C: Coach them to explore what other options they have, e.g. how they can widen their search	Where this may help them problem solve in the future Your thoughts?	Where they are in severe distress, unable to think independently and need immediate support Your thoughts?
D: Do nothing	Where they have developed good support networks and you recognize that helping could be perceived as "going above and beyond" your role as their line manager Your thoughts?	Where you feel their health is affected and offering your help is morally appropriate in the short term Your thoughts?
E: Something else	Your thoughts?	Your thoughts?

a good handle on our own emotional state so that we are not using other people's "issues" as a way of meeting our own needs. In this dilemma there could be a temptation to take on a parental role thereby impeding the individual's maturity and resilience. As a professional, we need to have boundaries to our role, which in turn helps the employee to take personal responsibility and develop their independence and life skills. A good test of an appropriate response is how you would feel if the scenario was on the front page of a newspaper!

Ethical category 3: Conflicts of interest

The dilemma here is recognizing organizational complexities that could hinder the coaching relationship: "How do you manage perceptions?"

One of your team has recently returned from long-term sick leave. You have weekly coaching conversations with them and you know how much effort they are putting in to getting back up to speed. Their resilience is fragile though and they often cannot work a full week. You have noticed that the level of patience in the team is wearing thin.

What could you do?

A   Talk to the team member about how they would like to keep their colleagues updated.
B   Brief the team member and bring it up in team meeting.
C   Speak individually to team members.
D   Do nothing.
E   Something else.

> **DISCUSSION POINT (SEE TABLE 6.11):**
>
> Which option are you most drawn to? What is influencing your perspective?

Further thoughts

This dilemma highlights the privileged position a line manager has where they have the fullest understanding of what is happening for individuals within their team. However, sometimes what they know has come from a confidential setting. At other times what they know is informed by multiple subtle and implicit messages but has not yet been expressed explicitly. So in this scenario while the line manager is likely to look for a solution that brings the team together, the confidential relationship with one individual precludes the sharing of information. If the manager were to offer feedback to the individual on behalf of the team, this might pass a sense of peer pressure to the individual concerned. This might not be wholly ethical if the individual is still in a vulnerable state. This might also pique the individual's curiosity in "who is saying what?" If a team member had shared something in confidence, you will need to protect their identity too!

Where this feedback relied on the manager "joining the dots," it could be that their own frustration with the speed of progress of the return might have skewed their perception of how the team was actually feeling. This would be an interesting challenge for leaders who take a paternalistic stance. An individual

Table 6.11 Line manager as coach – conflicts of interest: How do you manage perceptions?

Option	Likely to be appropriate	Less appropriate
A: Talk to the team member about how they would like to keep their colleagues updated	Coaching will give them the opportunity to think through how their situation might be impacting on the team Your thoughts?	Where this would divert their emotional energy away from their own recovery Your thoughts?
B: Brief the team member and bring it up in team meeting	Where they will have the opportunity with your support to talk to the whole team and communicate their situation in a safe space Your thoughts?	Where you are frustrated with the situation and you have no hard evidence that the team feels similarly Your thoughts?
C: Speak individually to team members	Where the team member has given permission for you to talk to others on their behalf Your thoughts?	Where you as a team have contracted to openly share the individual's circumstance and think that if you caveat the information as "confidential" it will be OK Your thoughts?
D: Do nothing	Where you want to support your team member to take ownership for dealing with their return to work Your thoughts?	Where the situation is likely to escalate in the team and cause bad feeling within the team about your team member Your thoughts?
E: Something else	Your thoughts?	Your thoughts?

may invite you to share information on their behalf, or you may feel compelled to share the information "confidentially" in their best interests. This can be political dynamite within a team. While a team member might be grateful for hearing information about a colleague to help them understand their situation more fully, they would see it as a breach of privacy if the roles were to be reversed.

Ironically therefore, despite a benevolent stance it could undermine the whole team's sense of trust in the line manager. In this particular scenario the line manager may do well to voice both concern for the individual and for the team from an early point in the "back to work" discussions. This would allow the individual to avoid sharing information with the team until they are ready to do so, but it also makes it easier for the manager to check this element each time without drawing undue attention to it.

Ethical category 4: Dual relationships

The dilemma here recognizes the impact and consequences of shared knowledge and of the need to be mindful of the origin of that knowledge: "How much is enough?"

You have a finance specialist in your team who is pinpointed as a successor to the CFO. They have been placed with you to get specific experience as part of their fast track progression as you are renowned for your ability to coach and develop talent in the organization. You are feeling conflicted. Their level of capability is clear and they are a delight to work with. However, you are giving them the lion's share of developmental opportunities that come up and you notice your existing team is beginning to feel sidelined.

What could you do?

A   Ask the finance specialist to teach other members of the team.
B   Raise it at the team meeting. Ask re. who is interested in developmental opportunities.
C   Reschedule your time so you can include development for other team members.
D   Do nothing, you see this as a short-term issue.
E   Something else.

> **DISCUSSION POINT (SEE TABLE 6.12):**
>
> Which option are you most drawn to? What is influencing your perspective?

Further thoughts

Here the challenge is around ensuring a sense of equity when as a line manager you have responsibilities to your team and to develop identified talent for the greater good on the organization. The dual relationship here is with the individual who is both a team member and part of the talent pool. It is likely that the progress of this talented individual will be more closely watched than the rest of your team. Therefore your reputation as a good people developer is wrapped up with your ability to help them succeed.

However, you are also aware that if you overdo this, then a sense of "them and us" will emerge within the team. Not only could this cause the talented individual some difficulties among their colleagues, it could also disaffect the team to the point where your reputation for coaching talent is sullied by a lack of

Table 6.12 Line manager as coach – dual relationships: How much is enough?

Option	Likely to be appropriate	Less appropriate
A: Ask the finance specialist to teach other members of the team	Where their experience, skill and attitude makes them a good prospect as a teacher Your thoughts?	Where the rest of the team are likely to see this as evidence of another "preferential" role Your thoughts?
B: Raise it at the team meeting and ask re. who is interested in developmental opportunities	Where this endorses a company culture that encourages individuals to take charge of their own development Your thoughts?	Where there is a high risk that everyone will want to take up the offer and you will not be able to manage expectations Your thoughts?
C: Reschedule your time so you can include development for other team members	When you want to reinforce that development is available for all Your thoughts?	Where this is a knee-jerk reaction and your capacity for sustaining this approach is minimal Your thoughts?
D: Do nothing – this is a short-term issue	Where you believe you have already set a constructive environment and you have empowered the team to manage their own development Your thoughts?	Where there is clear evidence that an "us and them" culture is developing Your thoughts?
E: Something else	Your thoughts?	Your thoughts?

engagement within the wider team. The team could be particularly sensitive to this if you have a succession of people "passing through" your team and they are constantly teaching and supporting high-fliers. Here the line manager may do well to share the dual relationship with the team – so that it is the whole team and not just the line manager who is credited with a reputation for developing others. Alternatively the line manager may want to pace how often they take on this coaching role so that the team feels like they have periods when they benefit more fully from the line manager's attention.

Section 4: Example dilemmas for mentors

Ethical category 1: Confidentiality

The scenario here considers the complexity of handling information when working with multiple stakeholders: "It's all hush, hush . . . or is it?"

You have an informal mentoring relationship with a team leader who regularly catches the same train as you to work. You are part of the talent board and recently you became aware that he was one of the individuals being discussed. Opinion was quite divided about him, with some behavioral examples being cited which suggested his values were not aligned with company culture. You have had no hint of this in your conversations with him.

What could you do?

A   Focus entirely on his agenda.
B   Explore whether he has ever sought 360 feedback.
C   Share with him that you have heard mixed feedback about him and get his reaction.
D   Invite an exploration of company culture and congruent behaviors.
E   Something else.

> **DISCUSSION POINT (SEE TABLE 6.13):**
>
> Which option are you most drawn to? What is influencing your perspective?

Further thoughts
This is an interesting dilemma when looked at through the eyes of a mentor compared to those of a coach. For many organizations there is an express understanding that the mentor might offer their experience about "how things are done around here." If a coach faced this dilemma, you may see it as less appropriate to offer a perspective on the organization, as it would contradict their objectivity.

We hope this dilemma has helped you think not just about confidentiality, but also about the non-directive or directive stance of the coach vs the mentor. In many of these scenarios, the apparently "open" questions are in fact informed from the mentor's view of the world. They would be guilty of "leading the witness"! The more non-directive the mentor (or coach) the more appropriate option A becomes. "Knowing what you know" can be hard to boundary and it

Table 6.13 Mentors – confidentiality: It's all hush, hush . . . or is it?

Option	Likely to be appropriate	Less appropriate
A: Focus entirely on his agenda	Where the talent board has a universal Contract for absolute confidentiality Your thoughts?	Where you have not contracted for challenge and he seems to be completely unaware of the disconnection between his own style and the company's values Your thoughts?
B: Explore whether he has ever sought 360 feedback	Where he has noticed that people are reacting differently to him, but doesn't understand why Your thoughts?	Where 360s are not generally carried out in the organization and where the timing is such that he is likely to link the suggestion to the Talent Board discussion Your thoughts?
C: Share with him that you have heard mixed feedback about him and get his reaction	Where you are in a position to have heard feedback from a variety of sources, not just the Talent Board. Where there is discretion within the Talent Board protocol to support individuals from a "process" rather than a "content" perspective Your thoughts?	Where it is the clear responsibility of his line manager or formal mentor or HR lead to provide this kind of feedback Your thoughts?
D: Invite an exploration of company culture and congruent behaviors	Where he is new to the business or the leadership role and you could help raise his awareness of what is generally considered appropriate in the organization without fear of divulging any specific information Your thoughts?	Where this would feel like a huge "topic shift" to your normal conversations and where it is likely to cause suspicion that "you know something he doesn't" Your thoughts?
E: Something else	Your thoughts?	Your thoughts?

may contaminate your questions even if that contamination comes with good intent!

We also have to be mindful that the client may indeed be aware of the mixed feedback; it may simply be that he is not choosing to share that with the mentor, in which case it could be worth exploring what the client sees as the purpose of the relationship. They may be seeing you as an ambassador for them and therefore only revealing their good side? Finally we hope this dilemma enables you to see some of the blurring that can happen when relationships are informal rather than formal. The more formal the relationship, the more likely the pair will have talked through how to manage these tensions between formal and confidential processes, and what is separate to or integral with the mentoring relationship.

Ethical category 2: Boundaries

The dilemma here explores values and when they are conflicted and compounded by cultural differences and how the mentor can stay authentic but respectful of diversity: "How do you accommodate cultural difference and personal values"?

You are mentoring a Norwegian leader who is overseeing a group of Chinese managers. He is frustrated by what he sees as their inability to take initiative. They are looking for clear and explicit direction from him. He feels that being directive would be inauthentic for him and would be contrary to his values as a leader. The leader seems to be seeking reassurance that continuing to be non-directive is appropriate.

What could you do?

A   Explore why they are asking you for reassurance.
B   Explore the cultural differences.
C   Explore what "authentic" leadership means to them in a global setting.
D   Decline to provide your solution until they have articulated theirs.
E   Something else?

> **DISCUSSION POINT (SEE TABLE 6.14):**
>
> Which option are you most drawn to? What is influencing your perspective?

Table 6.14 Mentors – boundaries: How do you accommodate cultural difference and personal values?

Option	Likely to be appropriate	Less appropriate
A: Explore why they are asking for reassurance	When you are concerned that they may not fully understand your role as mentor Your thoughts?	When the focus of the mentoring relationship is to deepen cultural sensitivity and you have contracted for sharing your global experiences Your thoughts?
B: Explore his understanding of the cultural differences	Where the client seems to have a genuine gap in understanding about cultural differences (either theirs or yours!) and may need additional information in order to co-create solutions Your thoughts?	Where you feel out of your depth exploring this issue and another mentor, with deeper international experience, might serve the client better Your thoughts?
C: Explore what authentic leadership means to them in a global setting	Where the mentoring goal is connected to his flexibility as a leader because his style tends to be an "all or nothing" approach Your thoughts?	Where it is easier to talk about this than cultural differences because one of you is not comfortable with conversations in this territory Your thoughts?
D: Decline to provide your solution until they have provided theirs	Where you believe they are capable of coming up with solutions Your thoughts?	Where you think they are so stuck they will not be able to progress and that continuing the current behavior would exacerbate the difficulty Your thoughts?
E: Something else	Your thoughts?	Your thoughts?

Further thoughts

We hope this dilemma served to illustrate the complexity of mentoring assignments. As a mentor you will have many choices about what the dialogue covers and about how much or how little of yourself and your experience you bring into the relationship. It is not unusual for someone to be selected as a mentor for one area of expertise and then to find that the mentoring need has strayed into different topics, of which they have little experience. It can often be tempting to continue, perhaps because you are embarrassed to admit what you don't know, or because you would like to learn about this topic for your own development. However, we need to keep in mind that unless you contract for this, your responsibility is to ensure that the client is the clear beneficiary of the work. On occasions a different mentor may be better placed to serve the client, either for all or part of the work.

In our experience although this dilemma is mentioned here for mentors it is equally challenging for other contexts. Increasingly we work across the globe and with multi-cultural and virtual teams, and all parties call for discussion and flexibility.

Ethical category 3: Conflicts of interest

The dilemma here is recognizing complexities that could hinder the mentoring relationship: "What's really going on here"?

The scheme administrator has allocated the mentee to you and the initial chemistry session seemed to go well, so you have both agreed to proceed. However as sessions progress, there is something odd in the comments they make, responses to your questions and their timekeeping. You are beginning to wonder if they respect mentoring and their motivation to continue to work with you.

What could you do?

A   Keep going and see how things pan out.
B   Terminate the contract. You don't want to waste yours or their time.
C   Raise your concerns with the scheme coordinator.
D   Share your observations and ask the mentee what's going on.
E   Something else?

> **DISCUSSION POINT (SEE TABLE 6.15):**
>
> Which option are you most drawn to? What is influencing your perspective?

Further thoughts

This dilemma highlights the difficulty of understanding the changing nature of human behavior. In this particular scenario the mentee's response to you seems to have changed since the chemistry session, so it is curious to consider why that might be. This dilemma prompts us to remember that as the mentor we need to have good self-awareness, as you will notice that in all of these options there

Table 6.15 Mentors – conflicts of interest: What's really going on here?

Option	Likely to be appropriate	Less appropriate
A: Keep going and see how things pan out	Where you feel more curious than disrespected and believe there is potential in the relationship Your thoughts?	Where your instinct tells you that you need to clarify the basis of the mentoring process before you proceed Your thoughts?
B: Terminate the contract. You don't want to waste yours or their time	Where the mentees behavior is seriously at odds with your values and you can communicate that in a constructive manner Your thoughts?	Where you feel that the disconnect you are experiencing is symptomatic of a wider issue and you could be well placed to offer this feedback Your thoughts?
C: Raise your concerns with the scheme coordinator	Where you can invite a discussion about what informed the matching process and are not inviting them to provide you with additional information about the individual that would fall outside of the process Your thoughts?	Where this could impact on the mentee's future career and was not "part of the brief" Your thoughts?
D: Share your observations and ask the mentee what's going on	Where it would be useful to explore the issues in order to raise the mentee's awareness of their impact on you and others Your thoughts?	Where you think the mentee may be in denial and not able to take the feedback at this stage of the process Your thoughts?
E: Something else	Your thoughts?	Your thoughts?

is an underlying assumption that the shift in the relationship is because of something connected with the mentee.

However, it could of course be that the mentor has somehow "shown up" differently in the chemistry session – perhaps they had been more charming or liberal with sharing their experience compared to how they have been in subsequent sessions. In which case the mentor's behavior may have been what caused the mentee to respond to them differently. For example, perhaps there is something confidential that the scheme administrator knows about the mentee

– if the mentor were to challenge the administrator that person may experience a sense of conflict around what to do for the best.

One also has to consider what benchmark the mentor is measuring their mentee's behavior against. This is particularly pertinent where the mentee is untypical in some way from the mentor's normal reference groups. For example a different culture, a different thinking style or different organizational function – here the difference may be unconnected to the relationship with the mentor, and simply reflect a different style of operating. One possibility is that the mentor themselves is overly sensitive to how people respond to them over time and therefore they may be inadvertently seeking out evidence that would suggest something has changed in the relationship. Under such circumstances, the mentor has to be careful that they are not using the mentoring relationship to help them work through their own developmental issues. Even if this were happening at an unconscious level, it raises an ethical concern as it would represent another conflict of interest around who would be the primary beneficiary of the relationship.

Ethical category 4: Dual relationships

The dilemma here recognizes the impact and consequences of shared knowledge and of the need to be mindful of the origin of that knowledge: "Is it possible for a mentor to be a friend too?"

Your client has contracted you as a mentor, because they know you well. They reported to you for several years and you have remained friends. They ask for your personal advice as they have a difficult working relationship with someone in the team that you used to work closely with.

What could you do?

A   Contract clearly for how this relationship will work.
B   Refer them to someone else who you think would be a good mentor.
C   Start mentoring and see how it goes.
D   Discuss with them where you see the difficulties.
E   Something else.

> **DISCUSSION POINT (SEE TABLE 6.16):**
>
> Which option are you most drawn to? What is influencing your perspective?

Table 6.16 Mentors – dual relationships: Is it possible for a mentor to be a friend too?

Option	Likely to be appropriate	Less appropriate
A: Contract clearly for how this relationship will work	Where you want to separate the friendship from the role of mentor Your thoughts?	Where you naturally take a non-directive approach and don't wish to formalize the mentoring role for risk of altering their expectations of you Your thoughts?
B: Refer them to someone else who you think would be a good mentor	Where you feel you know both them and the team too well and that the mentoring would create a sense of "divided loyalty" Your thoughts?	Where you are genuinely the most appropriate person to help them and you are avoiding the conversation about managing the complexities of supporting them in this way Your thoughts?
C: Start mentoring and see how it goes	Where you have prior experience of managing "multiple hats" in a professional setting Your thoughts?	Where you agreed to the idea without thinking through the possible complexities of your historical and current relationships Your thoughts?
D: Discuss with them where you see the difficulties	Where their request came with good intent and you feel this will help them appreciate the difficult position it could place you in Your thoughts?	Where you have a good grasp of how you will navigate the potential difficulties as they arise, and a difficult discussion might cause them to withdraw from the relationship through being overly sensitive to your needs Your thoughts?
E: Something else	Your thoughts?	Your thoughts?

Further thoughts

We hope this dilemma serves to reflect the reality of how many mentoring relationships evolve. Sometimes the most successful mentoring relationships originate from when the mentor was the line manager of the individual and the two had a natural rapport, which keeps them connected over the years. Of course the mentor may have many such relationships and therefore if issues arise directly with individuals where there is a shared history, the mentor may feel very torn as to how to respond with authenticity and loyalty.

When relationships evolve over a long period of time, two individuals can become very comfortable with each other – while this can enable the pair to have good, honest and frank conversations, there is also a lot to lose if something were to change that. Hence it could be that keeping things on an informal basis is the least risky thing to do. Conversely, if the pair is too familiar, it may prove really helpful to get more formal in order to approach a particularly difficult or political piece of work.

In this scenario it is quite possible that this particular person is best placed to mentor the individual. While transparency is often the best possible approach, a mentee who is particularly sensitive to not being "a trouble" to their mentor, may be prepared to walk away from good developmental support for fear of putting their mentor in a difficult position. Therefore assuming the mentor is adept at navigating the complexities (or perhaps welcomes the challenge of managing them?), it could be that the mentor may deliberately take a position of not burdening the mentee with the difficulties of their own position because they prioritize their mentees development over their own emotional labor.

Final thoughts

We hope these dilemmas and their explorations have given you food for thought and expanded your options for future discussions. You might like to consider your reactions to reading each dilemma and possible options, what your initial thoughts were and whether your ideas have changed over time. You might find it useful as you progress on your coaching or mentoring journey to collect your own scenarios in a log and bring them to future peer supervision meetings.

For further reference we mention the Professional Bodies' ethical codes in Chapter 7 and discuss how they might be applied.

Key learning points

1 Revisit a situation and challenge yourself to see it differently – for example look through all seven eyes of the seven-eyed model.
2 Reflect on your initial responses to the dilemmas – what (if anything) does this help you identify with regards to themes and/or bias in your thinking?
3 Listen to your instinct – and decode what it is telling you.

4   In a coaching dilemma every stakeholder is likely to see things differently, so consider the scenario from each person's point of view. When thinking about next steps again, actively consider how this will impact on each person involved.
5   It's important to consider the context and systems surrounding a situation including cultural differences – these will be having an impact.
6   It sounds obvious, but life doesn't fit into boxes. Reflect on how you can take the learning from similar, yet different scenarios, to aid your thinking and inform your actions into new circumstances.
7   Consciously capture your learning to broaden and develop your "ethical muscle."
8   Apply "new" knowledge and insights practically. Convert the learning through this chapter into your day-to-day coaching approaches and processes – for example, contracting, record keeping, CPD etc.

Reference

Whitaker, C. and Lucas, M. (2014) Risk Assessor. Road Test Feature: "The Coaching Dilemma Cards." *Coaching At Work*, 9(6).

Ethics

The elephant in the room

7

Definition: The *Oxford Dictionary* defines "ethics" as "moral principles that govern a person's behavior or the conducting of an activity." Accordingly, ethics refers to the morals and values a person holds, which determine her/his actions and behaviors. "Ethics aims to answer one big question. *How should I live?* Ethical beliefs shape the way we live – what we do, what we make and the world we create through our choices" (St. James Ethics Centre, 2017). De Jong (2010) says when helping others it's our ethical principles that we rely on, and which help us focus on the needs and interests of our clients.

What we mean by "ethics"

In this chapter we are going to discuss the importance of personal ethics. Ethics defines who we are as human beings and as a result help us to answer deep questions about how we live our lives (St. James Ethics Centre, 2017). As ethics are part of who we are as individuals, they are always present in coaching and mentoring! This is why we refer to ethics as "the elephant in the room." Ethics provides an internal moral compass. Relying on this compass supports you as a practitioner to better understand the choices you have. Examples could be negotiating the terms and conditions in the Contract or simply navigating the choice points which are made during the session with your client. Why? Because your ethics informs the choices you make. Reflecting upon what drives your choices is one of the key components of working with ethics.

In Chapter 6, we highlighted a number of client and/or practitioner dilemmas to discuss with your peers. We hope that sharing your insights and hearing others' perspectives on dilemmas has provided you the opportunity to begin to understand that the interpretation of a particular scenario is informed by your ethics. It may seem odd that we're devoting two chapters to what may seem like covering the same ground. However, one of the challenges in peer supervision can be the limitation in putting more emphasis on the client and the elements of the case. The blind spot for practitioners can be that they don't actually put themselves into the client–practitioner dynamic and are unconscious as to how their choices directly impact on their client work. This may also be further perpetuated by professional codes that stress the practitioner is judgment free, neutral and/or adheres to a code of ethics, which encourages more of a client focus.

As we have been trained to be judgment free, we often don't recognize that the elephant (the practitioner's ethics) is present in the client engagement. Only when you stumble across a dilemma which brings up your judgment, bias, preference or an emotional response, do you realize that it was there all along. As important as it is to be judgment free it is equally important to know and appreciate your judgments, as they're with you all of the time. Noticing your judgments may hold a clue as to which of your ethics may require further reflection.

Although ethics can be *related* to the client, the ethics from which we make decisions are within our control as the practitioner. To highlight what we mean, please read this *example scenario* and notice what comes up for you.

The organization is competitive in retaining its industry leading position and as a result, the sales manager is challenging himself and his team to work long hours. As a result he is experiencing stress and signs of burn out. The external coach has signed a Contract that incentivizes her to retain the sales manager in his role, reduce stress and if the sales team achieves their annual target, the coach will receive an additional 10 per cent bonus.

Brief reflection:

- What are some of the ethical issues you see in this case?
- How does the coach work with the client?
- How do you think the client will respond to the coach given the terms outlined in the contract?
- If you were the coach, how do you think you would approach this client?
- If a peer brought this case to peer supervision, what could you do?

Notice we start with reflection, which illuminates our thinking about our options and if we were actively looking for it, pinpoints our values and beliefs that inform how we make ethical decisions.

When you read this case, the way in which you view it is probably from a critical or judgmental mindset, which signposts you have a moral issue that has been triggered by your values and beliefs. It is your judgment (both positive and negative) that creates the moral compass from which you operate. This feeling of judgment, that sometimes includes a sense of "I'm right" creates the ethical position from which we make our ethical decisions, is also called bias. This "I'm right" feeling may also be an opportunity for reflection to test whether or not the position you've taken is suitable for the circumstances and/or you're comfortable with the choices available.

Consequently in this chapter, we delve a bit deeper into personal choices that require more consideration than those in Chapter 6. The situations described in this chapter are less straightforward and require careful internal reflection about your reactions and ethics. By identifying your core beliefs, values and/or morals you can become aware of and comfortable with, the elephant being in the room. This enables you to make more considered choices about how you practice. Through careful reflective practice, you uncover that within the client–practitioner relationship, you as the practitioner contribute to the dynamic as well. Both peer and professional supervision can be a helpful support to reflect with others to further explore both your bias and choices.

Why should you be interested in ethical issues at all?

If you have worked through the dilemmas presented in Chapter 6, or if you have worked with ethics previously, you are probably aware that the tension in discussing ethics arises because the person noticing an ethical issue is likely to hold a different bias and belief, than others. It is for this same reason that peers can have some degree of hesitation in raising their ethics in peer supervision, for fear of being judged. Again, as ethics are part of who we are as individuals, and are *always* present (the elephant in the room), we suggest acknowledging the elephant and welcoming it as part of your peer supervision discussions. By having open, honest conversations about ethics, everyone will benefit: You, your client, the client organization and the industry as a whole. We offer some tools and techniques to help you do this later in the chapter.

As we've previously mentioned, coaching operates in an unregulated market. As a result, it is left to the individual to consider how ethics and values pertain to their work and how their beliefs, ideas, and actions shape their working relationships. The development of the Global Code of Ethics (GCoE) (AC and EMCC, 2016) and similar codes of ethics by the ICF and/or APECS is very promising and highly welcomed in our field. The professional body's codes of ethics are typically a starting point when ethical concerns arise. However, given the interpersonal nature of coaching, Codes of Conduct may be too difficult or too vague to cater for the highly complex situations that can surface. We believe in subscribing to a code of ethics and supplementing this with individual reflective practice and supervision in order to articulate and maintain your personal ethical practice.

The ethical *example scenario* above squarely sits in a gray area. Having coaching and mentoring outcomes toward goal attainment is part of standard measurements during engagements. However, when areas like money and/or value for money are brought into the engagement, this creates a different scenario. The 10 per cent bonus creates an expectation on behalf of the client paying the invoice, and also perhaps the client receiving the coaching that the goal will be attained. Interestingly it puts responsibility onto the practitioner to be an integral part of the goal attainment, rather than the client. Depending on your professional body's code of ethics, this may or may not be specifically stated. However, you probably have an immediate opinion (judgment) about whether this is ethical practice. Indeed your rationale may differ from your peers' judgments, even if they too believe it is unethical. This is due to the fact that our personal ethics and values are shaped by the culture we grew up in (Iordanou, Hawley and Iordanou, 2017), and they are so much a part of who we are that we often fail to notice or question them.

In the fast paced, multi-tasking world of today, in which we cooperate with people of diverse cultural and professional backgrounds, many ethical issues may arise in both our work and within a peer supervision meeting, which we may not even have considered existed. Our life history shapes our biases and beliefs such that in each situation you are likely to respond from your own map of the world. You may find that issues such as race, ethnicity, gender, sexual orientation and beliefs impact on how you treat and think about others. Unwittingly that can mean that the default lens you apply may obscure your ability to be genuinely objective and respectful with your client or indeed your peers.

Biases (both positive and negative) are the foundation of our ethics. The purpose of this chapter is to highlight that as a practitioner you bring your own biases, beliefs and values in which you operate, thus informing the choices you make. This chapter is not meant to replace your reflective practice or supervision; rather to illustrate when ethical issues can arise, what things you may want to signpost for your reflective practice and to bring for conversation to both peer and professional supervision. We hope that by raising your awareness of ethics and by discerning your ethics that underpin your choices, you will have more consistency in your work.

How to spot ethical issues

If you haven't paid much attention to the ethical perspective of your work in the past it may take some effort to do so. Being able to spot ethical issues in both your own and your peers' work, and dealing with them effectively is imperative for safeguarding the client relationship, how comfortable you feel as a practitioner during the engagement and the quality of your work. However, most ethical issues occur at the edge of our awareness – few practitioners would deliberately engage with a client (or with their peers) with the intention of being biased! Therefore in order to spot an ethical issue we first need to acknowledge that they exist, and that we all have them, whether we notice them or not! Although we all have bias, the person holding their belief may be slow to recognize their bias. This is because fundamentally, bias stems from the individual fabric of who they are. We recommend having compassion for both yourself and others as you work with your biases as you reflect and discuss your ethical issues.

Referring to the *example scenario*, although the immediate ethical issue people recognize is the bonus there may also be a bias toward the practitioner being unethical. There may be other ethical considerations such as:

- The client organization may be unaware that incentivizing goal attainment is uncommon industry practice (and unethical in some professional body codes). Whose responsibility is it to educate the organization? The industry? The professional body? The practitioner? Human Resources?
- The client is under pressure. Is coaching an appropriate intervention? Who is responsible for assessing this? What happens if the client has a break down or goes on stress leave during the engagement?
- What legal considerations may the coach need to consider before taking on this client?
- If resiliency is part of the organizational imperative, could you stay judgment-free if you were the practitioner?
- If the practitioner has a strong belief in helping others, how might that bias the coaching?

As you can see, there are levels of complexity that are a result of individual preferences, understanding and knowledge that can be uncovered as a result of reflection and discussion as part of your peer supervision. The main goal of peer supervision is to provide a forum to explore your expectations and thoughts to see whether there is an impact on the coaching process directly or indirectly (Bachkirova and Jackson, 2011, pp. 230–231). Your peers can provide an outlet to explore the motives that lead you to manage situations in the way that felt right for you at the time. Talking about this honestly is an important aspect for both your personal growth and the growth of the peer supervision relationship. Some ethics may warrant further careful consideration. The following are compromising ethical issues that commonly arise in professional supervision. We suspect they will be present in peer supervision too, so we suggest being on alert for these or similar situations. As you become aware of them in your own choices, you are more likely to spot them as they arise and to be comfortable in discussing them during peer supervision.

Misrepresentation

A key ethical issue can arise where coaches, eager to grow their practice, may inadvertently compromise themselves and/or the way in which they represent their work. Think this hasn't happened to you? Well consider these common situations for a moment:

Scenario 1: Have you ever been asked to take on a client where the focus for the work lay outside of your core areas of expertise?
Scenario 2: Have you ever been tempted to embellish your skills to an individual client/organization in order to secure a piece of work?

> **REFLECTIONS:**
>
> - What would you do in this situation?
> - How would your decision impact on your work?
> - What clues does this give you about your ethics?

Most coaches would recognize being in this situation. An individual's sense of where the ethical boundary lies is likely to be highly unique. For example, knowing your strengths and limitations is important; however, if you only do what is precisely within your core competence, how do you ever develop and grow? How much does it matter if you exaggerate your skill set if you also have an intention to develop that skill set before you deliver the work? For some coaches, absolute transparency will be essential to set an appropriate expectation for what each coaching relationship requires. For others they will take a more commercial view and have strategies for managing difficulties should they arise rather than avoiding getting into the situation in the first place.

Integrity

Ethical behavior is sometimes described as "what you do when no one is watching." In your practice you may well act with the best intent in a particular situation, however, an independent observer could see those actions quite differently. Consider these situations for a moment:

Scenario 1: Have you ever charged more or less than your average fee for the services you offered because you are aware of the budget available?

Yet again, a coach's response to this is likely to vary widely. Some coaches will simply see this as a feature of the unregulated commercial market in which we operate. Others will worry that whichever client is paying more would feel short-changed if they were to discover another person/organization was getting the same service but for less money.

Scenario 2: Have you ever been hired to work with a client to gain promotion and discovered they have already made a career decision to leave the organization?

This scenario highlights the "who is the client" issue. Some coaches would rely on the non-directive nature of their work and trust that their decision would be seen in a wider context. Other coaches would be concerned that they had somehow failed in their duty to promote their loyalty to the organization that employs them both.

Scenario 3: Have you ever worked with a client who practices a different religion, comes from a different cultural heritage or has beliefs that are radically different from yours?

We probably have all made choices to take on clients who are different from ourselves. This scenario highlights the "how strong are my biases" issue. Some practitioners think they are judgment-free and can coach anyone. There is a danger in this perspective as we've highlighted in this chapter, we all have judgments that make us unique. Being accepting of others' differences is something that all professional bodies have in some way or another in their code of ethics. Yet being honest with yourself about your own values and what keeps you from being accepting of another's beliefs is useful to signpost here.

REFLECTIONS:

- What would you do?
- What values and beliefs interfere with or support your decision?
- How do you know when you cannot effectively coach or mentor someone?
- What clues does this give you about your ethics?

Reflecting on your choices such as these as they arise can be an important foundation for terms in your client Contract, who you choose to work with and how you talk about your work with others. Ongoing reflective practice is the first step for defining your integrity.

Competence

For the most part we would not be winning and delivering work with clients if we were not competent to do so. However, life is rarely that simple. Consider the following scenarios:

Scenario 1: Have you ever noticed signs of a clinical issue in one of your clients, but agreed to another session as you prepare yourself for managing a referral conversation? In this scenario you are torn between acting quickly and acting skillfully.

Scenario 2: Have you ever found yourself short of time to prepare for a session, and gone ahead with the session anyway? In this scenario you are likely to be weighing up whether cancellation at short notice is better or worse than not being fully prepared.

Scenario 3: Have you ever described yourself as a non-directive practitioner and then been surprised when your client thanks you for your "advice"? This scenario highlights how sometimes our intentions and behaviors can lack alignment.

> **REFLECTIONS:**
>
> - What would you do?
> - What values and beliefs interfere or support your decision?
> - What choices similar to these have you made within your current work?
> - What clues does this give you about your ethics?

In our experience these are common occurrences – as we all think we are competent to take on the work. Yet some assignments shift into areas where we no longer have the skills required or our resourcefulness may be suboptimal. Consequently we make a choice in the moment that may cause doubt, worry or anxiety. The reaction is a signpost to review our choices. It's not about judging our choice per se; it is better understanding what caused us to take the action. When we do this from a place of knowing ourselves, it leads to a sense of congruence. Reflective practice lends itself to understanding our choices so we can behave in the way we say we will.

Self-care

Ignoring the importance of self-care is sadly quite common in coaches. Recognizing your own needs and limitations as a coach or mentor helps ensure you can be fully present and be your best in all areas of your life and work. This is not only about safeguarding the quality of your work; it is also about recognizing the relevance of your wider life for you as a person, not just a coach. Consider the following situations:

Scenario 1: Has there ever been a time when you booked more appointments than you could sensibly handle in one day, despite knowing that you would feel jaded by the end?

Scenario 2: What if one of your peers was going through a divorce, travelling globally as part of their senior leadership position and continuing to commit to sessions with their portfolio of internal mentoring clients?

> **REFLECTIONS:**
>
> - What would you do in this situation?
> - How would your decision impact on your work?
> - What clues does this give you about your ethics?

Sometimes the desire to be of service to others overshadows the desire to look after our self. The context for the work also brings challenges. Self-employed practitioners often have peaks and troughs of work – they will therefore take on assignments as and when they can, even when it leads to a crazy schedule or converting annual leave into work days. The practical need to make ends meet can mean they neglect their own need for down time. Internal coaches and mentors are often managing busy day jobs and yet passionate about developing their coaching or mentoring work outside of their job. As a consequence they might be reluctant to rearrange a client session despite being given additional work and then find themselves working out of hours in order to keep the day job on track. Planning holidays, recovery time and daily activities that restore your health such as exercise, sleep, mindfulness and spending time with friends are necessary for career longevity. For more ideas, see Chapter 2. Openly sharing your plans with your peers and maintaining your boundaries about your self-care are sacrosanct. Sharing your concerns with your peers when they are out of balance in a compassionate way can benefit everyone.

Bias

In our experience our bias, habits and patterns tend to follow us around – how we are in one context will give us a pretty reliable indication of how we will be in another. For example, someone who would never tell a lie at work will most likely never tell a lie outside of work. Therefore how your ethical behaviors show up in your peer supervision relationship may well give you information about how your bias might show up with your clients. Consider the following situations:

Scenario 1: Your peer brings an issue to peer supervision that you have encountered previously. Keen to ensure they don't make the same mistake as you did, you feel compelled to share your opinion and tell them what they *should do*.

Scenario 2: You notice that your peer often turns up to your peer meetings with the smell of alcohol on their breath.

Scenario 3: You get the feeling that one person in the peer supervision group is being marginalized in small but significant ways.

Stopping for a moment to reflect, you may notice you already have formed an opinion about these ethical scenarios mentioned above. In the early stages of peer supervision your initial reaction may be "I can't believe that . . .," or comparisons "If I was in this scenario, I would . . . ." This may be the first indication that an elephant has arrived in the room, and a useful place for reflection.

> **REFLECTIONS:**
>
> - What would you do in this situation?
> - How do your decisions inform your ability to manage your bias?
> - What clues does this give you about your ethics?

Starting with your judgment of the situation is important because it immediately highlights your bias about a dilemma or situation. One of the unifying coaching and mentoring competencies is being "judgment free," so during your coaching or mentoring sessions you can be neutral with the client's decisions. If your bias is interfering during the session, the client can experience this as being judged. The conundrum here is that we *all* have bias! Unfortunately becoming a practitioner doesn't mean you become free of bias. What it does do, is allow you to better recognize your biases. Once you recognize your biases, you have choices about how you manage your reaction to the particular issue at hand.

By having self-awareness of our bias, it allows us to choose how we react to any situations as these are now under our own control. Effective self-management starts by being aware of our own bias and habit, stopping for a moment and consciously considering our response, thus opening up more options. When our reactions (resulting from our bias) lead us to quickly form opinions, judgments and solutions, we can manage and regulate how to respond wisely.

Peer supervision can be a safe environment to better understand your bias and observe others. A few things to signpost include:

- What judgments do you have about others' choices?
- What positive judgments do you hold of yourself or others? (e.g. I'm ethical. Evidenced-based approaches are the best way of getting outcomes. Ian is smart.)
- When do you or others feel confident in sharing observations quickly?
- When do you or others resist sharing observations?

We hope that these scenarios illustrate how bias appears and the opportunity you have to make choices when they arise. They may also highlight your ethical choices as to when to take action. The moment you have awareness of a potential action, you also have a moment of choice where you can give in to an impulse to speak or conversely impose some self-discipline and resist that impulse. What's interesting about these scenarios is that "doing nothing" or "waiting" may be colluding with unhelpful behaviors, and your silence may contribute to the perpetuation of what is occurring.

The tipping point to taking action for many people is often when the concern with the potentially unethical behavior is greater than the concern for potential damage to the relationship (should you be mistaken or if you were to handle the conversation clumsily). Tackling these sorts of situations requires courage, as the fear of rejection within peers can be powerful. Yet taking action can be an authentic way to give voice to what can be a fruitful conversation and better self-awareness and understanding.

Tools and techniques for discussing ethics in peer supervision

As unpalatable as it might seem, noticing ethical challenges as they occur, capturing your ethical choices within your reflective practice and bringing them to discuss in peer supervision is enriching. Within the context of this confidential setting, you can be supported to explore your ethics, to share different perspectives and be encouraged to re-examine your ethical choices. Approaching these potentially different perspectives may require careful consideration. Here we offer a few inter-related tools and techniques that can help peers have constructive discussions on potentially ethical matters.

Enquiry

Enquiry is only possible when you approach the process with openness, understanding and trust. Enquiry begins with a curiosity about whether or not an ethical issue exists and requires asking probing questions to ascertain where the work stems from. When done constructively, it opens up the possibility for knowledge and growth. As stated by Iordanou *et al.* (2017, pp. 85–89), "developing a stance of enquiry towards your actions within peer supervision can help spot any issues of unethical misconduct and come up with a solution, which will benefit your practice as a coach (and peer supervisor)."

As you've probably already discovered in working through some of the suggested reflections in this chapter, the process of enquiry offers the opportunity to question and challenge your own beliefs and perspectives about yourself, your client and your peer. Each reflection typically starts with the simple "What would I do?" and from here can open to a wider range of enquiry. When you review your enquiry with your peers, enquiry can enable you to come to new conclusions, which will improve the quality of your work and your peer relationship. In determining what to prepare to bring to peer supervision, we've adapted these questions from Lane (2011, p. 97):

- What are some of the elements in your coaching and mentoring which typify your ethics?
- What is it that you said or did in your coaching or mentoring that shows you treat your clients with respect, caring, integrity and responsibility?
- Does the way you perceive these principles help you evolve as a practitioner and enhance the client's experience?
- How do these principles show up in your work and become evident to you as a practitioner, your clients, peers and profession as a whole?
- Do your own beliefs enable or hinder your clients in the pursuit of their own principles?

Working through these questions may help shed more light onto different ethical perspectives and to understand how they manifest in your work. The more you work closely together as peers, the more adept you will become at spotting for yourself the nuances which your peers may more easily spot. As a result you will be able to pinpoint ethical choices that may affect the quality of your services and will give you more choice about how to move forward.

When you notice ethical areas arising during peer supervision, it can simply be stating "I'm noticing I'm feeling . . . ," sharing your observations and then asking your peers for a discussion about their perspective on the observation. Referring to Chapter 5 and using the skills of contracting can be helpful as well. If you or your peers find this challenging, engaging a professional supervisor for further discussion can be valuable. Either way, the awareness you gain will be the lens from which you develop your ethical perspective.

Feedback and discussion

Feedback is a truly valuable process in supervision because it allows for the growth and development of a coach or mentor (Long, 2011). For it to be constructive, it should be offered in a respectful, sincere, straightforward and direct manner. Offering and receiving feedback is a great tool that can help you strengthen, challenge and evaluate your work with your clients and your peers. For it to work positively it is helpful to explore how you will manage the feedback process as part of your peer supervision Contract. This will require continual updating, drawing upon the contracting skills that we outlined in Chapter 5. Here are some steps to help you use feedback productively.

Be self-reflective
We recommend you ask yourself the following questions:

- What do I feel curious yet nervous, ashamed or embarrassed about in my practice?
- Where might I have become habituated, presumptive or complacent in my practice?
- What filters was I aware of using as I managed a particular part of my practice – what lenses or perspectives were therefore not used?
- What do I need from my peers to have the courage to explore things more openly?
- How will I feel about myself if I receive difficult feedback?
- What support mechanisms could I turn to outside of my peer supervision?

Answering these questions will help you have clear expectations about how you might react to your peers' feedback towards your work and make it more likely that you will use that feedback in a productive and beneficial manner.

Ask for help
Peer supervision is there to help you unpick both easy and tricky situations to give you a fuller understanding of what was happening at the time. We are all

human, and there are times in our lives that we don't have answers to all questions. One way or another, most of us have at some point felt apprehensive in bringing issues to peer supervision. For example, thinking that the supervisor and/or group might think that we should have solved that issue by ourselves, or already know the answers to specific questions. Remember, it is OK to ask for help! Sometimes the most honest and noble thing to do is to say "I don't know the answer to this one." What if not knowing wasn't an expression of ignorance, but an expression of openness to learning? Not knowing how to deal with a specific situation can promote a deep discussion as to how to deal with it, which can ultimately benefit your coaching or mentoring relationships. When you give yourself permission not to know everything, you role model to your peers how you live with uncertainty or vulnerability and you may also inspire your clients to seek the answers they wish to know within themselves, for themselves.

Take risks

It may take a little time before you are ready to take this step with your peer(s) as it is important to have first built rapport and a trusting environment. However, given that peer supervision is a collaborative learning environment, if you don't take a risk here – where can you take one! By taking risks we mean asking direct questions such as "I notice that in our meetings you tend to make statements rather than asking powerful questions. Could this be something to explore further?" Or "There was something in the way you described that client situation that bothered me a little. Would you be open to analyze together why that might be?" Such direct approaches not only allow feedback to unfold but also promote honest discussions between the peers, which is likely to lead to a richer collective understanding and often leads to a positive impact on everyone's client work.

The peer supervision discussion is likely to have two stages. The first invites enquiry and feedback around what values, principles and beliefs may have drawn the practitioner to see what they saw and to work how they worked. In the second stage, the conversation focuses around a constructive way to formulate the responsibilities towards clients and articulates the ethical framework to guide and enable the practitioner's work.

When peer supervision stalls

On occasions, it may not be possible to find a way forward that is acceptable to all those involved. In Chapter 5 we provided an escalation process that outlines exactly how to use enquiry in peer supervision. We advise you to read through it carefully, as it can act as a helpful guide regarding the steps that need to be taken in peer supervision to resolve any ethical issues that may arise, and what to do should you find there is a lack of alignment between you and your peers.

Final thoughts

Ethics are always present in your work whether you realize it or not. Developing ethical awareness is essential but how we do it is a personal choice; it relates to the morals and values we hold as individuals and the extent to which we are willing and able to re-examine them. Discovering your preferences and where you fall into habits can be illuminating. Some can be freeing and others downright frustrating! Peer supervision is a great forum for reviewing what happened and reflecting on what options to consider for the future. Of course over time your experience of how to handle these circumstances will grow, and even as experienced practitioners, there will be a first time for everything, as each situation will undoubtedly have unique characteristics.

We would therefore encourage you to view your peer supervision as a laboratory for deliberating and exploring subtle differences in your own and your peer's approach to ethics. This implies sharing common goals for best practice, expanding on existing knowledge, valuing diversity and working together to safeguard the coaching profession as a whole (Brennan and Wildflower, 2014). Good awareness enables you to articulate an ethical framework that is both personally congruent and which would objectively be regarded as good practice.

Peer supervision can play a crucial role in the fulfillment of these goals: By allowing yourselves time to explore and consider your ethics in a safe and encompassing environment, welcoming constructive and reflective discussions, and creating space for your ethical compass to find its true north. This will generate a level of confidence that enables you to be aware of and open to a range of choices available to you.

Through reflecting upon your choices and bringing ethical issues for exploration with your peer supervision group, you can be genuinely of service to yourself, the client and the industry as a whole.

Key learning points

1   Ethical issues occur at the edge of our awareness, and are always present in our work as a coach or mentor. Our culture and life history shape our ethics, beliefs, biases and blind spots.
2   Noticing our judgments about our peers' dilemmas provides a trigger to explore our own ethics, biases, beliefs and values.
3   When the choices we make in our coaching practice cause us doubt, worry or anxiety, this invites us to be curious and reflective about the ethics in play.
4   Peer supervision can safeguard the quality of your work by providing a supportive relationship in which to spot areas of ethical consideration.

5. Ethics can be discussed deeply and courageously when there is honesty, respect, openness, non-judgment, trust and a constructive intent in the supervision relationship.
6. The tools of enquiry, seeking feedback, self-reflection and asking for guidance lead to insightful supervision conversations.
7. Putting Ethics on your agenda and including it in your contracting phase is useful.
8. Ethics are always the elephant in the room. Being mindful the elephant is there, pausing to noticing your reaction to it, considering your options and taking considered action to discuss it creates new awareness.

References

AC and EMCC (2016) Global Code of Ethics for Coaches and Mentors [Online]. Available from: https://actoonline.org/wp-content/uploads/2016/10/Global-Code-of-Ethics_2016.pdf [accessed 1 May 2017].

APECS (2006) Ethical Guideline [Online]. Available from: www.apecs.org/ethical-guidelines [accessed 16 June 2017].

Bachkirova, T. and Jackson, P. (2011) Peer supervision in coaching and mentoring. In: T. Bachkirova, P. Jackson and D. Clutterbuck (eds), *Coaching and Mentoring Supervision: Theory and practice*. Maidenhead, UK: Open University, pp. 230–231.

Brennan, D. and Wildflower, L. (2014) Ethics in coaching. In: E. Cox, T. Bachkirova and D. Clutterbuck (eds), *The Complete Handbook of Coaching* (2nd edn). London: Sage, pp. 430–444.

de Jong, A. (2010) Coaching ethics: Integrity in the moment of choice. In: J. Passmore (ed.), *Excellence in Coaching*. London: Association for Coaching, pp. 191–202.

Gray, D. and Jackson, P. (2011) Coaching supervision in the historical context of psychotherapeutic and counseling models: A meta-model. In: T. Bachkirova, P. Jackson and D. Clutterbuck (eds), *Coaching and Mentoring Supervision: Theory and practice*. Maidenhead, UK: Open University, pp. 15–27.

ICF (2015) ICF Code of Ethics [Online]. Available from: www.gtcoaching.net/wpcontent/uploads/ICF_Code_of_Ethics.pdf [accessed 16 June 2017].

Iordanou, I., Hawley, R. and Iordanou, C. (2017) *Values and Ethics in Coaching*. London: Sage.

Lane, D. (2011) Ethics and professional standards in supervision. In: T. Bachkirova, P. Jackson and D. Clutterbuck (eds), *Coaching and Mentoring Supervision: Theory and practice*. Maidenhead, UK: Open University, pp. 91–104.

Long, K. (2011) The self in supervision. In: T. Bachkirova, P. Jackson and D. Clutterbuck (eds), *Coaching and Mentoring Supervision: Theory and practice*. Maidenhead, UK: Open University, pp. 78–90.

Oxford Dictionary [Online]. Available from: www.oxforddictionaries.com [accessed 20 May 2017].

Pelham, G. (2016) *The Coaching Relationship in Practice*. London: Sage.

St. James Ethics Centre [Online]. Available from: www.ethics.org.au/about/what-is-ethics [accessed 14 August 2017].

Van Nieuwerburgh, C. (2014) *An Introduction to Coaching Skills: A practical guide*. London: Sage.

Managing pitfalls 8

Definition: The *Oxford Thesaurus* defines pitfall as a noun; a hazard, danger, risk, peril, difficulty, catch, snag, stumbling block, and drawback.

What we mean by pitfalls

As outlined throughout the book, there are many benefits of working with a peer for supervision; however, there are also a number of risks that may need to be considered and managed. A common occurrence is that peer supervision relationships can grow out of similar interests, training or background. However, this can create blind spots so it is good to aim for diversity where possible as this expands options and learning. Interestingly, whether you choose to work with one other peer in one to one supervision or work as part of a larger group, the types of risk you might encounter are similar. We will start the chapter looking at the common issues and then go on to look at some additional risks that arise when working in groups.

Perhaps the most critical question you can ask yourself when setting up your peer supervision relationships is "Why am I drawn to work with them?" There are a number of answers to this question, and each one will hint at different pitfalls that could arise as a result. The answers that we cover and the potential pitfalls that emerge are as given in Table 8.1 below.

In the first part of the chapter we explore how these risks play out more fully, give some hints about how you might spot these pitfalls within your relationships and offer some suggestions on how those risks could be managed. The second part of the chapter focuses on the potential pitfalls that arise in group work and are likely to be experienced whatever your motivation for joining the group. In the same way as the first section, we offer hints about how to spot these pitfalls and provide some guidance on how to manage the risks.

178 Managing pitfalls

Table 8.1 Motivations and potential pitfalls

Motivation for working with peers	Potential pitfall
Feeling safe	Collusion
They think differently to you	Disorientation/confusion
You think you can learn from them	Discounting your own experience
You trained with them	Developmental stagnation
They approached you	Minimizing your supervision needs
To benchmark your practice	Breeding competitiveness
Convenience and existing camaraderie	Dual relationships
Lack of alternatives	Dependency
You were allocated to them	Lack of ownership
You sought them out	Overinvestment in the relationship

Section 1: Pitfalls for any form of peer supervision

Pitfall 1: Collusion

If you are driven by feeling safe, it's probably because you are not yet ready to step outside of your comfort zone. Feeling safe may be a useful environment in which to build your confidence early on in your coaching journey, however, it may also slow your learning down. If confidence is the primary driver of supervision, perhaps investing in professional supervision or a coach mentor is a better option and/or an adjunct to peer supervision.

Examples of warning signs that you may be colluding:

- You don't want to challenge others.
- You say you agree when you don't entirely.
- You convince yourself the issue is less important than keeping the relationship positive.

Managing collusion

- When setting up your peer supervision relationships it can be helpful to have some diversity and some sameness between you and your peer(s).
- Remember we all need a bit of stretch now and again – it's a good idea to all contract to bring examples of when you are actively stretching your coaching practice.
- When contracting for your relationship, discuss how important comfort is to you and additionally what an appropriate level of challenge would be for you too.

- Discuss how you will notice when the relationship has slipped from comfortable to "cozy."
- Set time aside at the end of a session (or at the beginning of the next) to consider what the proportion of support and challenge was from your peer(s). If the balance is less than 50:50 (or whatever proportion you have agreed is right for you), consider what steps you can actively take in the next session to get the ratio back on track.
- Take responsibility for your own learning and prepare individually before each session.
- Take time to reflect on your reflections – what do you notice you are avoiding or looking for affirmation for?
- Contract to bring a challenge to the group and/or your peer in one to one supervision every third session or so.

Pitfall 2: Disorientation/confusion

If you are attracted to work with people who think differently to you, this generally feels like a positive move. The benefits are that it will open up your perspective, lead to some interesting debates and will actively expand your repertoire. These ingredients can help accelerate your development.

This arrangement is likely to be most beneficial when you are fully grounded in your own practice. Otherwise, when your peer supervisor(s) present a very different mindset to yours, it is easy for you to feel undermined or disoriented.

In our experience the perceived advantage of being able to learn a new perspective and have supervision on client issues is far more difficult to achieve than it sounds. Often the issues brought to supervision are just out of our awareness. Trying to process blind spots, while also trying to think differently, often means that one overshadows the other. Energy can go to understanding the theory and the client issue gets obscured. Alternatively the energy goes to resolving the client issue within the existing range of knowledge, which means the opportunity for new theoretical learning gets lost.

When disorientation occurs, professional supervision might be useful to understand the deeper cause and/or to get additional support to integrate the new learning received from the peer supervision.

Examples of warning signs that you may be feeling disorientation and confusion:

- You feel undermined by others.
- You don't know what to say and feel tongue-tied.
- You feel confused by what you hear but don't have the confidence to ask for clarification.

Managing disorientation and confusion

- No matter how early on in your coaching or mentoring journey you are, articulate your coaching or mentoring model and share this with your peer(s). Invite them to do the same.
- Before you begin to work on client issues, discuss your different approaches to understand where there are similarities, where there are differences and where there are subtle distinctions – for example, common terminology may mean different things.
- When discussing client matters, notice when a new frame of reference is causing you an unhelpful level of confusion. Return to something familiar to get grounded before exploring from a less familiar perspective or theoretical base.

Pitfall 3: Discounting your own experience

It could be an attractive prospect to partner with people who are longer in experience than you. It can also potentially stymie your own growth. For example, you might admire their track record and feel that you could learn a lot from them. However, if this is what is attracting you to a person, perhaps you would be better seeking out a mentoring relationship than a peer supervision relationship? To understand more fully how we differentiate peer supervision relationships from other helping relationships, please refer to Chapter 1.

Working with a range of experience levels could also be a positive choice. The more experienced practitioner(s) may enjoy sharing their expertise. By contrast for the novice practitioner(s) curiosity may be helpfully provocative. For example, naïve questions often cause an experienced person to consider how they have come to know something.

Interestingly this can be a trap for both the inexperienced and experienced practitioner alike. Where we choose to learn *from* others we are also choosing to diminish the value of working it out independently. For the more experienced person it is a subtle invitation to step into a more dominant role.

Examples of warning signs that you may be discounting your own experience:

- You feel in awe of others.
- You don't volunteer your experience.
- You caveat what you say.
- When someone offers a perspective different to your own, you automatically assume you are mistaken.

Managing discounting your own experience

- In coaching and in peer supervision our primary intent is to promote self-actualization. Therefore every time you feel drawn to asking your peer(s) "What would you do?"– pause and think through how far you could get without their input, but with their facilitation. This could easily form a part of your contracting discussions. For example, how will we know that sharing experience rather than problem solving is the most helpful thing we can do?
- Track what topics you bring for each session and try to ensure that there is an equal balance between the client cases that you bring where you became stuck and the client cases where you have had successes. This balanced approach will help you feel more grounded in your current level of capability, even if you have many fewer hours' experience than your peer(s).
- Be really clear on your development gaps. See Chapter 2 on how to do this. By being transparent and sharing how you want to develop, or your development goals with your peer(s), you can collaborate on providing targeted development support. Remember, it is important that each person can offer something to the other(s), otherwise equity is challenged.
- Although you may start out with the constructive intent of learning from your peers, if you overplay this you could find yourself feeling small and helpless. If this becomes a consistent pattern, a professional supervisor may be able to highlight areas for improvement and/or work with you individually to enhance your confidence within the peer supervision relationship.

Pitfall 4: Developmental stagnation

Working with people you trained with can seem like an obvious way of continuing your journey and embedding learning. The benefits are that you will have a common language and that you enter the peer supervision relationship on the back of a formative relationship. However, this also means that you are likely to see your professional world through a similar lens. There is a tendency to "feel good" about each other, so while this might be good for empathy, it is not helpful for considering multiple perspectives.

Examples of warning signs that you may have developmental stagnation:

- You assume you know what issues the other person(s) will raise.
- You find your peers help in very similar ways each session.
- You notice that your client work is no longer stretching.
- You cease to question anything.

Managing developmental stagnation

- First and foremost, gather some evidence on how your development is actually progressing. There are a number of models which articulate how coaches develop, provided as Appendices 8.1–8.4. Consider where each of you would place yourself at the outset of the relationship and then deliberately track whether or not this is shifting.
- Identify and explore your commonality and assumptions. For example, when common terminology arises, how do you know you mean the same thing? Check out each of your interpretations – your common language might be masking some interesting nuance. This can help raise awareness of unconscious bias both individually and collectively.
- If you have some common ground, also consider what you have that is different. By identifying both, each of you can share your specialist knowledge or different context or alternative application to actively change the shape or tone of the discussion.
- Anticipate the possibility of stagnation and actively seek ways of keeping things fresh, for example:
  o Play with taking a "devil's advocate" position – what would someone from a different training school do or say?
  o Introduce reading and/or new methodology. Reflect on the impact and bring to the sessions.
  o Where working as a group, you could invite new members to join either on a permanent or occasional basis.
  o Bring in a professional supervisor who can offer new ideas.

Pitfall 5: Minimizing your own supervision needs

We are all likely to feel a degree of flattery when we are approached by a peer to engage in a reciprocal relationship. The assumption is that there is a perceived complementarity between you. However, you need to consider whether agreeing would be a positive choice for you personally. If you do not deliberately think about what your supervision needs are and how they will be met by this particular relationship, you may find a degree of inequity in the relationship. Over time this can lead to feelings of resentment, obligation and avoidance. Sometimes the request to work together can be political – for example there may be a perception that you can help them commercially, to get a promotion or to learn how to run their business. This is particularly dangerous territory as it could result in exploitation of the relationship.

Examples of warning signs that you may be minimizing your own supervisory needs:

- When someone raises something similar but not the same as your issue but you don't want to bother them with your issue.
- Where you have the sense that you are giving more than you are getting.
- Where the input you received from your peer(s) does not extend your thinking.
- Feeling flattered to be invited and not being able to say no to the invitation.

Managing the minimization of your own supervision needs

- Before agreeing to the relationship, understand their motivation for approaching you. Should this hint at one or more of the risks mentioned earlier in this chapter, then agree how you might navigate these tensions.
- Be clear about what you need in your supervision arrangements. Agree to design in some "break-points" where you can objectively review the effectiveness of the relationship so that you have natural opportunities to conclude or continue the relationship.
- If you already have professional supervision, consider how this additional arrangement will fit in terms of frequency, content, separation etc. If you do not already have professional supervision, then address the matter from first principles. Given a blank sheet of paper, what would work for you? When you know that, you can determine whether the request is a good fit for you right now.
- One of the huge risks is that for some reason you feel it is easier to agree, than to have the "no thanks" conversation. This is probably a massive warning sign that agreeing is the wrong thing to do! In which case, you have a couple of options:
  o Agree to have a couple of practice sessions and see how it goes – you may be pleasantly surprised!
  o Agree to consider their request and then find another coach or mentor who can help you prepare for that conversation.

Pitfall 6: Breeding competitiveness

There is something "nice" about working with a peer – and yet there is also a human tendency to compare and consider how we rate in the peer relationship. At times we may feel better equipped than our peer(s) and at other times we might feel inferior to them. This is a sign that competitiveness may well be causing a distortion in the relationship. Of course, some level of comparison can be helpful in helping us evaluate whether our learning journey is progressing at an appropriate pace. However, we need to recognize that learning is rarely achieved in a straight line – some learning simply adds information and other learning seems to catapult our understanding to a whole new dimension. This is very difficult to predict or to engineer. There may be multiple reasons why two people are learning at different rates – we would argue that your efforts are better served by exploring what it is that helps or hinders your own learning rather than judging who among you is progressing fastest.

If you find yourself thinking that they have more (or less) interesting or lucrative work than you, this may result in jealousy and increased competitiveness. This could challenge your ability to be independent and objective, pushing you to be more or less critical. Similarly, if you feel in competition with others, especially for clients and interesting opportunities, this may lead to you not sharing your experience and to be less collaborative and less likely to open your work for inspection.

Examples of warning signs that you may be breeding competitiveness:

- A tendency to suggest that another model/technique/approach would have been better, without exploring first why your peer chose to approach it in the way they did.
- A private sense that you would have done it differently and you are certain that this would have been considerably more (or indeed less) effective.
- A tendency to drop into the conversation indicators of success – for instance – how many clients you have, how much you are able to charge, what fantastic feedback you have received.
- A desire to want to demonstrate that your learning is deeper, more transformational, more integrated than the other person's.

Managing breeding competitiveness

- This can be really tricky as often these behaviors and thought processes occur at the edge of our awareness. You may not be deliberately doing these things – but somehow they seep through. Alternatively, it could be that you are aware of them, but when you have these thoughts you experience some sense of guilt or shame.
- We would therefore encourage you to use your original contracting session and your regular review sessions to be explicit about how your coaching practice (both professionnal and commercial) is progressing. See Chapter 5 for tips on how to do this. There is no rational need to "hint" at how successful or unsuccessful you are feeling, as there will be a time and place for sharing that.
- When you notice a peer dropping this kind of information into the discussion, call them on it. However, rather than distract the focus of the current session, we would suggest the observation is noted as something to bring to a regular review session.

- When you notice yourself doing this (and your peer doesn't call you on it), consider what insecurity is behind this. Make a note of how this contributes to your self-awareness and ensure you bring this to your next process review for fuller discussion.
- Clearly these issues have the potential for a difficult conversation with your peer(s) – there may be a fear that it could cause tension within the working relationship. We offer some hints and tips on how to manage this within Chapter 5. This is therefore a good example of when you may want to involve another peer or a professional supervisor to help you prepare for the regular review.

Pitfall 7: Dual relationships

Setting up a peer supervision relationship with people you work with can be attractive, because of its convenience and the level of camaraderie that exists as work colleagues. In many larger organizations (especially in Europe and the UK) where internal coaching is common, peer supervision can seemingly be a convenient option as well. As we've previously mentioned, this can create politics, dual relationships, collusion and/or ethical difficulties if not managed appropriately. Additionally, if you intend to use peer supervision as part of the accreditation process, this may require explanation if there is a dual relationship. As you can see, the collegiate nature of peer supervision brings with it a number of added complications, for example:

- How can a work colleague be objective when they may be working with the same organizational client or clients within the same organization, and they may have witnessed your work?
- When you are part of the same system (whether as internal or external practitioners), there may be systemic blind spots that affect each of you.
- There may be times when you are in competition with each other for work, such as part of being on a panel or working in the same consultancy.
- How will you handle confidentiality in practice? Your peer(s), especially internal practitioners, may know who you are talking about and vice versa.
- If your colleague determines your next assignment or you report into them, how simple is it to reveal some of your vulnerabilities? Or to bring things that went awry in a session?
- Where you are delivering on the same project, if one of you appears to be struggling, how comfortable will it be to wax lyrical about how well your clients are doing?
- How will you manage pressing operational or political issues to ensure they give helpful context rather than taking precedence over the supervision work?

Examples of warning signs that you may have a dual relationship:

- Where you work together or in the same organization.
- You belong to the same groups (could be sports, children, school, family etc.).
- You are close friends and have the same circle of contacts.
- You have a shared history.

Managing dual relationships

- The quick answer here is – don't do it! Look for alternative peer supervision or go to professional supervision. Dual relationships are probably *the* most difficult thing to manage because of their complexity and potential for distorting the supervision relationship.
- However, if your situation means that this is your peer supervision relationship of choice, then we would recommend contracting to minimize risk. By reviewing in detail the possible conflicts of interest that you might encounter, you can contract carefully for each one. There is more guidance on this in Chapters 5 and 7.
- When there is a dual relationship, you will need to articulate clearly how you manage the dual relationship such that it does not impact upon the quality of the supervision and/or damage your confidence.
- Ensure that you protect the supervision time for supervision. Schedule separate catch-ups for talking as colleagues, or at the very least set a time boundary for when you switch into the peer supervision discussion.
- In these circumstances, we would highly recommend that each of you have access to a professional supervisor – ideally a different one to each other! This affords you an independent perspective, will raise your awareness of emerging challenges in the relationship and will support you to navigate the complexities in a proactive and assertive way. There is more information on how this works in Chapter 9.

Pitfall 8: Dependency

In some localities there may be very few coaches or mentors available to work with face to face, and therefore it may be that anyone feels better than no one. However, if we perceive that we don't have any alternatives it is highly likely that should one of you outgrow the other(s) you will start to feel trapped. Watching out for dependency is the responsibility of all parties as both parties have a role in creating it.

Examples of warning signs that dependency is occurring:

- You start to de-prioritize the supervision time in your diary.
- You start to feel you are "giving more than you are getting."
- You start to feel you are "getting more than you are giving."
- You feel obligated to continue even though you would like to move on.
- You feel you would like something different in your supervision relationship but can't find it anywhere.
- You notice that others seem to be becoming dependent on you.

Managing dependency

- Stress test your thinking – the assumption that "there is no one else" is likely to be faulty.
- Challenge your communication preferences. For example, rather than work on a face to face basis, consider working virtually. This opens up the possibility of working with practitioners who live in a complementary time-zone.
- Stretch your network as you may need to look beyond those practitioners you already know. We offer some ideas of how to address this in Chapter 3.
- As you become aware that others are depending on you, use your contracting skills to open up a conversation about it.
- Keep the relationship fresh by putting effort into careful contracting and by engaging in regular reviews or bring in a professional supervisor. All these activities help you stay proactive. How you do this is explained in more detail in Chapters 3, 4 and 5.

So far the significant risks outlined here have been connected with the fact that you already know the peer(s) you plan to engage with. In addition, there are some risks that arise when you engage in peer supervision with people you don't yet know.

Pitfall 9: Lack of ownership

This situation often arises on training courses where a central person "buddies" delegates up to work together either on a one-off basis or over the duration of the program. This opportunity creates diversity in peer relationships; however, we also might be connected with people with whom we feel uncomfortable. The problem is seen as externally generated and "not our fault" that the arrangement didn't succeed. This may generate frustration or resentment in us and yet we may not yet have the skills to bring it to the table for discussion. Or it may be that we feel so disenchanted with the relationship that we "can't be bothered" to work with it – it feels easier just to go through the motions than cause a fuss.

Examples of warning signs that there may be a lack of ownership:

- One or more of the members appear to be reticent to fully engage.
- Members bring something transactional or something that they already know the answer to and so learning is being minimized.
- Avoidant behaviors appear such as being late, forgetting appointments, not having much to bring.

Managing lack of ownership

- Where the situation is a one-off, journal the experience of your discomfort. Once you understand it more fully you are likely to be better prepared for next time and you could rehearse what you would hope to do.
- Where the situation is a longer-term arrangement, it may be helpful to get some additional support – perhaps the help of a trusted colleague or a professional supervisor. This will help raise your self-awareness and give you the confidence to manage the situation with your peer(s).
- Where challenging the situation directly feels too risky or you have tried and failed, then escalating it to the central coordinator is the final option.

Pitfall 10: Overinvestment in the relationship

In this scenario you will have been proactive in finding people to partner with. Typically this will mean that you have invested a significant amount of time checking out the complementarity of the partnership. The problem here is that having put so much time and effort into setting up the relationship, we can be reluctant to give up on it. We put further effort into getting it right, which means we deepen our investment into it. Sometimes we might be better off calling a halt and trying again. However, there is something disheartening about having done all the right things, and not getting it right! The result is we stay in an unproductive relationship longer than we should and it dents our belief that we could find something better. Indeed, the intimacy and intensity of peer relationships can result in it being emotionally difficult to challenge or end the relationship. If you find yourself in this situation, we suggest taking this to professional supervision.

Examples of warning signs that you may be overinvesting in the relationship:

- You feel you have to stick with it as you have already invested a lot of time in it.
- You don't like to give up.
- You feel that walking away will reflect badly on you.

Managing overinvestment in the relationship

- Ensure you engage in practice or "chemistry" sessions before embarking on a full contracting piece.
- Implement regular reviews of the working relationship (see Chapters 3 and 4 for more detail).
- Keep the contact details of the other practitioners who you encountered through the selection process, leaving the door open to come back to them in the future should you choose to.

Section 2: The particular pitfalls of peer group supervision

To set the group up for a strong start, before commencing in peer group supervision we suggest practitioners agree the ground rules that they will adhere to during the group meetings (Chapter 3). Being clear about roles, responsibilities and commitments creates psychological safety and underpins the success of the group. However, groups are curious things! Sometimes despite all our best efforts to keep things balanced, unhelpful group dynamics arise. Also difficulties within the group dynamics often highlight the things we need to work upon ourselves.

Group Pitfall 1: Groupthink

"Groupthink" is a term first coined by Irving Janis (1972), who noticed that individuals within groups (especially those with a similar background) often made faulty decisions because of the human desire to be part of a cohesive group.

Groupthink is caused by our need to belong. Additional complexities arise from being social creatures. For example, we will tend to gravitate to people like us, thereby creating sub-groups within the overall group.

Examples of warning signs that there is a risk of "Groupthink":

- There is a negative experience of what happens in this group when one or more of the members disagree with the majority of the group. For example, they may be talked over, ignored or forced to leave.
- Members feel pressure to maintain the unity of the group and exert pressure on one another to conform to group norms.
- Members self-censor the expression of their views in order to fit in with the prevailing thinking.

- A tendency to assume that there will be unanimity; the group goes along with a suggestion which receives some endorsement without fully checking if all members agree.
- Being comfortable that the group is self-sufficient without seeking objective or third party input from time to time.
- Individuals take risks outside of the group, because the group has endorsed its appropriateness and unforeseen consequences arise.
- The sense of pride in the group is tipping over into an inflated sense of their worth, feeling superior to others.

Managing Groupthink

- Contract specifically for how you want to challenge each other.
- Actively look for diversity in group membership and value difference.
- Work sometimes in smaller groups; seek input from each group independently. Importantly, the membership of these smaller groups needs to be different each time.
- Look at your behavior and how you operate in a group setting. How much self-censoring are you doing? When did you last take an opposite stance to the rest of the group? When do you seek to influence another member to see the group's perspective? Bring what you notice to a process review meeting.
- Develop mechanisms for bringing in fresh thinking. This could be as simple as using a technique like "Devils and Angels" where you deliberately invite affirmative and alternative feedback. You could also invite guest members, other practitioners or perhaps a professional supervisor to join the group intermittently.

Important note: When our anxiety is triggered our primal and automatic response is likely to be fight, flight or freeze. This in turn will provoke an emotional reaction (sometimes one that is outside our awareness) in both us and others in the group – and if this is not managed it can often divert attention from the supervision work itself. In our experience, when unhelpful group dynamics occur it is usually because one of three group principles is not being fully honored. The three principles to be mindful about in group dynamics are – parity, patience and power dynamics.

Group Pitfall 2: Parity

It is highly likely that within a group the levels of experience will vary. How the group manages the difference among them can have an impact on group dynamics. No matter what the intention, where experience is used as a differentiator it may cause some individuals to feel "more than" or "less than."

Some warning signs that there is a risk to parity:

- The group defers to the more seasoned practitioners to take up roles of responsibility first to role model how it should be done.
- The group deliberately takes a more developmental stance encouraging those with the least experience to engage with the opportunity for development first.
- The group tends to seek input from the "elders" of the group.
- The group works hard to ensure those with less experience are heard in the discussion, but fails to do the same for the more introverted and experienced members.
- Where there is not time for each member to bring a case to every session, you notice a tendency for some more than others to get the attention of the group.

Managing parity

- There are some key roles that will help the group function (for more detail see Chapter 4) and which can be shared among the group. Rather than play to people's perceived strengths or development areas, simply rotate them on a regular basis. Have fun with it, be creative – for example, go to everyone's birthday month order or those with blue eyes go last.
- Use deliberate facilitation strategies rather than allow group members to speak freely. Structure can help prevent the more confident or extrovert or experienced members going first. Similarly it can prevent the more reticent members from going last and waiting to see what the others say. Some simple methods include:
    o When working in a circle, invite the person sitting to the right of the member bringing an issue to go first and then go clockwise around the circle. When the next case is brought the person to the left of the member bringing an issue goes first and then the group works anticlockwise around the circle.
    o Use a "koosh" ball to keep the energy flowing. Here the facilitator or the peer supervisee throws the ball to one member inviting a contribution, that member then throws the ball to the person they would like to hear from, who offers their contribution before throwing the ball to whomever they would like to hear from, and so on.
- When you are contributing to a discussion, consider your personal responsibility for how your natural communication preference might influence the

group dynamics. Take opportunities to work both within and outside of your comfort zone. If you tend to share more than others, try sharing less often or last. If you share less than others, try contributing first or trusting a hunch and voicing it.
- Track what actually happens (this could be one members role) and analyze your data to see what happens. Maintaining parity over time is something you could incorporate into the group Contract. There can then be a group agreement to share any group dynamics in a review meeting, or indeed working with it in the moment if you notice that parity could be jeopardized.
- If despite your best efforts you discover that there are some habitual patterns within the group that are hard to manage, this is where bringing in a professional supervisor to review group process could be helpful.

Group Pitfall 3: Patience

Everyone will have a preferred pace to their communication and different level of tolerance for silence and for how deeply we like to explore matters. The contracting process is a good opportunity to explore those differences, though it will not eradicate them. So it can be interesting to observe when members get restless, or when they break a silence, or when they offer a contribution that actually moves the group onto a different matter. These behaviors can have the effect of diverting the peer supervisee's attention away from their own processing of the issue, and serves to keep the discussion at a surface level.

Some warning signs that there is a risk to patience:

- Some of the group gets fidgety when certain members present their case or make a contribution.
- Some members have different levels of tolerance for silence and make an intervention when other members would have been happy to sit with the silence a while longer.
- Having a tendency to rescue members who seem to be struggling to articulate something, by offering experience or interpretations rather than allowing the process of articulation to take place.
- Becoming obsessed with time slots, moving the discussion along or closing it down so as to keep to time. In fact the issue may only have needed a few more moments to reach a more natural pause.

Managing patience

- Start by noticing and analyzing your own behavior – what is it that causes you to be fidgety, to break silence, to move the group on? What might that be saying about you?
- For the more extrovert thinkers, try writing things down as they occur to you so that you reduce the likelihood of interrupting.
- There is often an assumption that when an issue has been brought to peer supervision that a conclusion needs to be found. If time is tight rather than rush to action, simply recognize that the issue might still need work and ask permission to move on. For example, "Can we leave this matter with you for more independent reflection?"
- Where patterns emerge, bring the behavior to the group's attention and talk about what is happening in the moment. It may be reassuring to know that sometimes these patterns are not simply a reflection of your peer group dynamics; they may actually hold clues about the case itself. This is known as "parallel process," and a professional supervisor would be able to work with the group to help you identify when this may be occurring.

Group Pitfall 4: Power dynamics

As outlined in Chapter 1, a key differentiator between peer supervision and professional supervision is the opportunity for genuine equity in the relationship. Therefore it is important to be vigilant to any clues that suggest that balance within the group is becoming distorted.

Examples of warning signs that there is a risk to a balance of power:

- One or more people monopolize the time available for discussing their work.
- Some people act as though they are a professional supervisor even though they are a peer, or act like the facilitator when it is not their turn.
- One or more group members give more attention to another member in the group, perhaps because of their stature in the market or conversely because of their apparent vulnerability.
- When there is conflict among the group there is a tendency to find a scapegoat or a rescuer thereby avoiding dealing with the issue collectively.
- On occasion alliances within the group form, perhaps holding a shared view which is in opposition to the majority of the group.
- Feeling as though you would be a lone voice and choosing to keep your thoughts to yourself.

Managing power dynamics

- Build in the principle that everyone will have equal airtime into your Contract (see Chapter 5).
- Observe your responses to how you contribute to power dynamics. Journal about it to help you notice your own patterns. What is it about this group that triggers your responses?
- Bring the behavior to the group's attention and talk about what is happening in the moment.
- If there are patterns of the same members and/or a dynamic appearing, have a specific session and/or amount of time for discussion about the dynamic.
- Where this feels awkward, difficult or you are simply curious, it may be helpful to bring in a professional supervisor to observe and facilitate a session.

Final thoughts

Whether you are working in a pair or part of a group, there are always challenges in managing peer relationships. One of the ways to avoid the pitfalls is to prepare adequately and raise your self-awareness to your own preferences, biases and how you like to learn. Having a clear focus of your aims for your peer supervision and/or overall continuous professional development (CPD) can help you stay on-track. Being flexible and re-contracting where necessary is also useful. Be prepared to voice concerns as well as give and receive feedback to ensure you get the best out of the time you have to invest.

Key learning points

1. A supervisee's appetite for expanding their perspective, being challenged and being open to learning might be uncomfortable at times, but will help them determine the most suitable form of supervision.
2. A supervisee's knowledge of their motivations for supervision can help them to choose the most suitable form of supervision: One to one, peer or professional supervision, mentoring or coaching.
3. In the supervision relationship it is important to balance the need for feeling good with being open to learning, being challenged, stretched and exploring multiple perspectives.

4   Understanding one's stage of development as a coach will help to avoid stagnation in learning and to find ways to keep things fresh in the supervision process.
5   Regularly review each person's motivations and needs for supervision to ensure that the best possible developmental and learning space is created in peer supervision.
6   Noticing when pitfalls arise in supervision provides a rich place for a discussion on the possibility of a parallel process that might be occurring in the supervisee's coaching or mentoring relationships.
7   Considering the potential pitfalls and ways to manage them can enhance the supervision contracting process.
8   Regularly review the supervision process, structure and roles to guard against habitual patterns which might inhibit effective supervision.
9   The qualities which underpin high quality coaching or mentoring are equally valued in minimizing pitfalls in supervision, e.g. tolerance, patience, flexibility, openness, curiosity and compassion.

References

Bachkirova, T. (2016) The self of the coach: Conceptualization, issues, and opportunities for practitioner development. *Consulting Psychology Journal: Practice and Research*, 68(2), pp. 143–156.

Janis, I.L. (1972) *Victims of Groupthink*. New York: Houghton Mifflin.

196 Managing pitfalls

Appendix 8.1

Hawkins and Smith (2006) developmental stages of the coach

For a full explanation see pp. 136–140 in Hawkins and Smith (2006). However, in summary they believe that as the coach matures in their work, the nature of enquiry when they reflect on their work also matures. They describe four stages: These are listed in the table below, along with the typical reflective enquiry that a coach at this level will often make.

When we first met this model, we weren't immediately clear about what Level IV was about. Our interpretation is that at this level we are concerned with the interplay of the client with their system and vice versa, and we are looking for "meaning making" as a whole.

Level	Focus	Core concern
Level I	Self-centered	Can I make this work?
Level II	Client-centered	Can I help this client make it?
Level III	Process-centered	How are we relating together?
Level IV	Process in context-centered	How do processes interconnect?

Figure 8.1 Peer supervisee developmental stages

It's important not to see this model as linear or as a one-way street! While generally speaking the more experienced we are the deeper our reflective questions become, we will not operate just at one level. Even seasoned coaches who are faced with a difficult client situation are likely to get moments of self-doubt and question whether or not they are the right coach. Similarly, relatively novice coaches may be curious about the ripple effect that exists around their client.

Reference
Hawkins, P. and Smith, N. (2006) *Coaching, Mentoring and Organisational Consultancy: Supervision and development*. Maidenhead, UK: Open University, pp. 123–124.

Appendix 8.2

Megginson and Clutterbuck (2009) four levels of coach maturity

This model was developed by Megginson and Clutterbuck in their work selecting coaches through assessment centers. You will notice that there are parallels with the earlier Hawkins and Smith model in that the style of coaching becomes increasingly more mature and free as the coach develops. The questions that the

Coaching approach	Style	Critical questions
Models-based	Control	How do I take the client where I think he needs to go? How do I adapt my technique or model to this circumstance?
Process-based	Contain	How do I give enough control to the client and still retain a purposeful conversation? What's the best way to apply my process in this instance?
Philosophy-based	Facilitate	What can I do to help the client do this for herself? How do I contextualize the client's issue within the perspective of my philosophy or discipline?
Systemic-eclectic	Enable	Are we both relaxed enough to allow the issue and the solution to emerge in whatever way they will? Do I need to apply any techniques or processes at all? If I do, what does the client context tell me about how to select from the wide choice available to me?

Figure 8.2 Four levels of coach maturity

coach is working with are less about reflection on their work and more about what will guide their work in the moment.

Reference

Megginson, D. and Clutterbuck, D. (2009) *Further Techniques for Coaching and Mentoring.* Oxford: Butterworth Heinemann.

Appendix 8.3

An explanation of the seven-eyed model

For an explanation from the original authors, take a look at pp. 159–174 of Hawkins and Smith (2006). Alternatively you could read an interpretation of the model in the context of the peer supervisee in the book by Clutterbuck, Whitaker and Lucas (2016), pp. 80–86.

However, as a starter for 10 we produce our own version of the model below, along with a quick explanation of what each of the seven eyes considers. Bear in mind that our coaching conversations are hugely complex and dynamic: Each of these eyes simply provides a different lens with which to review our work. In reality more than one aspect may be useful at any one point in time and indeed some aspects may not be relevant at all.

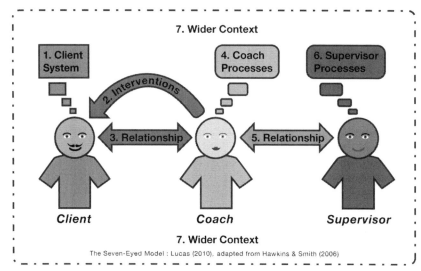

Figure 8.3 The seven-eyed model
Lucas (2010), adapted from Hawkins and Smith (2006)

Eye 1: The client system

Here we recognize that our client does not live in a vacuum. While we may be working on their here and now and moving into the future, they will also bring their history with them. This lens also reminds us to consider the huge range of individual differences. So we need to be aware of how things like the client's personality, culture and values might impact on their presenting issue.

Eye 2: The intervention

Here we review what question we asked, what tool we used and what model or theory informs our work. Remember it's difficult to see this eye in isolation as our choice of tool may well depend on our own (the coach) preferences and the level of relationship we currently have with our client.

Eye 3: The client–coach relationship

Here we consider the level of rapport that exists between ourselves and our client. It is generally our assessment of the relationship that helps us determine how challenging we feel we can be with our client and to assess what the client might be ready for. It can also be an indicator of how the client manages their relationships more generally, for example if we are finding it hard to get to know them, would others experience them in the same way?

Eye 4: The coach's processes

Just like Eye 1, the coach does not live in a vacuum either. And so this lens encourages us to heighten our own self-awareness so that we can make a conscious choice of how to be with the client. When we can do this we can be more confident our responses are based on our client's needs rather than our own.

Eye 5: The coach: Peer supervisor relationship
Here we consider the strength of the relationship between the coach and their peer supervisor – which could of course be yourself (if you are reflecting independently) or a colleague (if you are engaging in peer supervision). Just like Eye 3 – the strength of this relationship will determine how safe you feel to reflect. In addition this is where we have the opportunity to pick up on a parallel process in action. So for example if your client lacks confidence and constantly asks you for advice, when you bring that client to supervision you may also present with a lack of confidence and seek reassurance from your peer supervisor.

Eye 6: The peer supervisor's processes
As with Eyes 1 and 4 – the peer supervisor does not exist in a bubble! With a qualified peer supervisor you might expect them to have done a significant amount of work on themselves so that they can work cleanly with you. In addition, once they know you well, they are in a good position to pick up on nuances in how you are reflecting on your work with the potential of spotting the parallel process that we mentioned in Eye 5. In addition, with your permission, they may offer to share some of their "here and now" experiences as this could offer additional insights as to what is occurring in the relational dynamic.

Eye 7: The wider context
Here we look at what might be influencing the client beyond what they are stating is the presenting issue. This can be really useful in an organizational context, as we need to consider how the organizational culture, business security and change initiatives might be impacting on the client. This is also about remembering that whatever the issue for coaching, we are working with the whole person. So even when working with a career goal it is diligent to consider any knock-on impact to the client's family system. Similarly, when working with a personal issue it is also appropriate to consider whether this is leaking into their work life. This eye reminds us that any coaching topic is unlikely to be an isolated matter.

References
Bachkirova, T. (2016) The self of the coach: Conceptualisation, issues, and opportunities for practitioner development. *Consulting Psychology Journal: Practice and Research*, 68(2), pp. 143–156.

Clutterbuck, D., Whitaker, C. and Lucas, M. (2016) *Coaching Supervision: A practical guide for supervisees*. Abingdon, UK: Routledge.

Hawkins, P. and Smith, N. (2006) *Coaching, Mentoring and Organisational Consultancy: Supervision and development*. Maidenhead, UK: Open University, pp. 123–124.

Appendix 8.4

A template for developing your coach development plan

For a full explanation, see pp. 177–178 of the Clutterbuck, Whitaker and Lucas (2016) book – however, we have replicated the information in Figure 8.4 below which offers a detailed list of items which could inform your coach development plan. Depending on your level of experience you may want to give more emphasis to some of the sections. For example, early on in our coaching journey developing our range of techniques often takes priority. Later when we feel we have a rich toolbox, our interest shifts to heightening our self-awareness as we recognize and use our "self as instrument" (Bachkirova, 2016).

Knowledge	*Some questions to ask yourself could be:*
How you will expand your understanding in a range of important areas, including: • Coaching • Business • Related disciplines, such as psychology, counseling, neuroscience and so on • Industry context – what are the wider market forces that might be impacting on the clients that you work with?	• What tools, techniques or coaching constructs do I want to add to my toolbox? • How will I ensure I understand them in sufficient depth to apply them safely and wisely? • How will I integrate these with my existing toolbox?
Self-awareness	*Some questions to ask yourself could be:*
The better you know yourself the more confident you can be that your own "stuff" is not contaminating the coaching relationship. Looking inwardly to develop greater understanding of your motivations, thought processes, ambitions, strengths and weaknesses, personality traits is an essential element of being fit to practice	• How can I develop and more clearly enunciate my personal philosophy as a coach? • How can I become even more authentic? • When am I at my most/least effective as a coach? How do I know? Who holds up the mirror to me as a coach? • What is my vision for the coach I want to be in 1, 2 and 5 years' time? • How will I know I'm making progress?

Figure 8.4 Critical areas and questions to inform a coach development plan

Skills	Some questions to ask yourself could be:
The practicalities of being an effective coach – how you listen, question, give feedback, summarize, interpret and generally support the client	• What skills do I most want to improve in? • What skills improvements in me would be of greatest benefit to my clients? Skills might, for example, include listening/mindfulness; self-awareness; systems awareness; or use of silence • How will I improve the quality of my reflections on my practice? • How can I *reduce* my reliance on models, processes, tools and techniques?
Characteristics	Some questions to ask yourself could be:
Personal qualities that you wish to develop – for example, curiosity, empathy, presence, authenticity	• How can I build my self-confidence as a coach? • How much energy, time and other resources can I invest in making my vision happen?
Range of practice	Some questions to ask yourself could be:
Who you can work with and in what circumstances could you extend your portfolio by taking on clients who will stretch you and/or who come from a very different cultural background	• Where can I find appropriate challenges to my assumptions about coaching and my role as a coach? • In what ways do I want to stretch my boundaries of my coaching? • What kind of clients seem to gravitate to me and why? • What kind of clients do I not work with and why?
Context	Some questions to ask yourself could be:
How you will create a better environment for your coaching – through for example, network development and how you use supervision	• What do I need from my professional peer supervisor? Is it time to trade them in? • What resources are available to support my development as a coach (e.g. reading, social networks, role models, courses, supervision . . .)? Who can I rely on to help me?

Figure 8.4 *continued*

Context	Some questions to ask yourself could be:
	• What can I do to increase the quantity and quality of the feedback I receive on my coaching? • How can I extend my learning network? Who can I use as role models of good practice?
Your business as a coach	Some questions to ask yourself could be:
How you will build a business that aligns with your values and provides the income you want. How you market your services and ensure that the business is soundly managed	• How can I build my reputation? • How comfortable am I with my hourly rate? • How much of my time do I spend working "on" my business, i.e. business development and how much of my time do I spend working "in" my business, i.e. coaching
Contribution to the profession	Some questions to ask yourself could be:
What you will put back into the world of coaching, through research, writing, supporting new, less experienced coaches, contributing to social network sites and so on	• What kind of "pro bono" clients could you work with? • What could you blog about? • What social media discussion forums do you participate in? • Could you publish an article about elements of your work? • What lessons have you learned in your journey as coach so far – who could benefit from your learning?

Figure 8.4 *continued*

References

Bachkirova, T. (2016) The self of the coach: Conceptualisation, issues, and opportunities for practitioner development. *Consulting Psychology Journal: Practice and Research*, 68(2), pp. 143–156.

Clutterbuck, D., Whitaker, C. and Lucas, M. (2016) *Coaching Supervision: A practical guide for supervisees*. Abingdon, UK: Routledge.

Accessing professional supervision

9

Definition: Professional supervision is a reflective learning environment where the supervisor is hired by the practitioner(s) and is specifically qualified to look at the entire system in which the work is being undertaken. Although the reflective space is co-created, the professional supervisor is purposefully of service to the practitioner(s) and their clients. What is significant is that the supervisor's intention is to develop the practitioner's competence, capability and capacity to become a reflective practitioner of their own work.

What we mean by professional supervision

In a field that is largely based on experiential learning, it seems only natural that the professionally inclined would want to seek further depth and understanding of themselves and the way in which they work. However, to date, our community is still quite divided about the role of supervision in achieving that fuller understanding. We often encounter a systemic resistance to supervision, perhaps due to coaching and mentoring being unregulated industries and the radically different context of each regional market. As we have noted earlier in this book, this is particularly true for those regions where the separation between the work of a coach and that of a therapist may be more clearly divided. Within this context, the need for supervision could be seen as blurring that separation. Practitioners are highly influenced by their formative training provider. Consequently in training organizations that don't require supervision, it is unlikely to be seen as a valuable addition. Or perhaps as coaching and mentoring are largely delivered in an intimate one to one or small group forum, there is simply fear of being exposed. I'm sure we have all met practitioners who don't "walk the talk" and could benefit from feedback and supervision and risk damaging their own and others' reputations.

At the same time, increasingly there seems to be more complexity in coaching and mentoring assignments (or perhaps more awareness of the complexity!). In some markets we are seeing a trend toward consistent, regular supervision. Our observations were also found in an EMCC research paper, "Multi-stakeholder contracting in coaching" by Turner and Hawkins (2017), which showed of 428 coaches, 356 (i.e. 83 per cent) used supervision as part of their professional or self-development. The trend seems to stem from:

1 The organization requiring the practitioner producing a letter from a supervisor ensuring that the assignment is being reviewed by a qualified supervisor.
2 The professional bodies supporting supervision as part of the coach or mentor's continuous professional development (CPD).
3 The practitioner's personal commitment to good practice.

If you are reading this book, then we are going to assume that you most probably fall into the category of desire for personal improvement or have experienced the benefit of professional supervision, regardless of the norms of your own particular geography. In this chapter we want to help you understand how you can derive the most value from professional supervision. In addition, we hope to prompt those who have discounted professional supervision to consider what they are missing out on, and encourage them to be creative about how they might derive similar value given the constraints of their local market conditions.

As the business coaching industry is now exceeding thirty years, many practitioners are seeing the benefit of regular supervision and budget time and money earmarked specifically for it. However, regardless of the motivation for supervision, we are also seeing the intersections of complexity and maturity creating value for time spent in supervision. Yet what form of supervision is going to best support your growth, provide additional insights for the client system and enhance the overall delivery?

We will now look at this chapter in two sections. In Section 1, we examine the differences between peer and professional supervision: What makes peer and professional supervision different and who can provide the "professional" supervision. In Section 2 we will explore why professional supervision may be important at various junctures of your career or during an engagement. We outline opportunities to use both professional and peer supervision. In the second section, we will offer suggestions in choosing a professional supervisor, and signpost what issues to look out for and specifically take to professional supervision. Finally, we will consider how to balance peer and professional supervision as complementary development options. Our aim for this chapter is for practitioners to consider how they can use peer supervision and professional supervision appropriately for their unique needs.

Section 1: Comparing peer supervision to professional supervision

In Chapter 1 we outlined that *"Peer supervision* is a collaborative learning environment created between fellow coaches, mentors or other professionals (practitioners). It is of mutual benefit to the practitioners involved as well as being of service to their clients and the wider system. Peers often have comparable levels of expertise and are without supervision training. It is a self-managed arrangement where typically the major exchange is time rather than money. What's significant is that it is reciprocal, generates the power to reflect on practice together, and peers share vulnerability and support in equal measure." Above we suggest that the definition *"professional supervision"* is a reflective learning environment where the supervisor is hired by the practitioner(s) and is specifically qualified to look at the entire system in which the work is being undertaken. Although the reflective space is co-created, the professional supervisor is purposefully of service to the practitioner(s) and their clients. What is significant is that the supervisor's intention is to develop the practitioner's competence, capability and capacity to become a reflective practitioner of their own work. In comparing these definitions, on the surface the two supervision methods seem nearly identical, yet there are two standout features:

1   Whether or not the individual doing the supervising is appropriately qualified to do so and as a result effectively develops the practitioner's competence, capability and capacity to become a reflective practitioner of their own work.
2   Whether or not the supervision is carried out on a reciprocal basis or money is exchanged for the services.

Although these differences may seem minor, the way in which practitioners experience professional supervision creates a different psychological Contract as the qualified supervisor can adeptly create a generative learning environment to support the wider ranging supervision territory. To create this purposeful environment, it requires someone who has specific training to provide professional supervision and as a result will have the ability to view the entire system in which the practitioner works employing specific models, methodologies and techniques.

What makes professional supervision different?

Beyond the skills involved in providing professional supervision, the session itself will probably be quite different. The nature of peers supporting each other fulfills our human need to be appreciated and liked; peer supervision often has more of a collegiate feel. This is due to the fact that in order for peer supervision to work, there has to be friendship that underpins trust and the growth that takes place in a peer supervision context. Conversely the professional supervisor will have specific training and experience that you can learn from, and as a result you respect their contribution to your growth but you don't have to be friends with them for the dynamic to work. As the professional supervisor is hired to be an independent investigator of the coaching or mentoring work, the examination is wider than simply the practitioner alone, making the field wide open to explore areas such as the dynamic between the coach and the client, between the client and their line manager or organization; and as a result, more ground is covered. If the professional supervision is to support the practitioner through the accreditation or credential process, there is an expectation that the professional supervisor has the appropriate level of experience as outlined by the professional body. If your emphasis is psychological in nature, you may seek out a clinical supervisor for individual therapeutic support. Finally, regardless of the focus of the professional supervision, we would recommend that the professional supervisor has specific coach or mentor supervision training over and above their coach or mentor skills.

For example, in Chapter 8 we discussed some of the pitfalls of peer supervision such as at times peers perhaps feeling too comfortable, which can lead to minimizing or not giving honest feedback, colluding and/or unexpressed shame in peer relationships. During peer supervision discussing ethical gray areas can create tension from "Should I say something because I don't agree with it?" because the peer is often viewing the scenario from what they might do in similar circumstances. However, the qualified supervisor is specifically trained and hired to provide this useful feedback. Exploring ethics can be a growth area for you and help you to be vigilant about the client and the wider system. The professional supervisor can navigate these difficult areas of concern and as a result, the same content can be generative for both you and your peers. To highlight these differences, we've modified Brigid Proctor's *Interactive Model of Clinical Supervision* (Proctor, 1986), see Table 9.1 below, to more closely align to coaching and mentoring and include the depth that professional supervision covers beyond the peer environment.

In comparing peer to professional supervision, you will see that in the normative function the qualified supervisor is looking for blind spots, choice points and impact to the engagement and ethical concerns. Particularly with internal coaching and mentoring, team coaching and more complex adaptive

Table 9.1 Peer and professional supervision comparisons

Proctor's categories	Peer supervision	Professional supervision
Normative function: Professional accountability – supervision concerned with maintaining and ensuring the effectiveness of the practitioner's everyday work	• Continuous Professional Development (CPD) • Review interventions • Moral or ethical dilemmas • Problem solving and solutions identification • Increased understanding of professional issues • Confirmation of actions • Better understanding of role, responsibility and/or professional identity	• Continuous Professional Development (CPD) • Efficacy of interventions • Ethical considerations • Highlighting and working with blind spots • Exploration of choices within a systems lens • Extension of actions • Professional role and/or identity against industry standard
Formative function: Learning – supervision concerned with developing the skills, abilities and understandings of the practitioner through reflective practice	• Embedding techniques and/or models • Self-awareness • Critiquing and/or improving practice • Competence and creativity • Ideas support • Coaching communication skills • Understanding others' practices • Confirmation of knowledge and/or bias	• Consistent application of skills, techniques and/or models • Self-understanding both individually and within a client system • Professional feedback • Competence and flexibility • Feedback and/or contracting skills • Understanding of the supervision process
Restorative function: Support – supervision concerned with how the supervisee or practitioner responds emotionally to the stresses of everyday work	• Celebrating success • Listening and support • Empathy • Improved relationships • Sense of knowing where sitting – in peers or industry? • Reduced conflict within self and/or understanding others • Enhanced understanding of triggers • Reduced tedium	• Spotting and celebrating success • Listening, support and challenge • Enhanced coping and/or resiliency • Improved relational understanding • Sense of security within self • Improved understanding of where tension points arise • Reduced burnout

Source: Proctor (1986)

engagements, a professional viewpoint can be beneficial. Peer support can only go so far in the formative function and progress to the level of knowledge and experiences of the peers involved. The formative benefits of professional supervision will most probably include a supervisor with the skills and experience in the practical application of a range of psychological concepts and theories (Parsloe and Leedham, 2017, p. 189). We offer some suggestions on how to choose a supervisor later in this chapter. The restorative function, however, is probably well served through peer relationships and adds to the community and feeling of belonging. The additional benefits from professional supervision include a sense of security, and perhaps more challenge in a safe space. Some of this is due to conditioning – many practitioners have a deficit model and are specifically looking for what isn't working or deficits – and in peer supervision celebrating successes can be overlooked. These sorts of opportunities propel the supervision beyond problem solving and can develop the practitioner's competence, capability and capacity.

Being an unregulated industry offers us as practitioners the opportunity to self-regulate and uphold quality standards. The upside to this is that, in principle, we have the skills to have the difficult conversations and offer fulsome feedback to each other (see Chapters 5, 7 and 8). The downside, for professional supervision in particular, that tends to be a bit contentious, is whether the supervisor is "qualified" to uphold industry standards and/or quality assurance. Additionally ICF has different nomenclature (coach mentoring for credential purposes), which must be provided by a qualified coach mentor; although coaching supervision can be provided by anyone, including peers, this can only be used for CPD after the original credential has been attained. Although all professional bodies adhere to ethical codes and a robust accreditation or credential process, the specific training for all coach mentors and supervisors may not be sufficient to ensure quality assurance to the industry's: ". . . *reliance on competency frameworks oversimplifies coaching practice and expertise and stultifies more creative solutions for a meaningful 'right of passage'*" (Bachkirova and Lawton Smith, 2015, p. 128). These variances create inconsistent standards and make it difficult to ensure that quality assurance can be upheld as an industry standard, and this also creates a "buyer beware" dilemma for both the practitioner and the organization wishing to secure professional supervision. As a result, many practitioners are choosing peer over professional supervision.

When professional supervision may be an option

It is our opinion that it isn't until you've been in supervision that you understand what it is or can experience the benefits of how supervision adds value to your development. Given the unique nature of both the service and the practitioner, both peer and professional supervision are valuable and can be symbiotic. As we have already highlighted, peer supervision, due to its convenience and non-financial cost, is often the practitioner's first choice. This initial experience of sharing your work with someone else can be fruitful; however, the complexity underpinning the coaching or mentoring relationship means that professional supervision can be a useful support, regardless of where you're at in your career. So how do you choose when to seek out professional supervision?

Some practitioners find that peer supervision is their preferred option for their less complex client issues, skills practice and for ongoing collegial support, such as networking or practicing techniques. However, for more complex assignments, more in-depth exploration on client-specific issues, peer supervision-related issues and/or for more shame-producing issues, some practitioners find professional supervision delivered by a supervisor trained to look at the entire system is their preferred option. One of the additional benefits is that qualified and trained supervisors will also have their own regular supervision. You will also therefore benefit from knowing that you are part of a wider network of support and opportunities for referral. Some peer supervision groups routinely bring in a qualified supervisor on a quarterly basis to provide a systems lens to their peer work, introduce new techniques such as using constellations, pointing out group dynamics in the moment, psychological concepts such as Karpman's (1968) drama triangle and to keep a focus on ethical concerns or blind spots. The benefit of having a professional supervisor during peer supervision enhances their peer effectiveness and is particularly important for organizations where internal practitioners are supplying coaching and mentoring. Some practitioners may take a break from peer supervision and exclusively work with a qualified supervisor and then return to their peer supervision. Others work exclusively with qualified supervisors. In short, many possibilities exist and can be development options.

Section 2: Issues to bring to professional supervision

Supervision issues within Proctor's functions

Referring to the Proctor (1986) model (Table 9.1), any topic that could potentially benefit the supervisees' development or prevent them from feeling competent in delivering their work is appropriate to bring for exploration during a professional supervision session. However, in our experience, some topic areas are perhaps taboo and peers don't openly discuss these, including burn out, sexual attraction, bias and shame. Although coaching and mentoring are emotionally demanding, it is highly unusual for someone to say they're burned out as a result of their work. However, given the complexity of the work, managing self, client and/or organizational expectations as well as the metrics around "doing the work well" can create the ideal situation for burn out to occur. Being attracted to others and/or having bias is normal human behavior, but knowing when it is time to refer a client is a useful supervision topic. Furthermore, the "doing the work well" aspect when you're under-resourced, inherently self-critical and/or have high expectations brings up fear of failure and then shame is the prominent result. "Where perfectionism exists, shame is always lurking. In fact shame is the birthplace of perfectionism" (Brown, 2010, p. 81). Although you probably could talk about these issues in peer supervision, an inexperienced peer(s) may feel inadequately equipped. It is for these circumstances in particular we agree with Alison Hodge: "One to one supervision with a qualified supervisor provides a vital forum for coaches to reflect on their practice and attend to their wellbeing and development that helps to keep them fit for purpose" (Hodge, 2016, p. 102).

Once again, using Proctor's functions, here are some areas that you might bring to professional supervision where your peer(s) don't have the training to support your growth:

Normative function
Professional accountability – maintaining and ensuring the effectiveness of the supervisee or practitioner's everyday work.

- Feeling unsure about the impact of the interventions used in individual or team coaching assignments, especially in meaningful three-way contracting meetings, transformational assignments and/or if you're finding it beyond your capabilities.
- Receiving assurances and feedback that you're developing against your required professional body's competencies.
- Reviewing reflective practice to better understand patterns of behavior where blind spots may be creeping in and working through options.
- Having a sharpened perspective of what's happening within the clients' system.
- When you and/or your peer's abilities to make progress in enhancing the others ability to increase self-awareness due to blind-spots and/or other dynamics within the peer supervision.
- Clarifying your personal ethical position.
- Team coaching – coaching individuals within a group coaching assignment, brainstorming ideas for new interventions to lift the group and/or facilitate group process.

Formative function
Learning – developing the skills, abilities and understanding of the supervisee or practitioner through reflective practice.

- Inability to break habit of giving to your clients or asking questions for context rather than insight and awareness.
- Developing solid presence and/or "mind chatter" interfering with your work, such as judging yourself, your clients and/or your peers in the moment; planning or predicting; knowing the answer to a client's problem.
- Understanding yourself to spot your projections, work through transference and/or countertransference aspects within the system.
- Feeling unsure about the impact of the interventions used in individual or team coaching assignments.
- Using the same techniques, models and/or approaches to all coaching assignments, regardless of the client need due to lack of confidence.
- Having the feeling that what's happening to your client is also happening to you and/or other clients in your portfolio.
- Enhancing capabilities is limited by either you and/or your peer – sometimes referred to as developmental stagnation.
- Team coaching – consistent broken group agreements, developing more cohesive group contracts and when you're impacted by individual group members or dynamics within the system.

Restorative function

Support – supervision concerned with how the supervisee or practitioner responds emotionally to the stresses of work.

- Issues around confidence. For example, not feeling "good enough" to effectively coach a successful or domineering client, avoiding providing useful feedback or openly discussing what you consider failures.
- Receiving feedback on issues such as how your confidence limits your sense of self, patterns that could be shifted and/or strengths that are blind spots which could be enhanced.
- Developing solid presence and/or "mind chatter" interfering with your work, such as judging yourself, your clients and/or your peers in the moment; planning or predicting; knowing the answer to a client's problem.
- Dealing with erratic client emotions and being unsure about whether to refer or continue to coach.
- Celebrating successes – sometimes it's inappropriate and/or there may be ethical intersections to share with your peers – a client win, for example, which you could share in professional supervision.
- Being "fit for purpose," avoiding burn out and managing both emotional and financial considerations in your work.
- Team coaching – identifying triggers and/or tension points that arise for the practitioner and how parallel process impedes on the group's progress.

- Peer supervision – any issues you are interested in pursuing further that come as a result of peer supervision and/or your reflective practice can extend your growth.

General supervision issues

For completeness we offer the following list (in alphabetical order) including psychological aspects. In Chapter 8 we outlined some of the risks that can arise in peer supervision and which may benefit from discussion with a professional supervisor; you will notice that we mention those risks here. In addition, depending on your level of experience and the experience of your peer(s), some issues are simply better suited for professional supervision, such as:

Bias – prejudges and judgments that can be both positive and/or negative and form the foundation from which the mentoring or coaching is practiced.

Blind spots – when you uncover a pattern of behavior, habit or understanding something that prevents you being your best or your neutrality within your work. Things to be on alert to are: Passive–aggressive behavior, judgments toward others behavior and/or inflexibility.

Challenge and support – when you find giving or receiving feedback and peer comparisons beyond your capability.

Collusion – consciously or unconsciously agreeing with others even though you know inside yourself something somehow isn't "right."

Cultural defensiveness or diversity – this applies to when you're finding that racial, gender, cultural, theoretical and professional differences either interfere with your growth as your peer supervision is lacking in diversity, or bias is too ingrained in either you as a practitioner or with the peer context.

Defensiveness – close-mindedness, sharing only positive insights and/or what you've done well and can appear as comparisons such as "I'm better than . . ." or being the expert in the peer dynamic.

Discounting – is a form of denial or undervaluing and can be a marker for confidence issues. This is when you discount either your own experience "I'm not good at . . ."; especially after receiving a compliment. This can also be in the form of discounting others' experience "Despite being good at . . . , he's not good at . . ." This can show up in reflecting on your own work, during peer supervision and/or during client work.

Disorientation – feeling like you don't fit in, are insecure in sharing your reflections or observations.

Dual or multiple relationships – when a practitioner has various relationships between themselves and others. Examples are: Within organizations or educational schools, client and peers, client and associates, client and mental, clinical or pastoral carers, team or group coaching and mentoring engagements.

Ethics – we recognize that this is a large topic and have devoted Chapter 7 to this. Our recommendation is to begin the conversation with your peers. However, when issues cannot be discussed openly in the peer meeting and/or the practitioner feels uncomfortable, professional supervision either independently or in tandem can often be the circuit breaker.

Power dynamics – whether transparent or hidden, power dynamics can appear at any time. As discussed throughout the book, valuing everyone's contribution equally can be the litmus test. Whether in your work or during peer supervision, if retaining a solid sense of equality is challenging, power dynamics may be at play.

Team coaching – taking your work to the next level by having a professional supervisor can be essential to identifying power dynamics, parallel process, ethical issues, transference and countertransference, bias (both yours and within the client system) and collusion, and many other aspects can be addressed through reviewing your team coaching assignments.

Transference and countertransference – where the client or the practitioner transfers feelings, attitudes or beliefs formed in the past to the present, typically unconsciously. Either party can react to the transference in a way that keeps the client stuck in their old ways of being and limits their growth. If the practitioner is skillful in their understanding of transference, it can be possible to use this for an opportunity for growth.

Unconscious bias – judgments or beliefs about people or groups of people outside of the practitioner's conscious awareness. This can form stereotypes and categorization, making relating to the client or organization easier or preventing growth.

When you notice these issues in your reflective practice or peer supervision, this is the time to reach out for professional supervision. Regardless of your experience level as a coach, we recommend engaging a professional supervisor to partner with you for both your team coaching and complex assignments. Our experience is that rather than monitoring your work, working with a professional supervisor can make the work more interesting by engaging you in a different way to your work and sharing the burden with someone specifically trained to lift your view, point out blind spots, share techniques in working with power dynamics and/or reflect more deeply on your biases, habitual ways of working or ethics.

Defining and choosing a professional supervisor

How will I know if someone is the right supervisor for me?
Most supervisors will offer you a sample session before asking you to commit to a Contract with them. This allows you to find out whether you have good rapport and seem to communicate well. Remember however, that good supervision

requires a combination of support and challenge, and good rapport is not just about feeling comfortable. After an initial session you may wish to ask yourself:

- Do I feel safe enough with them to open up and be vulnerable? Or do I anticipate that there will be some things that it would be difficult to bring?
- Do I feel they will "call it" if I have missed something? Or do I sense they are likely to let me off the hook?
- Do I believe they will stretch my thinking at a pace that is appropriate for me? Or am I already worrying that I could quickly get out of my depth?
- Am I already identifying questions that I want to explore with them about my work? Or do I feel confused about how they will bring value to my practice?

When choosing a professional supervisor, the most important element is that we feel supported by the supervisor to have a conversation in which all areas of our work can be explored and in which we can develop, personally and professionally. Professional supervision will inevitably touch on your vulnerabilities. Choosing someone you trust and who is trained to challenge without threatening your development or learning is also significant. We suggest the delicate balance of developing your competency, capability and capacity; focusing on the client and the client's system for the ultimate goal of developing your reflective practice requires specialized expertise. Supervisor qualifications may include:

- Having a recognized qualification in coaching supervision, which follows the same guidelines established by the professional bodies for coach-specific training of a minimum of sixty hours.
- Working knowledge of corporate life and organizational systems and developments in coaching and mentoring.
- Having a significant level of psychological understanding, sensitivity to the learner's situation and ability to work with different coaching styles.
- Demonstrating the highest ethical and professional standards.
- Minimum of three years' practice as coach or coach mentor and have been in professional supervision over a number of years themselves.

Depending on what the supervisee is trying to develop, the supervisor may not have specific coach or mentoring training. However, as previously mentioned, the professional supervisor will be skillful in identifying psychological constructs of parallel process, transference and countertransference both within one to one and group coaching and mentoring, deep knowledge of ethics, a wide variety of techniques in facilitating supervision, experience in working with group and power dynamics, and/or adult learning. As suggested in Chapter 1, using Bachkirova and Jackson's (2011) suggested areas for effective supervision of coaching can be useful as well. If the supervisor is being hired to assess competency for accreditation, a solid background in the core skills under review is required. Often the supervisor will have been practicing longer than the practitioner, as the professional supervisor's role is to take the supervisee further than they could go in a peer supervision setting and to provide sharing experience as part of the engagement, if required.

During the vetting process, in addition to gauging how comfortable and supported you feel, we recommend asking the supervisor about their training, background, biases, reflective practice and ongoing development, including if they are currently in supervision themselves. We would caution against the "one discipline" supervisor – for example, someone who claims to be an NLP supervisor or an "expert" business coach or someone from your training school who only has their methodological foundation from which to supervise. Although they may be helpful for short-term learning of a technique, these supervisors tend to be subject matter experts and can be biased as a result, which can stunt your development for the longer term. Once you've selected a supervisor, in preparing for professional supervision we suggest reading Chapter 2 and following the suggestions as outlined in Chapters 3 and 4, for your professional supervision sessions. Over your lifetime, you may find many styles of supervisors with varying types of experience and backgrounds will bring a depth and grounding to your work that staying with a single supervisor will not provide.

Final thoughts

Our aim in this chapter is to help you to explore the value professional supervision can bring to you, your practice and the wider range of stakeholders. We have examined the differences between peer and professional supervision, when it might be appropriate and how to choose a professional supervisor now and in the future.

Your experience of supervision will be a never-ending journey and we hope we have raised your awareness about how it can support you at every stage of you career. Where you start is a choice and we hope we have demonstrated that there is a symbiotic relationship between peer and professional supervision.

Key learning points

1   The definitions of peer and professional supervision might seem similar; however, there are two main differences: A professional supervisor is qualified to develop the practitioners' competence, capability and capacity and views their entire system. In addition, money is exchanged for services.

2   Both forms of supervision are valuable and can be symbiotic.
3   There is tension between different approaches to supervision, especially where it might be seen as crossing the boundaries into counseling or therapy.
4   While peer supervision is cost effective and can be appropriate for less complex issues, more ground tends to be covered during professional supervision as the supervisor is an independent investigator who looks for blind spots, choice points, impact to the engagement and ethical concerns (normative function). The supervisor can furthermore apply a range of psychological concepts (formative function) and can provide a sense of security or more challenge in a safe place (restorative function).
5   Issues that can be brought to supervision include taboo topics such as burn out, sexual attraction, bias or shame, and include areas that range from maintaining and ensuring work effectiveness (normative) or developing skills through reflective practice (formative) to areas of general support (restorative).
6   The most important element when choosing a supervisor is the feeling of support so that the practitioner's personal and professional development is enhanced rather than thwarted.

References

Bachkirova, T. and Jackson, P. (2011) Peer supervision for coaching and mentoring. In: T. Bachkirova, P. Jackson and D. Clutterbuck (eds), *Coaching & Mentoring Supervision: Theory and practice*. Maidenhead, UK: McGraw-Hill, Ch. 18.

Bachkirova, T. and Lawton Smith, C. (2015) From competencies to capabilities in the assessment and accreditation of coaches. *International Journal of Evidence Based Coaching and Mentoring*, 13(2), pp. 123–140.

Brown, B. (2010) *The Gifts of Imperfection*. Center City, MN: Hazelden.

Hodge, A. (2016) The value of coaching supervision as a development process: Contribution to continued professional and personal wellbeing for executive coaches. *International Journal of Evidence Based Coaching and Mentoring*, 14(2), pp. 87–106.

Karpman, S. (1968) Fairy tales and script drama analysis. *Transactional Analysis Bulletin*, 26(7), pp. 39–43.

Parsloe, E. and Leedham, M. (2017) *Coaching and Mentoring: Practical techniques for developing learning and performance* (3rd edn). London: Kogan Page.

Passmore, J. (ed.) (2011) *Supervision in Coaching: Supervision, ethics and continuous professional development*. London: Kogan Page.

Proctor, B. (1986) Supervision: A co-operative exercise in accountability. In: M. Marken and M. Payne (eds), *Enabling and Ensuring*. Leicester, UK: Leicester National Youth Bureau and Council for Education and Training in Youth and Community Work, pp. 21–23.

Turner, E. and Hawkins, P. (2017) Multi-stakeholder contracting in coaching. *International Journal of Evidence Based Coaching and Mentoring*, 14(2), pp. 48–65.

Afterword

As a coaching or mentoring practitioner, the quality of delivery and the experience that the client has with you is entirely in your hands. As an unregulated industry, coaching and mentoring relies upon you as a practitioner to come prepared to your engagements with the competency to consistently apply your skills in the moment: The capability to deliver what your Contract states over time and the capacity to reflect about yourself and the system in which you're working. This involves regularly learning new skills, taking on board feedback, operating ethically, knowing your strengths and limitations and being adaptable to change in the moment. It is for this reason that we believe in the power of reflective practice and supervision. As professional supervisors, we bring this particular bias into our writing as it underpins our motivation for writing it.

The three authors first came together to collaborate on the book *Coaching Supervision: A Practical Guide for Supervisees* (Routledge, 2016). During the writing of *Coaching Supervision*, Sally Webb and Tammy Turner were contacted by the ICF Chapter New Zealand Northern (ICF NZN) to write a coaching-specific peer supervision handbook. ICF NZN had three face-to-face peer supervision groups in 2008. The branch wanted to enhance ICF coaches' professional development by providing peer supervision to all of its members. In 2014, ICF NZN along with Sally and Tammy ran a workshop on "How to run coaching peer supervision groups" using the newly printed handbook. As of September 2017, ICF NZN now has a total of six in-person and virtual peer supervision groups comprised of forty-one people out of a 140-person branch.

In 2015, the handbook was also tested by a University of Sydney Coaching and Mentoring Alumni (USCMA) group, which receives professional supervision on a quarterly basis in addition to their monthly peer supervision sessions. They reported the impact of the combination of both solid processes provided in the handbook to use during their peer meetings, and the addition of professional supervision has meant that peer members are clearer about sticking to process, naming issues in the moment and feeling increased capacity with their clients.

In conversations with those directly involved, having additional certainty provided through the processes outlined in the original handbook and to some, the addition of professional supervision, enabled a robust peer supervision experience and helped to establish credibility, professionalism and appreciation within their peer learning communities. Although we're highlighting examples specific to the antipodean geography, our experience in this is not an isolated incident. As referenced in Chapter 1, many practitioners have found benefit from either one to one or group peer supervision, which we call communities of practice.

There are also some examples of communities of practice extending beyond traditional boundaries of strictly coaches and mentors. We've found that practitioners such as psychologists, social workers, teachers and pastoral carers find value in joining the peer supervision community of practice. Some coaching peer supervision groups are extending invitations to the human resources community, and individual coaches are pairing with perhaps a clinical or an adult learning background practitioner. In all cases, we were encouraged to find that there was a specific purpose in enhancing themselves and the way in which they wanted to grow.

In gathering this anecdotal evidence about the value of peer supervision, we were captivated by the spirit of these individuals' commitment to crafting their trade and making a difference to themselves, their clients and the industry. The power of peer supervision created the energy for us to embark on the journey and write *Peer Supervision in Coaching and Mentoring: A Versatile Guide for Reflective Practice*, to support our belief that additional committed practitioners may be catalyzed into action with the support of the guidance in this book.

Reflecting in and on the practice of writing

Although activated by enthusiasm, we were perhaps also taking a bit of a risk. Documentation and research about peer supervision in the coaching and mentoring field is slim, so our writing has relied more on anecdotal evidence. To compile our content, we have talked to our peers and clients, read extensively, as well as used reflective practice to draw upon our own wisdom. As already mentioned, we also gratefully received feedback from peer supervision groups and other coaching and mentoring practitioners using peer supervision internationally. Though it sounds like a straightforward project, it was only through the process of writing we were able to uncover what we have shared with you. In short, writing was in fact a perfect example of reflective practice. We believe this descriptive approach is an important step towards creating an evidence base. We have provided a number of observed frameworks, which could subsequently be tested empirically and we have identified a number of areas for future research (see below).

Considerations for peer supervision

Given the gap in both research and literature about peer supervision, a key consideration as we developed our writing was how to best position our text. Given current industry, professional bodies, and laws within countries variances, we found this presented challenges as to where peer supervision fits and what value it may bring. It also opened up the difficult conversation about whether professional bodies should require supervision and who is qualified to provide that support. As much as possible, we tried to stay out of that confusion and instead focus on providing a duty of care, ensuring that we did not guide the reader into territory that is beyond their particular skill set as a coach or mentor, and into psychological or clinical aspects that many in the industry are concerned that supervision may stray into. We see reflective practice and being a peer contributor in peer supervision as a "life skill" and part of developing the skill of the individual practitioner.

To foster this habit, our hope is that coaching and mentoring training providers and universities will integrate peer supervision guidance and processes into their programs. We hope that more training providers will build supervision into their curriculum. Indeed, perhaps this book will act as a core text for these providers. We see this book as supporting depth in training by offering the addition of peer supervision for development purposes. As practitioners evolve, we anticipate that the benefits gained from reflective practice and supervision from the start will result in practitioners being clearer about where peer and professional supervision sit in their suite of reflective practice activities.

Another consideration was in regard to whether the contents in the book would replace or undermine the training required or need for professional supervision. We were concerned that by helping individual practitioners work with their peers in supervision and they became skilled at it – that when required, professional supervision may not be readily available or considered. Looking at the evolution of the more clinical helping professions, we were encouraged to note that even where professional supervision was regulated and a requirement for practice, peer supervision activities were also promoted, valued and supported.

We also wondered whether concern about the cost and/or requirements for professional supervision would increase. Certainly, there is some truth here. If peer supervision becomes more commonplace and more robust in the process, it will no doubt require all professional supervisors to continue to raise the quality of their own practice to remain relevant, which we believe is important. Rather than tackle that sticky issue here, we're hopeful that by providing guidance for peer supervision, the entire industry can benefit.

Overall, within the coaching and mentoring market, we currently see peer supervision largely as a diffuse activity for the independent practitioner with informal practices and contracts. However, in some parts of the world, organizations are starting to require their coaching providers to be in supervision. Currently that service is predominately provided by professional supervisors. Would peer supervision be a viable alternative? And could both internal and external practitioner benefit from sharing their reflective practice in peer supervision? In our opinion this may provide cross pollination and support that individual professional supervision alone may not provide. Some organizations are paying for their human resource personnel to attend coach training or complete university master's degrees in coaching and, as a result, we're seeing an increase in peer supervision post graduation. Additionally we have noticed a small but growing trend within corporate mentoring programs to encourage peer supervision between experienced mentors and new mentors. What started out as simply buddying has now in some cases evolved into a more precise role, with brief training for the experienced mentor in how to "supervise" a colleague new to the role. These trends mean potentially an increased need for peer supervision processes for the internal coach or mentor. Given these requirements, our intention was at a minimum to provide some guidelines for ethical considerations, potential pitfalls of peer supervision and best practices for this growing community of practitioners.

Looking ahead

Regardless of the context, the adoption of peer supervision is growing. In part this is because it is a practical solution. The continuing expansion of internal coaching and mentoring and the desire to contain costs also serves to increase peer supervision activity. The advance of technology has an impact on all forms of coaching and mentoring; making both peer and professional supervision more accessible across the globe and the differences between actual and virtual diminish. Group peer supervision is proving especially valuable as it generates the opportunity for a positive impact on the environment in which people work, highlighting systemic influences, sharing knowledge and building networks alongside building practitioners' skill sets and capabilities. Peer supervision offers practitioners the opportunity to build long-term relationships and to receive feedback and support within their community.

We support these communities of practice. We've witnessed the heightened gratification from having peer support as well as the enhanced quality of delivery to their clients as a result of their efforts. Our intention with this book was to provide a framework for peer supervision activities so practitioners around the world could share their reflective practice with others, wherever and whenever required throughout their career.

Currently, we see both peer and professional supervision as being separate and complementary. The growth of peer supervision in the market is likely to be organic and dependent on the perceived value that professional supervision and peer supervision bring for the individual. We suggest that by offering students the opportunity to work with peers during their coach or mentor training, they will realize the benefits of reflecting on their work while learning their skills.

This first experience of reflective practice and developmental supervision can extend to ongoing opportunities, enhancing practitioner wellbeing and enabling them to be fit for purpose throughout their careers. Over time when individuals feel they need more or different stretch than they get from their peers, and/or they may recognize the additional insight that professional supervisors can bring, we will expect to see an increase in the uptake of professional supervision. By seeing peer supervision as a strategic partner to professional supervision, together they can add value in a number of ways:

1 Peer supervision can be a useful preparation ground for determining what could be solved independently and what needs to be explored in more depth through professional supervision.
2 Peer supervision can be a useful digestion space for reflection on what has been explored further through professional supervision.
3 Peer supervision can supplement professional supervision by bringing in additional and alternative perspectives.
4 Peer supervision can bring additional variety to individual reflective practice. Where a practitioner has one to one professional supervision, this could be augmented with group peer supervision and vice versa.
5 Peer supervision can be targeted to support a particular area of practice. For example, professional supervision might focus on a team coaching engagement and group peer supervision could focus on individual career transition clients.

When the two activities are seen together in this way we hope that effectively generates an integrated, virtuous and upward cycle of continuous improvement creating a community of coaches and mentors with increased competence, capability and capacity.

Questions for further research

For peer coaching and mentoring to continue to be viable, research needs to be continued as to what constitutes best practice and how to measure it. The same is true on the subject of peer supervision. As many of you may be interested in research, we encourage you and your peers to collect data for future projects. Each chapter discusses a number of issues that could benefit from future research. We've compiled a list below, which we hope fosters consideration and publication:

1. How and when do practitioners use peer supervision and professional supervision?
2. What is the correlation between the success of the practitioner's business, the perceived value of supervision and the level of investment made in reflective practice?
3. What factors enable or hinder effective one to one peer supervision?
4. What factors enable or hinder effective group peer supervision?
5. How do contracting skills develop and mature over time?
6. What conditions need to be present in peer relationships to facilitate discussions about ethical issues?
7. How can you develop your ability to recognize when you become biased?
8. How do you raise awareness of the risks and potential pitfalls of working with peers?
9. How will technology impact on peer and professional supervision?
10. What is the correlation between the rate of coach maturity and their use of reflective practice (independent, peer supervision or professional supervision)?
11. How many coach-training organizations teach students how to organize and leverage peer supervision?
12. Where is peer supervision taught and what impact does it have on the individual practitioner's professional practice?

Parting comments

The co-creation of this book has been quite a journey for us, which has been both an exciting and challenging project. As peers we had moments of laughter and moments of gritting teeth. Like many of you, we needed to bridge time zones, cultural and professional backgrounds as well as working style preferences. As a result we gave and received feedback from each other, which created the opportunity to clarify how we work and this has shaped our perspective about peer supervision. This process has accelerated our learning through the affirmations and challenges from each other. We became aware of multiple parallel processes occurring as we worked together, including engaging with each other to reach a final outcome. To some extent this mirrored peer supervision and we had the unique opportunity to test our professional supervision capabilities.

What the result has been, though, is a more comprehensive amalgamation of our collective knowledge to support and enhance the processes in the book. In writing the book we have also noticed an impact on our practice: We have become more studious observers of ourselves. It's had the effect of moving us back into "conscious competence," revisiting why we are doing what we do in our individual reflection and our peer and professional supervision and fine-tuning things as a result. As a result of this collaboration we have gained a deeper understanding of different cultures and approaches. We recognized that when you make meaning of something the awareness raised never goes back to its original position.

Our hope is that through sharing our journey in writing this book, you realize that we are all reflective practitioners. By reading this book, you too have the opportunity to develop a clearer sense of the part that reflective practice, peer supervision and professional supervision can play in your own journey towards mastery. Our aspiration is to support and inspire practitioners to come together, enjoy and be purposeful with their reflective practice and this in turn will benefit the entire community.

Tammy, Michelle and Carol

Reference

Clutterbuck, D., Whitaker, C. and Lucas, M. (2016) *Coaching Supervision: A practical guide for supervisees*. Abingdon, UK: Routledge.

Index

Locators in **bold** refer to tables and those in *italics* to figures.

academic context 218–223
accountability 210
accreditation: masterful practitioners 26–27; non-qualified supervisors 17–18; peer supervision 19–20; quality of supervision 217; regulatory context 12
annual reviews: group peer supervision 93; one to one peer supervision 61–62
Association for Coaching (AC) 27, 58

Bachkirova, T. 13, 22, 23, 215
bias: Contracts **116–117**; ethical context 164, 170–171; professional supervision 212, **213**; reflective practice 217
blind spots 212
book clubs, finding a peer supervision partner 58
boundaries: coaching and mentoring dilemmas 129–130, **130**, 137, **138**, 145–146, **146**, 153–155, **154**; contracting **120**; Contracts **108**, 111–112; group peer supervision 82–83; one to one peer supervision 52–53, 66
buddy relationships 18, 220

capability, three Cs 27, 28–29
capacity, three Cs 28–29
client case reviews: group peer supervision 92, 93, 100–105; techniques 60, 68–71; *see also* coaching and mentoring dilemmas
Clutterbuck, D. 13, 48, 72, 196–197, 199
coach development plans 199, **200–202**
coaching: context 7–9, 19; experience level for supervision 22, **22**; global context 1–2; masterful practitioners 26–27; purpose of book 3–6; regulatory context 12; review form *43*; *see also* peer supervision
coaching the coach 15, 58
coaching and mentoring dilemmas 125–127, 159; boundaries 129–130, **130**, 137, **138**, 145–146, **146**, 153–155, **154**; confidentiality 127–129, **128**, 135–136, **136**, 143–145, **144**, 151–153, **152**; conflicts of interest 131–133, **132**, 139–141, **140**, 147–148, **148**, 155–157, **156**; dual relationships 133–135, **134**, 141–143, **142**, 149–150, **150**, 157–159, **158**; ethical context 161–162; independent coaches 127–135; internal coaches 135–143; line manager as coach 143–150; mentors 151–159; *see also* pitfalls
coaching supervision 2, 8, 12, 18, 19, 23, 111, 208
coach mentor 35, 53, 83, 178, 208, 214
coach mentoring 16–17

Index

co-coaching: confusions around 14–15; finding a peer supervision partner 58; reflective practice 35–36
collusion 178–179, 212
competency: conscious 17, 60–62, 223; ethical context 168; International Coaching Federation 2; masterful practitioners 26–27; one to one peer supervision 60–62; three Cs 27, 28–29
competitiveness 182–185
confidence, supervision 20
confidentiality: coaching and mentoring dilemmas 127–129, **128**, 135–136, **136**, 143–145, **144**, 151–153, **152**; contracting **120**; Contracts **112**; group peer supervision 84; one to one peer supervision 53–54; professional or peer supervision 21
confirmation bias **116**
conflicts of interest 131–133, **132**, 139–141, **140**, 147–148, **148**, 155–157, **156**
confusion/disorientation 179–180, 212
conscious competency 17, 60–62, 223
continuous professional development (CPD): finding a peer supervision partner 57–58; group peer supervision 94; masterful practitioners 26–29; peer supervision 7; three Cs **29**
contracting: defining 106–107; process of 122–123; skills of 117–122
Contracts: defining 106; development of 107–114, 122–123; group peer supervision 77, 81–87, 97; one to one peer supervision 51–52, 56–57, 66–67; templates 66–67, 97
convenience of supervision 20–21; see also practicalities
costs, professional supervision 20
countertransference 13, 213
cultural context: coaching and mentoring dilemmas 137, **138**, 153–155, **154**; confusion/disorientation 179–180; contracting 119–120; professional supervision 212

dependency 186–187
developmental stages model 196
dilemmas see coaching and mentoring dilemmas

discounting 180–181, 212
disorientation/confusion 179–180, 212
documentation: need for Contracts 107; reflective practice 32, 33–34, 41–46; see also Contracts
dual relationships: coaching and mentoring dilemmas 133–135, **134**, 141–143, **142**, 149–150, **150**, 157–159, **158**; pitfalls 185–186; professional supervision 212
duration of session see length of session

endings: group peer supervision 82, 95; one to one peer supervision 63
enquiry, ethical context 172–173
escalation: ethical issues **112**, 124; group peer supervision 83
ethical context: awareness 175; Contracts 108; defining 161–163; discussion techniques 171–174; escalation **112**, 124; group peer supervision 86; how to spot 164–171; importance of 163–164; one to one peer supervision 55; professional supervision 13, 212; see also coaching and mentoring dilemmas
ethics 11, 55, 86, 161–176, 212; see also ethical context
European Mentoring and Coaching Council (EMCC) 27, 38
experience level: Contracts **114–115**, **115–116**; discounting your own experience 180–181, 212; for peer supervision 22; group peer supervision 91
experiential writing 34

feedback: contracting **121**; Contracts 113–114; ethical context 173–174
fees, professional supervision 20
finding a supervisor see supervisors, finding the right people
formative supervision 11, 206–208, **207**, 210–211
frequency of meetings: contracting **109–110**, **120**; group peer supervision 78; one to one peer supervision 51
future research 218–222

geographical context: global context 1–2, 26; peer supervision 18–19; where to meet 52
Gibbs, G. 31
Global Code of Ethics (GCoE) 163
global context 1–2, 26
goals of supervision: Contracts *118*, 118–119; ethical context 162, 164, 165; group peer supervision 85; rewards 21–22; template *65*
group peer supervision: benefits and limitations **76**, **95**; defining 75–77; facilitating the meeting 88–92; forming a group 77–87; maintaining and sustaining 92–94; managing endings 95
groupthink 189–190

Hawkins, P. 51, 72–74, 195–196, 197
Holder, Jackee 34

indemnity insurance 56, 87
independent coach dilemmas 127–135
independent thinking 68, 130
insurance 56, 87
integrity 166–167
internal coach dilemmas 135–143
International Coaching Federation (ICF): coach mentoring 16; core competencies 2; handbook 217; masterful practitioners 27
intervision 9–10

Jackson, P. 13, 215
Johari window 36, *36–37*
journaling, reflective practice 32, 33–34; *see also* documentation

Labyrinth writing tool 34, *46*
lateness for meetings 89, **109–110**, **120**
learning function 210–211
legal context *see* regulatory context
length of session: Contracts **109–110**; group peer supervision 78; one to one peer supervision 52
line manager as coach dilemmas 143–150
LinkedIn 57
location: contracting **120**; Contracts **110–111**; one to one peer supervision 52

Lucas, M. 48, 72, 199
lyrical reflection form *44–45*

markets: global context 1–2; regulatory context 12
mastery, reflective practice 26–29
maturity model 196–197
medium of interaction 47, 75
meeting structure: contracting **120**; Contracts **108**; group peer supervision 78, 86, 88, 90–91, 98, 99–105; one to one peer supervision 59–60, 68–71; *see also* frequency of meetings; punctuality for meetings
Megginson, D. 196–197
members *see* supervisors, finding the right people
mentor coach 16–17
mentoring: context 7–9, 19; dilemmas 151–159; global context 1–2; and peer supervision 18; purpose of book 3–6; reflective practice 35–36
mentoring supervision 1–2, 8–9, 18
metaphor: one to one peer supervision 70; reflective practice 45
mindfulness 37–38
misrepresentation 166
morality *see* ethical context
multiple relationships 212; *see also* dual relationships
mutuality 13–14

normative supervision 11, 206, **207**, 210
note taking, reflective practice 32, 33–34; *see also* documentation

objectives *see* goals of supervision
one to one peer supervision: benefits and limitations **48**, 63–64; client case reviews 60, 68–71; Contracts 51–52, 56–57, 66–67; defining 47–48; facilitating supervision 58–60; goals *65*; maintaining and sustaining 60–62; managing endings 63; relationship forming 48–58; seven-eyed model 70–71, 72–74
overinvestment in the relationship 188–189
ownership 187–188

parallel processes 213
parity, group peer supervision 191–192
patience, group peer supervision 192–193
peer groups *see* group peer supervision
peer learning groups 4, 9, 218; *see also* group peer supervision
peer supervision: academic context 219; accreditation 19–20; cautions about 22–23; confusions about 14–18; context 19; defining 7–10; differences to professional 10–13, 18–19, 20–21, 205–209; ethical context 174; geographical context 18–19; global context 1–2; in practice 20–21, 219–221; quality of 219–220; reciprocal nature 13–14; rewards of 21–22; shortcomings 2–3; *see also* group peer supervision; one to one peer supervision
perfectionism 210
personal ethics *see* ethical context
pitfalls: collusion 178–179; competitiveness 182–185; defining 177; dependency 186–187; developmental stagnation 181–182; discounting your own experience 180–181; disorientation/confusion 179–180; dual relationships 185–186; group peer supervision 189–194; groupthink 189–190; overinvestment in the relationship 188–189; ownership 187–188; parity 191–192; patience 192–193; peer supervision 178–189; power dynamics 193–194; supervision needs 182–183; *see also* coaching and mentoring dilemmas
political context 115, 182
power: Contracts **115–116**; pitfalls 193–194; professional or peer supervision 20; professional supervision 213; roles 13–14
practicalities: contracting 109, **109–117, 120**; Contracts 108; group peer supervision 78–82; location 52, **110–111, 120**; medium of interaction 47, 75; one to one peer supervision 51–52; *see also* meeting structure; time management in meetings
Proctor, B. 11, 206, **207**, 209–210
Proctor, G. 13–14

professional context, contracting 111, **120**
professional indemnity insurance 56, 87
professional supervision 203–205, 215; defining 9; differences to peer 10–13, 18–19, 20–21, 205–209; and group peer supervision 83; how to choose a supervisor 213–215; issues to bring to 209–215; qualifications required 13, 208; value of 5, 205–209, 219, 221; *see also* accreditation
psychological matters: Contracts 112–113; professional supervision 212–213; *see also* coaching and mentoring dilemmas
punctuality for meetings 89, **109–110, 120**

qualifications *see* accreditation
quality of supervision 217, 219–220

rapport: Contracts **113**; dilemmas **128**, 137, **138**, 158–159; ethical context 174; one to one peer supervision 60–61; professional supervision 214; seven-eyed model 72
reciprocal relationships 13–14, 60; *see also* one to one peer supervision
"reflection in action" 30–31, 37–38
"reflection on action" 30–35
reflective practice: becoming a reflective practitioner 30–31, 38–39; cycle *31*, 31–32; defining 25–26; form *41–42*; group peer supervision 84; "in action" 30–31, 37–38; masterful practitioners 26–29; "on action" 30–35; with others 35–37; peer supervision 29–30; professional supervision 30; this volume 217, 218, 223; three Cs 27–29, *29*
regulatory context: coaching 12; professional supervision 208; *see also* accreditation
relationships, between peer supervisors: competitiveness 182–185; contracting 117–122; Contracts 107, 109, **112**; dependency 186–187; ethical context 161–162; group peer supervision 90, 91–94; one to one peer supervision

48–58, 60–62, 73; overinvestment in 188–189; seven-eyed model 197–199; *see also* rapport; supervisors, finding the right people
relationships, client–coach 72, 197–199; *see also* coaching and mentoring dilemmas
restorative supervision 11, **207**, 208, 211
reviews *see* annual reviews; client case reviews
role power 13–14
roles: group peer supervision 84, 88–90, 91–92, 98; one to one peer supervision 58–59

Schön, D. 30–31, 39
self-care 169
sense-checking 21
seven-eyed model 70–71, 72–74, 197–199
shame 20, 210
skills enhancement, as purpose 21
Smith, N. 51, 72–74, 196, 197
social media 57
spot contracting 119–120
stagnation 181–182
stakeholders, one to one peer supervision 56
standards: ethics 163; masterful practitioners 26–27; *see also* accreditation
Standards Australia Handbook 22, **22**
study enhancement, as purpose 21

supervision: defining 8–9; non-qualified 17–18; *see also* peer supervision; professional supervision
supervisors, finding the right people: group peer supervision 77–87, 98; how to choose a professional 213–215; one to one peer supervision 57–58
support function 211

team coaching 213; *see also* group peer supervision
Thinking Environment training 68
time management in meetings: Contracts **109–110**; punctuality for meetings 89, **109–110**, **120**; timekeeper role 89, 99; *see also* frequency of meetings; meeting structure
training programs, finding a peer supervision partner 58
transference 13, 213
Turner, T. 217

unconscious competency 17
University of Sydney Coaching and Mentoring Alumni (USCMA) 217

Webb, Sally 217
Whitaker, C. 48, 72, 199
working alliances: contracting **120**; Contracts **108**; group peer supervision 84–85; one to one peer supervision 53–54, **67**

Taylor & Francis eBooks

Helping you to choose the right eBooks for your Library

Add Routledge titles to your library's digital collection today. Taylor and Francis ebooks contains over 50,000 titles in the Humanities, Social Sciences, Behavioural Sciences, Built Environment and Law.

Choose from a range of subject packages or create your own!

Benefits for you
- Free MARC records
- COUNTER-compliant usage statistics
- Flexible purchase and pricing options
- All titles DRM-free.

Benefits for your user
- Off-site, anytime access via Athens or referring URL
- Print or copy pages or chapters
- Full content search
- Bookmark, highlight and annotate text
- Access to thousands of pages of quality research at the click of a button.

REQUEST YOUR FREE INSTITUTIONAL TRIAL TODAY

Free Trials Available
We offer free trials to qualifying academic, corporate and government customers.

eCollections – Choose from over 30 subject eCollections, including:

Archaeology	Language Learning
Architecture	Law
Asian Studies	Literature
Business & Management	Media & Communication
Classical Studies	Middle East Studies
Construction	Music
Creative & Media Arts	Philosophy
Criminology & Criminal Justice	Planning
Economics	Politics
Education	Psychology & Mental Health
Energy	Religion
Engineering	Security
English Language & Linguistics	Social Work
Environment & Sustainability	Sociology
Geography	Sport
Health Studies	Theatre & Performance
History	Tourism, Hospitality & Events

For more information, pricing enquiries or to order a free trial, please contact your local sales team:
www.tandfebooks.com/page/sales

The home of Routledge books

www.tandfebooks.com